USING
windows® 8

J. Peter Bruzzese
Wayne Dipchan
Nick Saccomanno

Using Windows 8

Copyright © 2013 by Pearson Education, Inc.

ISBN-13: 978-0-7897-5051-8

ISBN-10: 0-7897-5051-1

Library of Congress Data-in-Publication data is on file.

First Printing November 2012

Trademarks

All terms mentioned in this book that are known to be trademarks or service marks have been appropriately capitalized. Que Publishing cannot attest to the accuracy of this information. Use of a term in this book should not be regarded as affecting the validity of any trademark or service mark.

Warning and Disclaimer

Every effort has been made to make this book as complete and as accurate as possible, but no warranty or fitness is implied. The information provided is on an "as is" basis. The author and the publisher shall have neither liability nor responsibility to any person or entity with respect to any loss or damages arising from the information contained in this book.

Bulk Sales

Que Publishing offers excellent discounts on this book when ordered in quantity for bulk purchases or special sales. For more information, please contact

U.S. Corporate and Government Sales

1-800-382-3419

corpsales@pearsontechgroup.com

For sales outside of the U.S., please contact

International Sales

international@pearsoned.com

Editor-in-Chief
Greg Wiegand

Executive Editor
Loretta Yates

Development Editor
Todd Brakke

Managing Editor
Sandra Schroeder

Project Editor
Seth Kerney

Copy Editor
Geneil Breeze

Indexer
Tim Wright

Proofreader
Debbie Williams

Technical Editor
Alan Wright

Publishing Coordinator
Cindy Teeters

Cover Designer
Anne Jones

Compositor
Trina Wurst

Media Table of Contents

To register this product and gain access to the free Web Edition and the audio and video files, go to **quepublishing.com/using**.

Table of Contents

About the Authors

J. Peter Bruzzese (co-founder and CIO of ClipTraining) is a Microsoft MVP, an internationally published technical author, a well-known tech speaker, and a journalist. Over the past 15 years, Peter has worked with Goldman Sachs, CommVault Systems, and Microsoft, to name a few. His focus has been, and continues to be, enterprise environments with a special focus on Active Directory, Exchange, SharePoint, and desktop operating systems. He holds the following certifications:

- Microsoft: MCSA 2000/2003, MCSE NT/2000/2003, MCITP: Messaging with Exchange 2007/2010
- Microsoft Exchange MVP
- Microsoft Certified Trainer (MCT)
- Novell: CNA
- Cisco: CCNA
- CIW: CIW Master, CIW Certified Instructor
- CompTIA: A+, Network+, iNET+

Peter and ClipTraining are partnered with TrainSignal to create powerful admin-oriented training videos that revolve around Exchange, SharePoint, and Lync.

Peter is also a contributor to *Redmond* magazine, *WindowsITPro* magazine, TechTarget, MSExchange.org, and other tech sites. He is a regular speaker for TechMentor Conferences and the FETC Conference. He has also spoken at Microsoft TechEd, the IT360 Tech Conference in Canada, the TEC Conference, and Connections. Last but certainly not least, he writes the Enterprise Windows column for InfoWorld.

Wayne Dipchan is the owner of AriLex Technologies LLC, an IT consulting company, and is a Windows Systems Engineer for Staten Island University Hospital, which is part of the LIJ Healthcare System. Wayne has had the opportunity to work for such companies as New Horizons CLC, St. Peter's Healthcare System, and Barclays Capital. At Barclays Capital, he was part of a team that managed more than 25,000 Windows servers, focusing on Active Directory and Citrix. Currently at Staten Island University Hospital, he is involved in an Active Directory migration and utilizes PowerShell to automate many functions. This real-world experience helps him understand what end clients want and deliver real solutions. His training background enables him to discuss and explain technology to a wide range of audiences. He is also the co-author of *Windows Server 2008 How To*.

Nick Saccomanno is a Microsoft Certified Professional (MCP) and is a professional screencaster and technical author with an emphasis on Microsoft technologies. On the forefront of the latest technologies, Nick simplifies the learning curve in trying to help the everyday user get the most out of them. Nick has created screencasts for ClipTraining relating to Windows XP, 7, and 8, as well as Office 2007/2010, and coauthored *Using Windows 7*. His unique style is due mostly to his love of technology and the gift of learning it quickly. When away from training, Nick enjoys playing guitar and traveling to new places with his wife, Marie.

Dedication

We dedicate this book to the Microsoft developers and others at Microsoft who put their hearts into their work each day to continue to develop the OS we've known and loved for years.

Acknowledgments

Although we've dedicated this book to Microsoft (something I do for all of my books that relate to the Windows operating system), my heart and appreciation go to my wife, Jennette; our son, Lucas; and our daughter, Bethany. My life as a husband and father brings me greater joys and blessings than anything else I've done or accomplished.

In addition, on a personal level, I have many others, both family and friends, to thank for their support—too many to number. On a professional level, the list is a bit shorter (but not much). I'd like to thank Nick Saccomanno and Wayne Dipchan for working with me on this book. I'd also like to thank Alan Wright, our technical editor, and others, both directly and indirectly, who have contributed to my personal success and to the success of this project.

I have many I work with who I would like to mention at this time, including Tim Duggan, my friend, business partner, and CEO of ClipTraining. I'd like to thank John Duggan, Director of Sales and traveling partner to every conference I speak at. We eat well though, don't we John? I'd like to thank John Van Horn, lead developer for ClipTraining, for being an amazing powerhouse genius developer.

I'd like to mention those I work with at InfoWorld, including Galen Gruman, Ted Samson, Eric Knorr, Doug Dineley, and others; the folks I work with at Techgenix, including Barbara Matysik-Magro, Michael Vella, Sean Buttigieg, and Bob Hanson; Eva Ciganova and others at GFI who care for the ExclusivelyExchange.com site; and Jay Gundotra of Enow, who continues to push me to stay true to my Exchange roots by working on Mailscape.

I would especially like to thank Scott Skinger and all the folks at TrainSignal, including Gary Eimerman, Iman Jalali, Brian Green, Ed Liberman, David Davis, Gosia Niklinkski, and the whole TrainSignal team. Never have I worked with a better group of people.

And I certainly want to thank my acquisitions editor, Loretta Yates, and everyone who assisted with the creation of this book, including Todd Brakke, Seth Kerney, Geneil Breeze.

—J. Peter Bruzzese

I would first like to acknowledge the love and support I receive from my wife, Davora, and two precious daughters, Ariana and Alexandria; without their support and patience, I would not be able to achieve so many of my goals in life. Every effort I make with regards to my profession is motivated by my love for them.

As far as my career in technology, I owe it all to good friend and coauthor J. Peter Bruzzese, who many years ago helped me to enter the information technology world. Thank you for your continued friendship, and including me in exciting projects such as this book.

I would also like to acknowledge the team at Staten Island University Hospital: John Gelsomino, Afroz Bakht, Igor Kucheryavy, Kamran Nasrullah, Richard Loeb, and CIO Kathy Kania. The opportunity to work with such a great group of people who are focused on utilizing technology to improve healthcare is certainly rewarding.

—Wayne Dipchan

I am grateful to the following for their unique contributions to this project: Thanks to lead author and project manager, J. Peter Bruzzese, a true professional and guide throughout the entire collaboration process. Thanks to my family, who gave the love, support, motivation, and inspiration needed to complete this work. And special thanks to my loving wife, Marie, who patiently endured and lovingly supported me every step of the way—a helper I couldn't be without. Thanks to all involved for making this a success!

—Nick Saccomanno

We Want to Hear from You!

As the reader of this book, *you* are our most important critic and commentator. We value your opinion and want to know what we're doing right, what we could do better, what areas you'd like to see us publish in, and any other words of wisdom you're willing to pass our way.

We welcome your comments. You can email or write us directly to let us know what you did or didn't like about this book—as well as what we can do to make our books better.

Please note that we cannot help you with technical problems related to the topic of this book.

When you write, please be sure to include this book's title and authors as well as your name, email address, and phone number. We will carefully review your comments and share them with the authors and editors who worked on the book.

Email: feedback@quepublishing.com

Mail: Que Publishing
            ATTN: Reader Feedback
            800 East 96th Street
            Indianapolis, IN 46240 USA

Reader Services

Visit our website and register this book at www.informit.com/title/9780789750518 for convenient access to any updates, downloads, or errata that might be available for this book.

Introduction

A touch-oriented, tablet ready system that promises better performance, newer features, and an enhanced user experience—that's what Microsoft has brought to its latest operating system, Windows 8. *Using Windows 8* provides an introduction to all the new features and shows you how to get the most out of them. For users coming from Windows XP, the transition will be smoother than ever. Vista users will be just as impressed with the ease of transition; they will also enjoy several new or improved features. Even Windows 7 users will find a whole new interface and new manner of working that requires assistance to get started.

This book has been designed to give you, the reader, more than one method of learning. Some can read a book and look at a few screenshots and that is all they need. Others like a step-by-step approach to learning so they can follow along with the process laid out. Others like to see a task demonstrated because they are visual learners. We have taken all of this (and more) into account when preparing this book. *Using Windows 8* is not only a book, it's an adventure in learning.

Using This Book

This book allows you to customize your own learning experience. The step-by-step instructions in the book give you a solid foundation in using Windows 8, while rich and varied online content, including video tutorials and audio sidebars, provide the following:

- Demonstrations of step-by-step tasks covered in the book
- Additional tips or information on a topic
- Practical advice and suggestions
- Direction for more advanced tasks not covered in the book

Here's a quick look at a few structural features designed to help you get the most out of this book.

Important tasks are offset to draw attention to them.

LET ME TRY IT   These tasks are presented in a step-by-step sequence so you can easily follow along.

 SHOW ME video walks through tasks you've just got to see—including bonus advanced techniques.

 TELL ME MORE audio delivers practical insights straight from the experts.

We encourage you to learn Windows 8 in the way you feel is most comfortable. Perhaps you might want to start with installing it and getting a feel for this new OS from Microsoft, and then explore the many features.

About the *Using* Web Edition

More than just a book, your *Using* product integrates step-by-step video tutorials and valuable audio sidebars delivered through the **Free Web Edition** that comes with every *Using* book. For the price of the book, you get online access anywhere with a web connection—no books to carry, content is updated as the technology changes, and the benefit of video and audio learning.

The Web Edition of every *Using* book is powered by **Safari Books Online**, allowing you to access the video tutorials and valuable audio sidebars. Plus, you can search the contents of the book, highlight text and attach a note to that text, print your notes and highlights in a custom summary, and cut and paste directly from Safari Books Online.

To register this product and gain access to the Free Web Edition and the audio and video files, go to **quepublishing.com/using**.

In this chapter, we will go through the various features of Windows 8 and help you locate where you can find those features to learn more within the book itself.

1

What's New in Windows 8

Ah…the first chapter of a new book on the latest OS from Microsoft. Fear, excitement, wonder—these may or may not be the feelings you have at this very moment. Windows 8 is a major overhaul from Microsoft, and it embraces a new direction in computing. It's amazing that on the one hand monitors have gotten larger and flatter, indicating people want desktop systems that have larger than life displays (and touch capability as well), while at the same time netbooks and tablets of both 10-inch and 7-inch form factors have been selling by the millions in recent years. Microsoft, in an attempt to embrace both concepts, has decided on an operating system to suit all needs. One OS to bind them all, so to speak.

In this chapter we provide an overview of features and point you in the right direction within the book so that you can quickly jump to those topics that interest you the most.

A New User Interface

The Windows 8 UI is probably the most talked about feature in Windows 8. It is more than just a new look, but an entirely new method and manner of working and navigating your system.

Microsoft originally referred to this new Windows 8 UI as Metro. However, toward the RTM of Windows 8, a German company wanted to fight about the use of the name, so Microsoft has discontinued using it to describe the new Windows 8 UI. Where we use the term in the book, we are simply referring to the style and not using it as a label.

"Metro" is based off classic Swiss design that focuses on International Typographic Styles that use a clean and readable approach over graphics. The principle of "content over chrome" is often touted in that your content should be the main focus with the OS itself fading into the background. So typography is relied on more so than graphics. This new Windows 8 UI can be seen in a variety of different Microsoft products like the Windows Phone, the Xbox 360, and even on the Microsoft website itself (see Figure 1.1).

Figure 1.1   *The new Windows UI is everywhere in the Microsoft world*

 SHOW ME   **Media 1.1—An Initial Tour of Windows 8**
Access this video file through your registered Web Edition at
my.safaribooksonline.com/9780789750518/media.

A New Start Screen

Windows 8 also sports a new Start screen, shown in Figure 1.2, that utilizes what are called Live Tiles to display information on your screen through the tiles. So a weather tile shows you the weather and a stock market tile shows you your chosen stocks, and so on.

There has been a bit of controversy on the new UI for Microsoft and the new forced Start screen approach to working with the OS. Although Microsoft doesn't appear to be budging on the subject, plenty of third-party tools can help you restore your OS to a more legacy or classic mode that may work better for you.

You can learn more about navigating your new Windows 8 OS in Chapter 2, "Navigating the Windows 8 User Interface."

Figure 1.2   *The Start screen is the home base for almost everything you do in Windows 8*

A New Windows Desktop

Some of you may be wondering what was wrong with the old Desktop? Well, with the new Start screen handling much of the functionality of the Start button/orb, the folks at Microsoft have decided to remove the Start menu altogether and provide a Windows Desktop that includes a Charms bar for access to other elements, shown in Figure 1.3. Part of that "content over chrome" mentality no doubt.

The missing Start button and menu may be the heart of the UI controversy but as mentioned here there are two options. Either learn to adopt the new UI fully or reach out to third-party solutions; there are several worth considering, including Start8, Classic Shell, and ViStart (all searchable online).

SHOW ME   **Media 1.2—The Windows Desktop**
Access this video file through your registered Web Edition at
my.safaribooksonline.com/9780789750518/media.

Figure 1.3   *The new Windows Desktop*

Windows Apps

If you have ever installed an application on your Desktop and then installed an app on your phone, you may have wondered "Why is it so much easier to install an app on my phone?" or even "Why are apps on my phone so much cooler looking than my Desktop apps?" Well, Metro-style apps, shown in Figure 1.4, are part of the new Windows 8 OS, and many of these are located right on the Start screen. In addition, you can use the Windows Store to locate and download additional apps, as I discuss in the next section. Not to worry, though; you can still install traditional Desktop apps on your Windows 8 OS.

Figure 1.4   *Metro-style apps*

A New Windows Store

For a convenient way to locate and download your favorite apps, you can use the Windows Store. The Store, shown in Figure 1.5, shows both free and paid-for apps that you can install in much the same way you do on your smartphone devices. They also have the capability to check for updates, so you can make sure your apps are the latest versions.

Figure 1.5   *All native Windows 8 apps are available in the Windows Store*

 SHOW ME   **Media 1.3—Windows 8 Store**
Access this video file through your registered Web Edition at
my.safaribooksonline.com/9780789750518/media.

A Tablet-Friendly OS

Windows is now going to be able to compete in the "Tablet Wars" that have been dominated by Apple and Google OS products (with a slight nod to BlackBerry). Tablets typically use one of two competing, and incompatible, architectures: x86, which is the same architecture your PC is based on, and ARM, which is built around the ideas of mobility and power conservation. Each architecture is supported with a different version of Windows 8, and although they look the same overall, the functionality differs slightly. One example of this is that ARM-based tablets are not able to join a domain and be controlled by the Group Policy settings that many system administrators use to manage large network environments.

Along with the excitement that Windows 8 will be tablet-friendly (which means it is a universal OS, operating on desktops, laptops, netbooks, tablets, and slates), Microsoft also announced that it is getting into the hardware side of the tablet game with the release of a Windows 8 tablet called Surface (see Figure 1.6). Surface comes in both x86 and ARM architectures so that they can be used in both a work and home environment.

Figure 1.6   *The new Surface tablet*

Ribbons Everywhere

When Microsoft first introduced the Ribbon UI with Office 2007, many hoped this was just a fad that would disappear. Others embraced it wholeheartedly and found the Ribbon to be much better to work with than the menus of old. Well, it's obvious the Ribbon UI is here to stay, and now we can see the Ribbon everywhere, even in File Explorer (previously called Windows Explorer), shown in Figure 1.7.

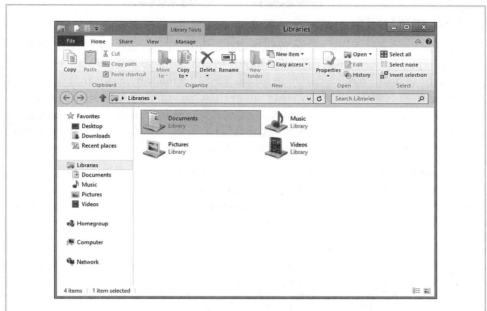

Figure 1.7   *File Explorer with the Ribbon UI*

Windows Essentials 2012

In this book's predecessor, we discussed the Windows Live Essentials suite of tools because, starting with Windows 7, some of the features traditionally built into the Windows OS were pulled out and had to be downloaded and installed instead. This remains the case with Windows 8. It's true, Windows 8 still has tools like Windows Media Player along with modern apps like Music. There are also Parental Control options built in, although the Windows Essentials version provides Internet protection. However, if you want a Blogging tool application or a Messenger IM application, for example, you should check out and download Windows Essentials 2012 (http://windows.microsoft.com/en-US/windows-live/essentials-home). Keep in mind that Essentials works on both Windows 7 and 8 and includes the following: Microsoft Mail, Microsoft Messenger, Microsoft Movie Maker, Microsoft Photo Gallery, and Microsoft Writer.

Learn more about both built-in and Essentials tools in Chapter 4, "Mail, Photos, Video, and Music."

Cloud Focused

You hear the term "cloud" all the time, and the easiest definition for it is the Internet. Everything from email to family photos to complete applications are in the cloud these days. That is a common expression. All it really means is that you access those elements through the Internet rather than having them stored on your PC. Truth be told, nothing exists literally in a cloud. Although you may use the super-highway to access your data (pictures, files, whatever), that data is stored on a server (or servers) located in some physical location.

Windows 8 shows a cloud focus by allowing you to use both a local login account or a Windows account. This Windows account is free. The value is that you can configure your system, and it remembers those settings and keeps them "in the cloud" so that if you log into another system, it carries them over.

You might have a Live email account with Microsoft because you have worked with other tools that required you to set up one of these in the past. The Live account is the same as the Windows account; it's just a name change.

You also have the capability to have your other credentials stored and used for access to Gmail, Facebook, and Microsoft's SkyDrive solution.

Learn more about SkyDrive and other Windows 8 built-in features in Chapter 5, "Additional Windows 8 Features."

Internet Explorer 10

Actually two different versions of Microsoft's Internet Explorer (IE) web browser are available in Windows 8. There is IE 10, the Windows Desktop version (which is the upgrade to IE 8 and 9 you may be using already), and then there is IE 10, the Metro-style app, shown in Figure 1.8, which is more for your tablet and touch-friendly devices.

Figure 1.8   *Internet Explorer Metro-style app*

Learn more about Internet Explorer 10 in Chapter 6, "Internet Explorer 10."

Networking Enhancements

On the networking side are enhancements to the ease of use for both home and office workers. We see improvements to preexisting features such as AppLocker, BitLocker (which can encrypt drives faster), BranchCache, and Direct Access (both of which have become easier to deploy).

There is added support for new network authentication types such as WISPr (Wireless Internet Services Provider roaming) protocol, which allows users to roam from one WiFi spot to another (similar to cell phone roaming capability). There are also EAP-SIM, EAP-AKA, and EAP-AKA Prime protocols for mobile broadband network connectivity option, as well as the EAP-TTLS protocol for campuses and enterprises that use this authentication type.

Learn more about networking features in Windows 8 for both home and work in Chapter 7, "Home Networking Features," and Chapter 8, "Domain Networking."

Security Enhancements

Security is always a big concern with an operating system, and each new flavor of Windows must bring with it major changes to keep up with the threats end users face each day. Windows 8 brings with it a new secure boot feature (for UEFI-based systems) to ensure the OS hasn't been tampered with, a new picture password feature (see Figure 1.9), an enhanced Windows Defender that goes beyond spam protection and also includes antivirus/antimalware protection, and more.

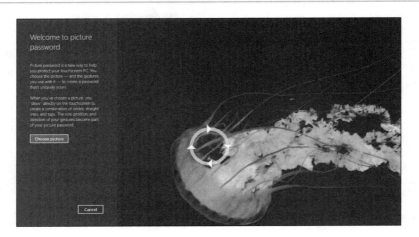

Figure 1.9   *Picture password capabilities*

Older PCs use built-in software code called a BIOS to get the system started and boot your OS (Windows in this case). However, Microsoft is promoting a new boot solution called Unified Extensible Firmware Interface (UEFI). The UEFI boot not only improves boot times but ensures safer boot experiences because unauthorized systems are not allowed to boot. New early launch antimalware (known as ELAM) also protects you from boot loader attacks.

Another security enhancement is the fact that Windows Defender (shown in Figure 1.10) has been revamped to include both antispam and antivirus malware protection. Now your system comes out of the box with more protection.

Learn more about new security features in Chapter 9, "Security Features."

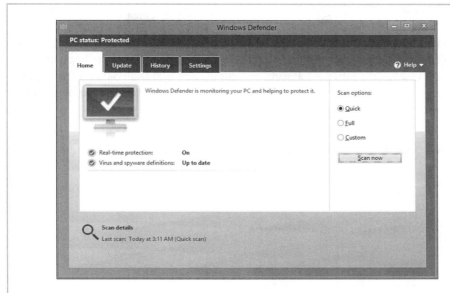

Figure 1.10   *Windows Defender*

Improved OS Features

Several improvements to the Windows operating system are worth noting. These include the following:

- **Storage Spaces**—Storage Spaces help to protect you from drive failure by allowing you to create storage pools of two or more drives and then create the Storage Space from the free pool capacity. This allows you to have multiple drives that are fault tolerant, in that if one drive goes down, your data is not lost.

- **File History**—This solution saves copies of your files so you can get them back if they are lost or damaged. Every hour the system scans files stored in Libraries, Desktop, Favorites, and Contacts (unless directed otherwise), looks for changes, and stores these changes to allow users to revert back to older file versions.

- **Portability with Windows-to-Go**—You can make a copy of your OS, put it on a USB thumb drive, and take it with you. You can then boot your particular OS from the key on a different system if that system supports the USB boot. You need at least a 32GB USB drive. This can really help telecommuters, temporary contractors, and others who need to travel with their system into different environments. It's great for admins who consult because they can travel with their system and all their tools right on their key.

- **Recovery**—The ability to recover your system has never been easier. You can "Refresh" your PC or "Reset" your PC (both shown in Figure 1.11). Refreshing your PC puts your PC settings back to their defaults but doesn't change files and personalization settings. Apps from the Windows Store are kept, but all other apps are removed. Resetting your PC obliterates all data on the system and allows you to recycle the system in that you start back at the beginning with everything else removed.

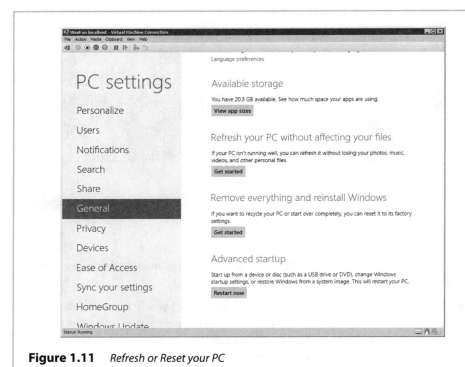

Figure 1.11   *Refresh or Reset your PC*

Learn more about these features and others in Chapter 10, "System Configuration Settings," Chapter 11, "Performance and Monitoring Tools," and Chapter 12, "Managing and Troubleshooting."

Administrative Feature Improvements

Whether you are a power user, a help desk expert, or an IT admin, features in Windows 8 can help you better test, monitor, and troubleshoot your OS.

- **Hyper-V (Microsoft's hypervisor solution)**—This virtualization software is built right into the OS, meaning you can run virtual systems on your Desktop. This replaces the Windows Virtual PC solution and the XP Mode options we used in the past. Whereas these other options were type-2 hypervisors, having Hyper-V brings the virtualized systems closer to the bare metal. If you are wondering "Why would I use a hypervisor?" it might be to perform testing and evaluation, to work with other tools, and more.

You have to enable Hyper-V in your Windows Features dialog, located through the Programs and Features item in Control Panel. In addition, your PC must support virtualization, and you may have to enable the virtualization features through your BIOS or UEFI firmware.

- **Enhanced Admin Tools**—The easiest tool to point out here is Task Manager, which now sports a crisper look with more information at your fingertips (see Figure 1.12). You'll see some effort to include features that we used to have to find elsewhere, such as the charting options in the Performance tab (that we used to have to use Resource Monitor for) and the Startup control options (that we used to reach out for the System Configuration tool).

For those of you who like using the System Configuration tool (msconfig) you can still find it, but the Startup tab now tells you to use Task Manager to configure options.

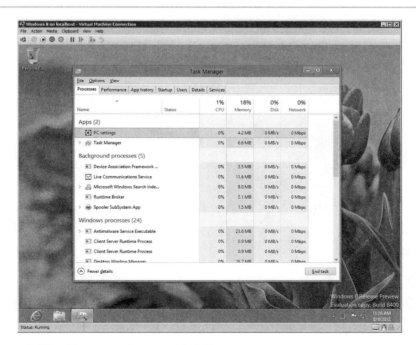

Figure 1.12   *The new and improved Task Manager*

- **Remote Desktop** —There are two ways to work with Remote Desktop. One is a new app that is easier and cleaner. Many prefer to use the full remote Desktop application that is also available.

To learn more about the system configuration, monitoring, and troubleshooting aspects of Windows 8, check out Chapters 10-12.

 TELL ME MORE   Media 1.4—A Discussion of the New Features in Windows 8

Access this audio recording through your registered Web Edition at
my.safaribooksonline.com/9780789750518/media.

In this chapter, we look at the brand new interface in
Windows 8 and how to navigate through it.

2

Navigating the Windows 8 User Interface

Logging In to Windows

Without a doubt the new Windows 8 Start screen represents a radical change from previous versions of Windows. Improving on the Start menu from prior releases, the Start screen takes up the entire screen and provides quick access to applications and information at a glance. But while the new Start screen represents one of the most obvious visual changes to the operating system, equally as impressive is what's not seen—Windows new navigation commands.

For users who have created a password, the Lock screen is the first interaction you will have with Windows (see Figure 2.1). At first glance it's not apparent what to do. A nice picture appears on the screen. The date, time, and network connection status are displayed in the lower left. Instinctively your reaction is to click somewhere on the screen and see what happens. Do that and the picture on the Lock screen scrolls up quickly to reveal a more traditional Windows login with username and password fields. Think about your password too long and the Lock screen rolls right back down to cover the username and password fields, once again hiding them. Let's log in to Windows 8.

Figure 2.1   *The Windows 8 Lock screen*

 **LET ME TRY IT**

Logging In to Windows 8

1. From the Lock screen click anywhere on the screen.

2. Select a user if multiple users are displayed and then enter a password.

3. Click the right arrow at the end of the password field or press Enter on your keyboard to log in to Windows.

> To make Windows easier to see, hear, and use, Windows contains several features that help make your computer more accessible. These features are located in the lower left of the Lock screen and include Narrator, Magnifier, Onscreen Keyboard, High Contrast, Sticky Keys, and Filter Keys. These features are explained in more detail in Chapter 3, "System Setup and Personalization."

Another feature located on the login screen is in the lower-right corner and looks like a power button. Selecting this button gives you three options for shutting down the machine:

- **Sleep**—This powers down the machine to slow power consumption. Only the memory is powered to save your system's current state, which is then quickly restored when turned on again.

- **Shut Down**—As expected, this turns the machine completely off.

- **Restart**—This restarts the PC without fully powering it off.

After successfully logging in you're greeted with an interface from Windows unlike anything you've ever seen before in previous versions of the OS. As you look over the new interface, observe the account name that you logged in with in the upper-right corner of the screen. From here you have the opportunity to change the account picture, return to the Lock screen, or sign out. Take a moment to learn how to return to the Lock screen.

 **LET ME TRY IT**

Using the Start Screen Account to Lock the Machine

1. On the Start screen left-click on the account name that appears in the upper right (see Figure 2.2).

2. Left-click on Lock.

Figure 2.2   *The Start screen account menu*

If you have just completed this exercise, log back into the Start screen. There you'll find colorful boxes, called tiles, lighting up the center of the screen. These tiles are the shortcuts to launch Windows 8 apps, a new style of application in Windows 8. Visually stunning, the new interface represents an entirely new way of working in Windows.

Not everyone likes the new look at first. In fact, for many, the first glance at the Windows 8 interface may have some wishing for the days of Windows XP, Windows Vista, or Windows 7. Another cause for concern is the question new users often ask first—Where is the Start button? Sad to say the beloved Start button has not made it into Windows 8. Instead it has been replaced by the more powerful Charms bar.

Understanding Charms

Windows has had a familiar Start button or Start Orb in one form or another since the days of Windows 95. To look at Windows without it almost gives the impression that this is *not* Windows that is running, but some other operating system. However, spend a little time with charms, the Start menu's replacement, and soon it will become an almost antiquated notion.

Undoubtedly one of the most important pieces to navigating Windows 8, charms are actually not visible until a command to show them is given. So without further ado, let's see the charms (or Charms bar as it's frequently called).

 **LET ME TRY IT**

Show and Hide Charms

1. Press the Windows Key + C on your keyboard to show the five charms.
2. A set of charms appears on the right side of your screen (see Figure 2.3).
3. Click on the screen to the left of the Charms bar to hide it.

Or:

1. Move your mouse pointer to the upper- or lower-right side of the screen.
2. A transparent set of charms appears. Slide your mouse toward the charms to fully activate the bar (which becomes black).
3. Move your mouse to the left until the Charms bar disappears.

When you activate the charms a separate black box also appears on the lower left. This is an information only box that gives you quick details on your network status, battery state (if working on a mobile device), and the date and time. Click or tap all you like on it; nothing happens with it.

Figure 2.3   *The Charms bar*

The ability to show or hide charms illustrates a powerful concept of Windows 8 navigation that is seen (or better yet not seen) throughout: navigation commands that are invisible until you need them. This can be a blessing, or for some users, a curse if they know little about this concept. Not understanding that your navigation commands are invisible until called for leaves most users scratching their heads or maybe even calling Windows 8 the worst operating system from Microsoft since Windows Vista! On the other hand, users empowered with the understanding that not every command is visible onscreen quickly realize there is more than meets the eye when they look at the screen.

Because they'll be a standard feature in Windows going forward, you should get to know these five charms well: Search, Share, Start, Devices, and Settings. Devices such as Microsoft's Surface actually contain keyboard keys on its integrated covers that activate each of these charms. You can find these keys at the top of the keyboard above the numbers.

Using the Start Charm

We start at this charm, located in the middle of the Charms bar, since it most likely will become the charm you access the most. The purpose of the Start charm is to switch from the Start screen to the last app viewed or vice versa. Do this just once, and you've uncovered a powerful method to navigate through Windows 8.

It's important to remember that charms are available from any interface within Windows 8—whether the Start screen, an app, or the traditional Desktop view. Keep this in mind as you start using Windows 8. If you get lost in Windows 8 at any time and don't know where to go next, bring up the Charms bar and select the Start charm to head back to the Start screen.

 LET ME TRY IT

Use the Start Charm to Switch Between an App and the Start Screen

1. On the Start screen, locate the blue tile that says Internet Explorer and left-click on it.

2. After Internet Explorer opens, show the Charms bar.

3. Left-click on Start.

4. Once the Start screen reappears, show the Charms bar again.

5. Left-click on the Start charm to return to Internet Explorer.

Using the Search Charm

A powerful search tool, the Search charm can look through files, apps, PC settings, Desktop applications, and the Control Panel to find what you're after. At the same time, the Search charm can be activated from within an app to reveal app-specific searches. This makes the Search charm (like other charms) context sensitive and thus a valuable part of the app experience. Let's take a look at how the Search charm works.

 LET ME TRY IT

Use the Search Charm to Locate the Control Panel

1. Show the Charms bar.

2. Start typing the word "control."

3. Locate the search result Control Panel on the left side (see Figure 2.4).

4. Left-click Control Panel to open it.

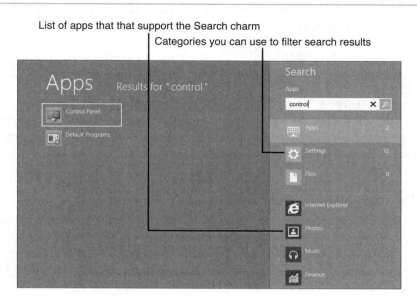

List of apps that that support the Search charm

Categories you can use to filter search results

Figure 2.4   *Use the Search charm to locate the Control Panel or pretty much any other tool, app, or document in Windows 8*

Notice how Search did not provide an exhaustive list of results, just the most relevant ones enabling you to find the Control Panel result quickly. If you want more results from your search, repeat the search, but this time underneath the white Search form, select from available results in Apps, Settings, or Files.

An even more powerful approach is to leverage the Search charm to locate Internet-based or app-based results. For example, type in the name of your favorite musician or group. If no results are found, select from one of the apps on the right side such as Internet Explorer or the Music app. Quickly you are taken to results from that type of app.

One of the best secrets to using the Search charm requires surprisingly little know-how. From the Start screen, just start typing and your search results automatically appear onscreen!

If you are within an app you can often search for results relevant to that application. Here is a look at a few examples:

- **News**—A great way to find almost anything, this search is performed like a web search returning only news results.

- **People**—Locates matches from your contacts and related information such as email addresses.

- **Store**—Find new apps, within the Store.

- **Weather**—Look for weather conditions in a specific area.

As a reminder Search is only available in supported apps. To get a look at these supported apps, open the Search charm from the Start screen and all the apps supporting Search are listed. Remember, this list will likely *not* include all apps on your system, just those supporting Search.

Using the Share Charm

Often when we're using a computer or mobile device there is information that we want to share with others or even refer to later ourselves. In a typical scenario, a user might visit a website, want to share it with someone else, and have to go through the steps of copying the website, pasting it, and then sending it off to its intended recipient. Windows 8 simplifies this process by integrating sharing capabilities throughout several apps through the Share charm. After launching the Share charm, you have the capability to share the info from your app such as a web link directly into a mail client or to one of your contacts and not open other apps or applications to complete this process. It's a smooth, fluid process that stands head and shoulders above previous methods of sharing in Windows.

Keep in mind that before you use the Share charm, you have to have someone to share it with (such as a contact in the People app) or have the Mail app configured. These topics are discussed later in the book. Let's look at the Share charm now.

 LET ME TRY IT

Open the Share Charm from Within Internet Explorer

1. On the Start screen, locate the blue tile that says Internet Explorer and left-click on it.

2. After Internet Explorer opens, show the Charms bar.

3. Left-click on Share.

4. Notice the menu on the right that appears with links to the Mail app or People app (see Figure 2.5). (The apps that appear here will vary based on what you're using or have installed.)

5. If you have already configured Mail or added a contact in the People app, select the appropriate app to continue. If you have not done this yet, close the Share charm by left-clicking anywhere to the left of the Charms bar.

Figure 2.5   *The Share charm viewed from Internet Explorer*

In Internet Explorer 10 you can share more than just web page links. You can highlight information and then using the Share charm send the HTML portion of your selection instead of the entire page.

Keep in mind sharing is not limited to only the Mail and Contact apps. Your favorite social networking sites like Facebook and Twitter and other social networking platforms can all utilize this Share charm to post information. Look in the Store for popular sharing apps like Tweetro, FlipToast, StumbleUpon, and many more.

Using the Devices Charm

The Devices charm is the place to go when you want to access devices for printing, playing to or otherwise connecting devices from a Windows app. So if you have browsed to a website in the IE10 app that you want to print out, head over to the Devices charm. Need to connect a Bluetooth wireless speaker to your Windows 8 mobile device? Again, go to the Devices charm. If you plug in a second screen, or a TV, use the Devices charm to set it up. Let's see what it takes to print something off the Internet using a printer connected to your system.

LET ME TRY IT

Print a Document Using the Devices Charm

1. Open Internet Explorer from the Start screen.

2. Browse to a page you want to print.

3. Once there open the Charms bar and select Devices.

4. Choose from the list of Printers the one you want to print to.

5. Left-click the Print button (see Figure 2.6).

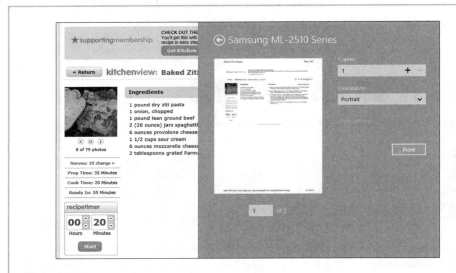

Figure 2.6   *Using the Devices charm to print a page*

Note that the devices listed are context-sensitive for the charm. To illustrate that, follow the same procedure as just outlined but use the Music app instead of Internet Explorer. The option to print won't exist, but if you have a DLNA-capable device on your network you can send content to it through this charm.

In previous versions of Windows we might have gone to the Control Panel, Device Manager, Printers, or other areas to check on our devices. Now, the Devices charm presents a first place to look when searching for devices to utilize Windows 8.

Using the Settings Charm

This charm contains quick access to important system settings and perhaps most importantly, the location where we can put our computer in Sleep mode, restart it, or shut it completely down. In fact, before we go any further let's take a look at these features on the Settings charm.

 **LET ME TRY IT**

Locate the Power Options on the Settings Charm

1. Show the Charms bar.

2. Left-click on Settings.

3. Left-click on Power to show available options.

As explained earlier in the chapter, these power options provide different methods of powering down the system.

The Settings charm is divided into three sections, an upper part consisting of links to various items based on context, a lower section of six icons, and a bottom section that links to the new PC settings (see Figure 2.7).

Figure 2.7   *The Settings charm*

Just like some of the other charms, information presented in the Settings charm is context–sensitive. The dynamic portion of the charm is the upper area with the links. The lower and bottom areas stay the same regardless of where the charm is opened.

Windows 8 Help is located in the upper links of the Settings charm.

SHOW ME   Media 2.1—Using the Charms Bar
Access this video file through your registered Web Edition at
my.safaribooksonline.com/9780789750518/media.

Windows 8 Start Screen

The center area of the Start screen is filled with multicolor customizable tiles that serve as a shortcut to open a specific app. Most of the tiles have one word names that make their use obvious such as Mail, Video, People, Weather, Finance, and Music. Opening and closing the apps is intuitive and easy to do. Since most people know how to use the Internet, let's open the new Internet Explorer app.

Open a Windows 8 App

1.   On the Start screen locate the blue tile that says Internet Explorer (see Figure 2.8).

2.   Left-click this tile to open Internet Explorer.

Figure 2.8   *Notice the first tile—Internet Explorer*

After launching Internet Explorer, you are greeted by the new Internet Explorer 10. The first thing you may notice is that this app uses the full screen to show you the browser. This fully immersive look is the guideline for all Windows 8 apps—a full screen viewing experience that has very little "chrome," that is, tool bars or menus, showing onscreen. Once you've had a good look at Internet Explorer it's time to return to the Start screen.

LET ME TRY IT

Return to the Start Screen from an App

1. On your keyboard press the Windows Key.

> Another option using touch gestures to return to the Start screen would be to press the Start charm located on the Charms bar. This command is discussed later in the chapter.

In the world of Windows some of the basic commands taught from the very beginning may include opening and closing applications. This is important to understand since open applications in previous versions of Windows could use system resources simply by being open. So for many it has become second nature to close applications completely down after finishing working with them so that system resources are not used unnecessarily. While the same principle still holds true when using the traditional Desktop version of Windows 8, the native Windows 8 apps found on the Start screen behave differently than Windows Desktop applications when they are not onscreen and do not need to be closed down.

> Windows 8 apps are the new kid on the block when it comes to Windows, and these apps play by different rules when it comes to leaving or closing the application. Unlike traditional Desktop applications that keep running in the background when they are not visible onscreen, apps are suspended when not visible onscreen.
>
> The idea of leaving a bunch of apps open, even if they are suspended, makes some uneasy, bringing back reminders of older versions of Windows crashing because of too many applications running or slowing down to a crawl and becoming unusable. To help overcome this trepidation to leave multiple apps open, here are some things to keep in mind. First, you can view the resources being used by opening the Task Manager. In some instances, you will notice that under the Status column, the app will be listed as Suspended. This is a low resource mode that keeps the app available and in its last used state when you return to activate it again by showing it onscreen. Even if the app is not listed as Suspended, take note of the other system resources it's using. They will likely be minimal or even listed as 0%.

Second, if you really feel the need to close an app, you can just go ahead and do that. While it's not prominently featured, the ability to close an app still exists for those who feel the need to do so or if a problem occurs and the need arises to restart an app that is misbehaving. Here are four ways to close a Metro app:

- Go to the Switcher list and right click the app; then select Close.
- Use the Task Manager to end the app by selecting the app and then choosing End Task.
- From within the app itself, press Alt + F4 on your keyboard.
- If you are using a mouse, move your mouse pointer to the top of the screen until it becomes a hand and then drag it to the bottom of the screen until it is completely off the screen.

Different Ways to View the Start Screen

Take a look at all your apps on the Start screen now.

 LET ME TRY IT

Navigate Through Start Screen Tiles

1. Move your mouse over the Start screen. Notice the scrollbar that appears at the bottom (see Figure 2.9).

2. Drag this bar to the right to scroll or use the scroll wheel of your mouse (if equipped) to navigate through the tiles.

Of course, as you install applications and apps you may find that you have many tiles that are located on the Start screen. Or you might look at your apps on your Start screen and think that some of them are missing. A feature called Semantic Zoom allows you to see multiple pages of tiles on one screen (see Figure 2.10). Use this to get a bird's eye view of all your apps.

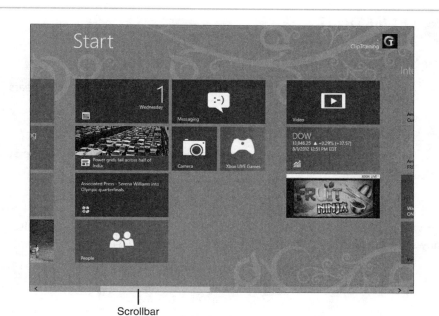

Scrollbar

Figure 2.9   *Scrolling through the Start screen*

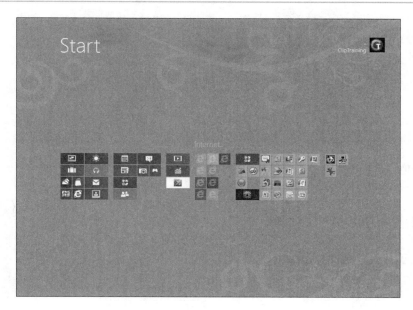

Figure 2.10   *Viewing the Start screen through Semantic Zoom*

 **LET ME TRY IT**

View Start Screen Tiles Using Semantic Zoom

1. Move your mouse over the Start screen. Notice the scrollbar that appears at the bottom.

2. Select the minus sign that appears on the very right of the scrollbar.

3. To return to normal view left-click anywhere on the background of the Start screen.

A different way to view your apps is by using the All apps command. Viewing apps this way shows you more than just the shortcuts from your Start screen; it also shows you all apps available on your system (see Figure 2.11).

Figure 2.11 *Viewing all apps*

 LET ME TRY IT

View All Apps at Once

1. Press Ctrl + Tab.

Or:

1. On the Start screen, right-click and notice the bar that appears at the bottom.

2. Select All Apps in the lower-right corner.

Or, if you are using a touch enabled device:

1. Swipe up from the bottom of the screen.

2. From the bar that appears at the bottom tap All Apps in the lower-right corner.

Keep in mind that when viewing all apps, you are viewing both the Start screen apps and regular applications that are viewed on the Desktop.

By default, administrative tools remain hidden on the Start screen. To see these tools as well, go to the Settings charm from the Start screen and select the link for Tiles in the upper section. Change the switch for Show Administrative Tools from No to Yes. Now head back to the Start screen and scroll to the end to see your system tools.

Now that you know you can see shortcuts for your apps as tiles on the Start screen, let's find out what it takes to modify these same tiles.

Modifying Tiles on the Start Screen

The location of each tile on the Start screen is customizable, meaning you can change your tiles around in almost any configuration you want. Just like shortcuts on the Desktop, tiles can be moved, grouped, and resized. Let's begin by looking at how to resize a tile.

Start screen tiles come in two different sized squares: large and small. Some, but not all, tiles can be resized. Here's how to resize the Desktop tile.

 LET ME TRY IT

Resize the Desktop Tile

1. On the Start screen, locate the Desktop tile and right-click it.

2. From the menu that appears at the bottom of the screen, left-click Smaller (see Figure 2.12).

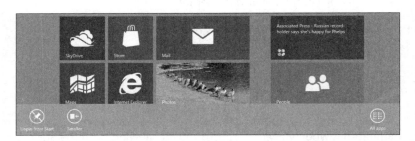

Figure 2.12   *Resizing the desktop tile*

If you're using a mouse and keyboard and change your mind after right-clicking on an app and decide not to resize it or utilize any of the options that appear on the toolbar at the bottom, simply right-click the app tile again to return to the Start screen.

Resizing your tiles in this way can make organizing your Start screen much easier. Take the time to find out which tiles you can resize by selecting the tile as shown here and looking for either Larger or Smaller.

Another aid to organizing the Start screen is moving Start screen tiles. Since Windows logs into the Start screen first each time, you want to have your most frequently used apps front and center. Moving your tiles on the Start screen is as easy as moving shortcuts in the Desktop. Here's how it's done.

 LET ME TRY IT

Moving Start Screen Tiles

1. On the Start screen left-click and hold down on any tile.

2. While still holding down the left-click drag the tile to a different location on the Start screen.

Windows 8 adds an additional layer of organization to the Start screen. If you look carefully as you scroll through the Start screen, you can see divisions between groups of tiles. These divisions help break the tiles into different groups. Can these groups be named, too? They certainly can and here's how to do it.

LET ME TRY IT

Renaming Tile Groups

1. On the Start screen, left-click the small minus sign that appears at the end of the scrollbar on the bottom.

2. Move your mouse over groups of tiles to highlight them.

3. Select a group to rename by right-clicking it.

4. Choose Name Group from the bar that appears on the bottom of the screen.

5. In the white dialog box that appears in the lower-left corner of the screen, create a name for the group (see Figure 2.13).

6. When finished, select the Name button.

7. Swipe down over a group of tiles to select them.

8. Tap Name group from the bar that appears on the bottom of the screen.

9. In the white dialog box that appears in the lower-left corner of the screen, create a name for the group.

10. When finished, tap the Name button.

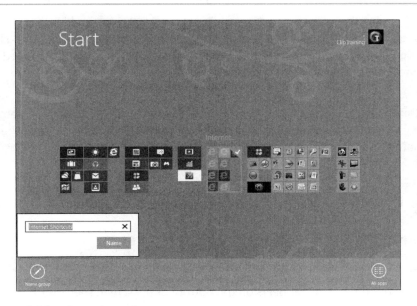

Figure 2.13 *Renaming a tile group*

If you take advantage of this capability to name groups, your Start screen will begin to take shape as an organized, efficient tool. Consider calling your tile groups names such as Internet Shortcuts, Business Tools, or Fun and Games to help differentiate one from the other.

The next feature builds on naming tile groups by offering you the capability to move these groups in one fell swoop.

 LET ME TRY IT

Moving Tile Groups

1. On the Start screen, left-click the small minus sign that appears at the end of the scrollbar on the bottom.

2. Move your mouse over groups of tiles to highlight them.

3. Select a group to move by left-clicking it and dragging it to its new location.

On Internet connected PCs and devices, Windows 8 makes good use of the Start screen by providing *live tiles*. These are tiles that contain updated information from the Internet. By providing this information at a glance, tiles such as Weather, News, Sports, Travel, Finance, Calendar, and Mail can quickly feed you information without you ever having to open the app. This enables you to see the latest info on a variety of interests without ever opening an app or getting on the Internet!

On the other hand, too much data coming at you all at once could lead to "information overload" for you. To balance this out, you have the option of turning live tiles off and then back on later. Keep in mind that not all tiles come equipped with this feature. Let's look at one that does.

In this next example, we use the Weather app to demonstrate how to turn off a live tile. If you have not done so already, open the Weather app and configure a location for it to complete the following steps.

 LET ME TRY IT

Turning a Live Tile Off for an App

1. Locate the Weather app and select it by right-clicking it.

2. From the bar that appears on the bottom of the screen select Turn Live Tile Off (see Figure 2.14).

Or if you are using a touch enabled device:

1. Locate the Weather app and select it by tapping it.

2. From the bar that appears on the bottom of the screen tap Turn Live Tile Off.

Figure 2.14   *Turning off a live tile. Note the command Turn Live Tile Off.*

 SHOW ME   Media 2.2—Working with Live Tiles
Access this video file through your registered Web Edition at
my.safaribooksonline.com/9780789750518/media.

Removing Tiles and Apps

Tiles are added automatically as you install apps and traditional applications. There may be times when you want to remove tiles from the Start screen as well.

> After some applications install, they can bring with them several tiles to the Start screen with features you may rarely if ever use. I recently installed Office 2007 Ultimate onto Windows 8 and to my amazement more than 17 tiles appeared on the Start screen!

You can remove a tile in one of two ways. Uninstalling an app will automatically remove the tile from the Start screen. However, there is also a way to remove the tile without uninstalling the app. This is called unpinning it from the Start screen. You can think of this as if you are deleting a shortcut.

LET ME TRY IT

Unpin a Tile from the Start Screen

1. Locate an app tile you want to unpin from the Start screen.

2. Right-click it.

3. From the bar that appears on the bottom, select Unpin from Start (refer to Figure 2.14).

Follow similar steps to unpin multiple apps from the Start screen.

LET ME TRY IT

Unpin Multiple Tiles from the Start Screen

1. Locate an app tile you want to unpin from the Start screen.

2. Right-click it.

3. Locate other app tiles you want to unpin from the Start screen and select them the same way. You see check marks appear in the upper-right corners of the tiles you select (see Figure 2.15).

4. From the bar that appears on the bottom, select Unpin from Start.

At times you may want to do more than just unpin an app from the Start screen; you may want to uninstall it completely. When removing Windows 8 apps, gone are the days of heading over to the Control Panel and searching for an application you want to remove from your computer from a long list of applications and then waiting for a sometimes tedious uninstall process. (Sad to say, this still exists for traditional Desktop applications in Windows 8, but we talk about that later.) On the Start screen, removing an app makes this process a whole lot easier.

In this next exercise, we go through the steps to uninstall an app. You can select any Windows 8 app and then reinstall it again from the Store. The exception here is if you choose applications that are not Windows 8 apps. In that case, following the steps here takes you to the Uninstall or Change a Program screen in the Control Panel.

Figure 2.15   *Unpinning several tiles at once. Note the command Unpin from Start and the check marks in the selected tiles.*

 **LET ME TRY IT**

Uninstalling an App

1. On the Start screen, locate an app you want to uninstall.

2. Right-click the app and notice the bar that appears at the bottom of the screen.

3. Left-click Uninstall (refer to Figure 2.14).

4. From the box that opens in the lower left, select Uninstall.

Working with the Start Tip

Perhaps one of the first things you did when you started using Windows 8 was move your mouse down to the lower-left corner of the screen looking for the Start button. Were you disappointed in finding a small box instead? Take heart, this small box is actually a useful button called the Start tip (see Figure 2.16).

> Sorry touchscreen users, you won't see the Start tip or Back tip unless you have a mouse connected to your device.

Start Tip

Figure 2.16   *Showing the Start tip*

 LET ME TRY IT

Show the Start Tip

1. From any screen in Windows 8, move your mouse to the lower-left corner until a small thumbnail appears.

2. Click on this to go to the Start screen or the previously accessed interface.

It is interesting to note that the Start tip duplicates the action of pressing the Windows key. In many instances, it will be a fast way to return to the Start screen. In other cases you are launched back into the last app or screen you viewed.

Power users pay attention! Right-click the Start tip to access a powerful menu of commands like Event Viewer, System, Device Manager, Disk Management, Computer Management, Task Manager, Elevated Command prompt, and more.

The Start tip serves another important role. It leads the way to the Switcher interface, which I cover later in this chapter, in the section "Using Switcher." A similar feature, the Back tip also points to the Switcher interface. The Back tip serves in many ways like the Start tip.

Using the Back Tip

Like the Start tip, the Back tip shows the previous experience you were working in with one notable exception: The Start screen will never appear in the Back tip. That also means for the Back tip to be available, there has to be a screen to actually go back to. So if you have just logged in to Windows and have not opened anything, there is nothing to go back to and thus the Back tip isn't available.

 LET ME TRY IT

Show the Back Tip

1. From any screen in Windows 8 (remember you need to open an app to go back to), move your mouse to the upper-left corner until a small thumbnail appears (see Figure 2.17).

2. Click on this to go to the previously accessed interface.

Figure 2.17   *Showing the Back tip*

If you like keyboard shortcuts, then you can think of the Back tip, Start tip, and Switcher as cousins of the shortcut Alt+Tab. The tips and Switcher work in a similar way.

Using Switcher

The purpose of Switcher is to show open apps on a bar that swipes in from the left edge of the screen (see Figure 2.18). How does this work? First, for Switcher to become visible, you need to have multiple apps open. If nothing has been opened, then it behaves like the Back tip and quietly stays invisible until there is an app or interface to present.

Figure 2.18   *Showing Switcher*

Switcher also works with mouse, keyboard, or touch commands, though they can be challenging to execute.

 LET ME TRY IT

Using Switcher to Alternate Between Open Apps

1. Open the Back tip thumbnail and left-click while dragging it down the left side of the screen.

2. A black bar appears showing your open apps. Release the left-click over the black box and Switcher appears.

3. Left-click on an app to launch it.

After Switcher has been opened using the mouse or touch, it stays open on the left side of the screen until a command is given.

Of all the touch-based commands, the ones for Switcher seem to be some of the hardest to master. The back and forth motion is not intuitive and usually takes a few tries to figure out. An alternative option for touch users is using a quick tap and drag motion from the left side of the screen. You can quickly cycle through your apps this way and open just the one you want.

At first glance it may seem that you can only launch an app from Switcher, but you can do more with it. Here is a look at a couple of other features of Switcher:

- **Close Windows 8 Apps**—For mouse users, just right-click on the app and select Close. For touch users, tap an app and drag it to the bottom of the screen until it disappears.

- **Snap Apps**—Mouse users, right-click and select either Snap Left or Snap Right to multitask between apps. (Requires minimum screen resolution of 1355×768.)

What, never heard of Snap? Let's find out what it's all about.

Using Snap

One of the most glaring productivity drawbacks for tablets is their inability to multitask. Not being able to run multiple applications simultaneously onscreen can be a deal breaker for businesses or individuals that require this. Microsoft wanted to make sure that this important feature was not left out of Windows 8 and thus Snap was merged into the OS.

Aero Snap first appeared in Windows 7 and was an easy way to dock two applications side by side. In Windows 8, Aero Snap has been renamed to Snap, and it has slightly different functionality. While it still allows for applications to dock together onscreen, now it's used in conjunction with Windows 8 apps or an app and the Windows Desktop.

If you're thinking of purchasing a computer to run Windows 8, give serious consideration to the screen resolution. Even though Microsoft states that the minimum resolution for Windows 8 is 1024x768, if your screen uses this resolution you'll be missing out on features such as Snap. Why? The minimum screen resolution for Snap is 1366x768. So while screen resolution was not a major factor for many users in purchasing hardware for previous versions of Windows, the new features of Windows 8 like Snap should have you taking a closer look at screen resolution before you purchase.

LET ME TRY IT

Use Snap to Show Two Apps Onscreen

1. Locate and open the Music app by left-clicking it.

2. Select an artist or music and begin playing it.

3. Bring your mouse pointer to the top of the screen until it turns into a hand.

4. Left-click and drag the app over to the left side of the screen.

5. A bar will appear dividing the screen in two vertically. Drop the app on the left side of the bar.

6. Click on the right side of the screen to return to the Start screen.

7. Open Internet Explorer.

8. Drag the vertical bar over to the right side of the screen to switch where the app snaps to (see Figure 2.19).

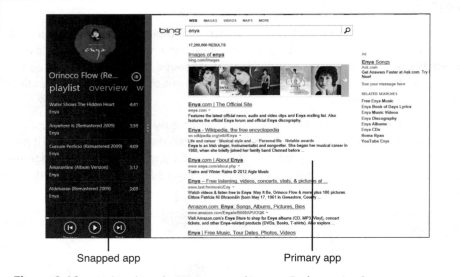

Snapped app   Primary app

Figure 2.19 *Multitasking the Music app and Internet Explorer using Snap*

Using the Desktop

With an eye to the past, Windows 8 offers an app that simulates the look and feel of Windows 7 called Desktop. Selecting this launches Windows 8 into a different look- ing computing environment altogether. One look at it and you can almost hear a collective sigh of relief when new users see familiar sights: We have a Desktop, we have a Recycle Bin, we have a taskbar at the bottom and a Notification Tray to the right side with our clock and other notification items that can be hidden or dis- played. Simply click the Desktop tile to be taken to it.

How do we return to the Start screen? Remember the Charms bar we talked about earlier in the chapter? Let's put the Start charm to good use.

 **LET ME TRY IT**

Return to the Start Screen from the Desktop

1. Show the Charms bar.
2. Left-click the Start charm (see Figure 2.20).

Figure 2.20   *Returning to the Start screen from the Desktop*

Of course this is just one way to do this. You could also use other onscreen interfaces like the Start tip, Back tip, or Switcher. Keyboard users can press the Windows key on their keyboard, and tablet users can press the Windows key if present on their device.

Back in the Desktop, the greatest cosmetic change is the disappearance of the Start button. Its replacement, the Start screen, is a worthy successor and should grow on you quickly the more you use it. Couple that with the functionality of the charms and it's apparent that Windows 8 offers a more powerful solution that surpasses the older Start buttons and orbs. Despite this improvement, some will still no doubt lament the changes that have taken place. Instead of focusing on that, let's see what the Windows 8 Desktop has to offer.

Using the Taskbar and Jump Lists

From within the Desktop app look at the bar at the bottom. This is called the taskbar. Here you see applications, folders, and other items displayed. Note a few existing icons on the taskbar that you can use to quickly access those applications or folders. On the right-hand side of your taskbar is the Notification Area. Here you see your date and time, your network connectivity, and other items that you can choose to continue to display or turn off.

One of the more exciting features of the taskbar is the inclusion of jump lists. To see a jump list you can right-click an icon on the taskbar (or you can left-click the icon and push upward to slide the jump list into view). Jump lists include lists of commonly used actions associated with the application you are selecting (see Figure 2.21).

Figure 2.21   *The Video library pinned to a jump list*

The purpose of jump lists is to quickly take you to items in an app you frequently visit. Small pushpins let you store links to previously visited items so you can access them again with a quick click. This works with websites, documents, presentations, spreadsheets, media, photos, and more.

Obviously applications that are Windows-savvy will be designed to work with jump lists a little better than legacy apps, but that doesn't mean that legacy applications will not receive jump lists too. They just will not be as populated with application-specific functionality.

 LET ME TRY IT

Pin a Location to a Jump List

1. Right-click the File Explorer folder icon located on the taskbar.

2. Note the jump list options. Select one of the Frequent locations like Videos.

3. Left-click the pushpin to pin this to the list.

FINDING THE START MENU KILLER: JUMP LISTS

Offering interesting insight into why Microsoft chose to eliminate the Start Menu, Principal Program Manager Chaitanya Sareen has this to say:

"The Start menu is one of the most visible parts of Windows, and so we don't take any changes we make to it lightly. The environment around Windows has changed immensely since we first introduced the Start menu, and we want to make sure we're still delivering an experience that is both relevant and tuned to the dynamic computing world we live in today. The evolution of the Start menu is inextricably linked with the development of several other related, but disparate concepts, such as application launching, application switching, system notifications, and gadgets."

"The evolution of the Windows taskbar directly impacted the Start menu. What once was locked behind a menu suddenly came closer to you. The most obvious advancements were the introduction of Quick Launch by Internet Explorer 4.0's Windows Desktop Update in 1997, as well as the more recent taskbar pinning in Windows 7." She continues, "85% of people have three or more items pinned to the taskbar compared to a mere 23% who have the same number pinned to the Start menu. Although the taskbar and Start menu have different pinned defaults, many people do customize both of them when they want to. The message is clear that the majority of people want most of their apps on the taskbar rather than having to dig into Start."

"When we visit IT pros, it's not uncommon for us to see a taskbar filled with icons for standard corporate desktops. We even see items like Control Panel pinned to the taskbar to save people a trip to Start. Pinning is also increasing in popularity because you can now also pin websites to your taskbar with IE 9. Fortunately, there's plenty of room on the taskbar—even at 1024x768 the taskbar can hold 22 small icons. Add the power of jump lists, and theoretically, you can also have access to 220 files, folders, and sites at that same resolution! This means that for those who wish to just use Desktop apps, the taskbar provides the room to quickly access the things you need every day without going to the Start menu."

"In summary, the taskbar has evolved to replace many aspects of the Start menu. You can even say the taskbar reveals many of the weaknesses of the Start menu and that the menu is no longer as valuable as it once was long ago. Search and access to All Programs are still unique strengths of the Start menu that we know you depend upon, but when it comes to the apps you use every day, one-click access from the taskbar is hard to beat. You, and many like you, are the ones who gave us this strong feedback over the years, which pushed us to make the taskbar a powerful primary launcher and switcher for the Desktop. In fact, we sometimes even referred to the taskbar in Windows 7 as the "Start bar," since it became clear that most people now start with the bar, rather than with the menu."

Source: http://blogs.msdn.com/b/b8/archive/2011/10/03/evolving-the-start-menu.aspx

Using File Explorer

You might note that File Explorer has changed slightly from Windows 7 (and it has certainly changed from Vista and XP), where it was still called the Windows Explorer. The address bar up at the top is not a static location showing you where you are in the file system. Rather it presents drop-down arrows to allow you to move forward in the structure (if there are more folders to delve into) or backward. That is why it is also known as a breadcrumb bar.

You will note four menu choices at the top of the File Explorer window. These choices expand to open a tab and Ribbon style menu first introduced in Office 2007. The Ribbon tabs are

- **File**—Also known as Backstage view, the File tab contains the following commands:

    - Open New Window

    - Open Command Prompt

- Open Windows PowerShell

- Delete History

- Help

- Close

To the right of the File tab is a "frequent place" list allowing you to pin items there for fast access like taskbar jump lists.

- **Home**—The most frequently used commands are found on the Home tab. They are divided into five groups:

  - **Clipboard**—Contains Cut, Copy, and Paste commands.

  - **Organize**—Contains Move to, Copy to, Delete, and Rename commands.

  - **New**—Contains New Folder, New Item, and Easy Access commands. (See the following Note.)

  - **Open**—Contains Properties, Open, Edit, and History commands.

  - **Select**—Contains Select All, Select None, and Invert selection commands.

Easy Access contains several tools to manage files and folders such as Include in Library, Map as Drive, and Sync. However, one tool may turn out to be a real timesaver; it's called Pin to Start. While not a new name, what it does is completely different than a similar feature in Windows Vista and Windows 7. With Pin to Start, you can pin an app, folder, or drive to the Start screen and have access to this feature quickly on startup without opening any menus.

- **Share**—Three groups make up the Share tab:

  - **Send**—Contains commands such as Email, Zip, and Print.

  - **Share With**—In this group choose between who you want to share items with such as members of your HomeGroup or specific people, or go here to stop sharing something.

  - **Advanced Security**—Offers advanced sharing configuration options.

- **View**—This tab lets you customize File Explorer and equips you to navigate it how you like. The four groups are

  - **Panes**—Modify Explorer to show the Navigation pane, Preview pane and Details pane.

  - **Layout**—Choose from various layout styles such as Icons, Lists, Tiles and Details.

- **Current View**—In this group, you can modify options such as the sort order of items within a column or resizing columns.

- **Show/Hide**—Allows you to show or hide features like file extensions, check boxes and hidden items.

As in the Office Ribbon, you have the option to expand or collapse the Ribbon entirely to a reduced state of just the four tabs appearing onscreen. Look for the up or down arrow in the upper-right corner of File Explorer to do this.

A simple Quick Access Toolbar in the upper left of the screen gives you the opportunity to pin some commonly used commands to the top-left corner of File Explorer. Look for the small dash with a drop-down under it that when clicked reveals these commands.

In a throwback to Windows XP the up arrow has once again been included near the address bar. Click this blue up arrow to quickly jump up a level of system navigation.

Libraries

First introduced in Windows 7, libraries do not replace folders per se. Rather, while you still have folders that hold documents on the traditional side of your system, some of your main locations (like Documents) have been changed into libraries. A library provides you with the ability to see more than one folder's worth of content in one location.

There are default libraries created for documents, downloads, music, pictures, and video. In the case of libraries created by the OS, content styles are programmed in. This means that the library is designed to provide you with a style appropriate to the supposed content.

Creating your own libraries is a great way to store and organize your content. Here's how to make your own library.

 **LET ME TRY IT**

Create a New Library and Add Folders To It

To create a new library in File Explorer:

1. From the Start screen open the Desktop.

2. Open File Explorer by clicking on the folder on the far left of the taskbar.

3. Right-click the Libraries link from the pane on the left.

4. Select New and then choose Library. This creates the new library and gives you the option to name it. At this point you have a library with no folder connecting points.

5. Double-click on the library link and you notice the library is empty (see Figure 2.22).

6. Click on the Include Folder button to navigate to your folder structure and add the folders you want for this library.

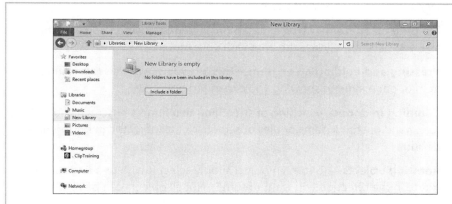

Figure 2.22   *Adding a new library*

You can delete a library you have created without any fear of deleting the folders that make up that library. The library is more of a view of aggregated data from multiple locations. It is not the "folder" itself but a view of the content within that folder aggregated together with data contained in other folders as well.

This brief overview of the Desktop shows that several features have carried right on over from Windows 7. Users coming into Windows 8 from Windows 7 should only experience a minimal learning curve when using File Explorer. And if you've come from Windows Vista, XP, or earlier, the changes you encounter are evolutionary in nature typically requiring little explanation.

Desktop help is available by selecting the little white question mark enclosed in a blue circle located in the upper right of File Explorer. This opens context-sensitive help (though you can navigate to the Help home page or search Help and Support from here as well).

Touch Navigation

Touch commands in themselves are not new to Windows, yet Windows 8 integrates touch into the operating system in a way unheard of in previous versions of Windows. Of course being able to use these touchscreen commands requires a device capable of recognizing touches. Leading the way with these types of devices are tablets, smartphones, and PCs with touchscreens.

There are some differences between the Windows 8 touch paradigm and other touch devices. So to help you get on the right track, here's a look at a few touch commands that work with Windows 8:

- **Tapping on an item**—When you tap on an item such as an app or a link, it is as if you have left-clicked the item with your mouse.

- **Pressing and holding on an item**—This lets you see details regarding an item or open a menu showing you expanded options.

- **Zooming in or out**—Pinching or stretching two fingers onscreen allows you to expand or shrink items or tiles onscreen. Not all objects can be zoomed in or out.

- **Rotating objects**—To turn an object simply select it with two fingers and rotate in the direction you want to turn it. Not all objects can be rotated.

- **Sliding to drag objects**—Frequently this command is used to scroll or pan through pages or lists; however, it can be used for other tasks, such as moving an item or when writing or drawing.

- **Closing apps**—Drag the app from the very top of your screen down to the bottom of your screen. (The app closes itself if you don't use it for a while.)

Windows 8 also offers these same touch gestures for PCs that contain supported trackpads. (Trackpad gestures support varies greatly between devices manufactured prior to Windows 8. Contact your specific hardware manufacturer to see whether your device is supported.) That means that your device is capable of a multi input experience such as mouse, keyboard, touchscreen, trackpad gestures, pen and digital ink notation, and more!

If a certain command is not working for you in a particular app it may not be your fault. Windows 8 apps are not required to support every touch gesture. It may be the specific app you are running does not use that feature. Try the touch gesture again in an app that is likely to support it.

Undoubtedly, Microsoft feels touch will play an important role in the future computing experience. By featuring touch-based gestures in Windows 8, the Windows computing experience takes a new turn into previously uncharted territory.

 SHOW ME　Media 2.3—Touch Navigation
Access this video file through your registered Web Edition at
my.safaribooksonline.com/9780789750518/media.

Keyboard Shortcuts

Advanced Windows users understand that keyboard shortcuts can make quick work out of common commands. Windows 8 continues the use of keyboard shortcuts and readily expands on them.

Many new keyboard shortcuts use the Windows key on the keyboard. At the same time, many Windows 7 keyboard shortcuts have been merged into Windows 8. The lists presented here show Windows 8 keyboard shortcuts that feature the Windows key. Additionally, keyboard shortcuts that are brand new to Windows 8 are highlighted in bold print.

Windows Key—Flips from Start screen last running app or the Windows Desktop

Windows Key + 1, Windows Key + 2, etc.—Go to the app in the given position on the taskbar

Windows Key + B—Switch to the Windows Desktop and choose the tray notification section

Windows Key + C—Open charms

Windows Key + D—Switch to Desktop

Windows Key + E—Switch to File Explorer

Windows Key + F—Go to files in Search charm

Windows Key + H—Show Share charm

Windows Key + I—Show Settings charm

Windows Key + J—Switch focus between snapped and larger apps

Windows Key + K—Show Devices charm

Windows Key + L—Lock PC

Windows Key + M—Minimize Desktop windows

Windows Key + O—Switch screen orientation on supported mobile devices

Windows Key + P—Show the Project pane (for projection options)

Windows Key + Q—Show Search charm

Windows Key + R—Show the Run box

Windows Key + T—Focus on taskbar and cycle through running Desktop apps

Windows Key + U—Show Ease of Access Center

Windows Key + V—Cycles through Notifications

Windows Key + W—Go to Settings in Search charm

Windows Key + Tab—Show Switcher

Windows Key + PrtScrn—Takes a screenshot of the screen and automatically saves it in the Pictures folder

Windows Key + Enter—Launch Narrator

Windows Key + Pause—Show System properties

Other shortcuts that do not use the Windows key on your keyboard are also available. Keep in mind that in many instances, these commands work only in the Desktop app. Listed here are some common ones:

Alt + F4—Shut the current window

Alt + Spacebar—Open the Shortcut menu for current window

Alt + Esc—Switch among open programs in the order that they were opened

Alt + Enter—Show the Properties dialog box for the selected item

Alt + PrtScn—Creates a screenshot of the active Window and saves it to the clipboard

Alt + Up Arrow—Move up one folder level in File Explorer (Like the Up Arrow in XP)

Alt + Left Arrow—Show the previous folder

Alt + Right Arrow—Show the next folder

Shift + Delete—Permanently delete item

Shift + F6—Cycle backward through objects in a window or dialog box

Shift + F10—Show the context menu for the selected item

Shift + Tab—Cycle backward through objects in a window or dialog box

Shift + Click—Choose a consecutive group of items

Shift + Click on a taskbar button—Open a new instance of selected application

Shift + Right-click on a taskbar button—Access the context menu for the selected item

Ctrl + A—Select all

Ctrl + C—Copy the selection

Ctrl + X—Cut the selection

Ctrl + V—Paste the selection

Ctrl + D—Delete the selection

Ctrl + Z—Undo

Ctrl + Y—Redo

Ctrl + N—Open a new window in File Explorer

Ctrl + W—Shut current window in File Explorer

Ctrl + E—Go to the Search box in the upper-right corner

Ctrl + Shift + N—Create a new folder

Ctrl + Shift + Esc—Open Task Manager

Ctrl + Alt + Tab—Use arrow keys to cycle through open windows

Ctrl + Alt + Delete—Open Windows Security screen

Ctrl + Click—Choose multiple individual items

Ctrl + Click and drag an item—Copy an item in the same folder

Ctrl + Shift + Click and drag an item—Make a shortcut for that item in the same folder

Ctrl + Tab—Cycle forward through tabs

Ctrl + Shift + Tab—Cycle backward through tabs

Ctrl + Shift + Click on a taskbar button—Open a program as an Administrator

Ctrl + Click on a grouped taskbar button—Switch through programs in a group

Ctrl + Esc—Switch between Start screen and the last accessed application

Home—Go to the top of the active window

End—Go to the bottom of the active window

Delete—Delete a selected item

Esc—Shut a dialog box or closes a charm

Press Shift 5 times—Turn StickyKeys on or off

Hold down right Shift for 8 seconds—Turn FilterKeys on or off

Hold down Num Lock for 5 seconds—Turn ToggleKeys on or off

Page Up—Scroll left on the Start screen

Page Down—Scroll right on the Start screen

 TELL ME MORE   Media 2.4—A Discussion of Windows 8 Navigation
Access this audio recording through your registered Web Edition at
my.safaribooksonline.com/9780789750518/media.

This chapter helps you make your system an extension of your personality.

3

System Setup and Personalization

System Setup Configuration Options

When setting up your system during the install process you come across a few screens that ask you to begin the personalization process. For example, in Figure 3.1 you can see the Personalize options where you can choose a color and provide a name for your PC.

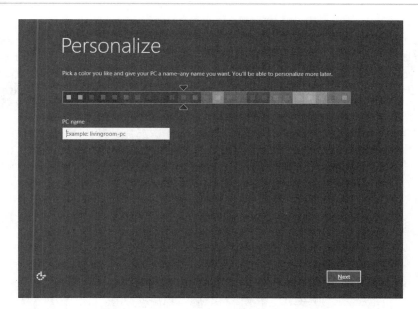

Figure 3.1   *Personalize during the install process*

Once you choose and move forward by selecting Next you are taken to a Settings screen where you can opt for express settings or customize your settings. It is up to you whether you choose to customize your settings now or later. Configuring the settings during the system setup process may be easier than going back and working through each option. However, to move through the install process quickly you might just choose express, which configures the following settings for you:

- Automatically install important and recommended updates.

- Help protect your PC from unsafe content, files, and websites.

- Help improve Microsoft software, services, and location services by sending Microsoft info.

- Check online for solutions to problems.

- Let apps give you personalized content based on your PC's location, name, and account picture.

- Turn on sharing and connect to devices on your network.

If you choose to customize your settings you are asked whether you want to turn on sharing between PCs and connect to devices on the surrounding network. If the network is a home or work network you might choose Yes; however, if it's a public place you might select No.

The configuration of settings in Windows 8 is now much more touch friendly as you learned in Chapter 2, "Navigating the Windows 8 User Interface" (see Figure 3.2). Adjusting settings is handled through drop-downs or on/off switches. You can choose your Windows Update settings during the customization process and also help to protect your PC from unsafe content. The default settings are already chosen for you, so if you don't feel the need to change any of them, you can go ahead and click Next.

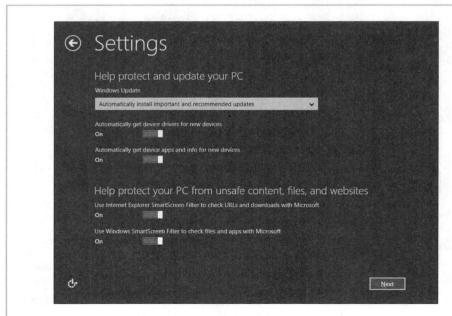

Figure 3.2   *Protection settings during the install process*

Microsoft wants you to help make Windows and apps better by sending information into Microsoft and being part of the Customer Experience Improvement Program and the Help Experience Improvement Program. However, they don't want to force you to be part of these programs so you can see that you have to opt in with a swipe of your mouse or finger to turn settings on or off. Click Next to continue.

During the setup process you can choose to use Windows Error Reporting to check for solutions to problems and use the Internet Explorer Compatibility lists for improved surfing performance. You can also determine whether the apps you are using can share information (that is, your name, picture, and location). Click Next to continue.

The Sign in to your PC screen (shown in Figure 3.3) gives you the ability to configure your system to use an email account to log in. If you sign in with an email it creates a Windows account. If you have one already you should use it to log in to your system. The value in doing this is that it automatically downloads purchased apps from the Windows Store, gets your online content in Microsoft apps automatically, and synchronizes settings online so that your systems automatically look and feel the same (that is, browser history, account picture, and color).

Figure 3.3 *Sign in to your PC*

You might decide to sign up for a new email address (if you don't have one or want to create a new one at this time). Selecting the Sign in Without a Microsoft Account link takes you to an explanation screen that helps to map out the two options for signing in—the Microsoft Account option and the Local Account option. At that point you can choose to use the Microsoft account or local account.

Putting in your Microsoft account has the system check to see whether such an account exists and then asks you for a password for that account.

Upon entering your password you are shown security information that you would have provided within your account profile for your Microsoft account. If that information is accurate, click Next. Your account will be established on your Windows 8 system and an email will be sent to the email address you indicated to confirm your system is trusted and that you made the request. You confirm the system by selecting the link within the email and signing in with your password through the Microsoft Live site.

After your system is all set and ready to begin use you are brought to the Start screen.

For every set of steps in this chapter we will be looking at setup and personalization from either the Start screen or the Windows Desktop. We indicate which in Step 1 of each group of steps.

Customizing Your System

In the event you took the express route through the system configuration options, you can always go back and make adjustments. In this section, we work through the methods and step-by-steps you need to follow to alter your Windows 8 settings in different ways.

 **LET ME TRY IT**

Changing Your Account Picture

There is more than one way to change your account picture. All methods lead you to the same group of settings, however.

1. From the Start screen select (either with mouse or finger) your avatar in the top right-hand corner.

2. Select Change Account Picture.

3. Note you are now taken to the Personalize options under Account Picture settings in your PC Settings options (see Figure 3.4).

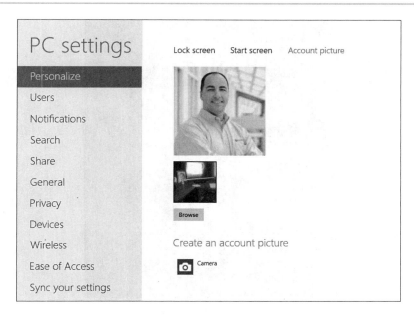

Figure 3.4   *Changing your account picture*

4.   Select the Browse button to choose a new picture.

5.   Choose the picture you wish to use and click Choose image.

> You can see any pictures you've previously used for your account on this screen, so you can choose one of those if you want. If you have a tablet with a camera or a webcam, you can click the Camera button and take a picture for your account.

An Alternate Path

There's another way to access common account settings like those that control your account picture. In Chapter 2 you learned about the Charms bar. From the Charms bar, which you can access from both the Start screen and the Desktop, you can select the Settings charm. Down at the bottom you can select Change PC Settings, as you can see in Figure 3.5. This takes you to the list of settings you saw in Figure 3.4.

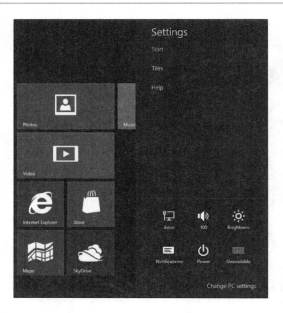

Figure 3.5   *Change PC settings*

 **LET ME TRY IT**

Changing the Look of the Start Screen

You might not like the color scheme you chose originally for your Start screen or the pattern that appears with it. It's easy to change both of these items through your PC Settings options:

1. From the Start screen (or Windows Desktop) bring up the Charms bar.

2. Select the Settings charm.

3. Select the Change PC Settings link.

4. From the left-hand menu select the Personalize option and choose the Start Screen link from the middle working pane.

5. You can change the pattern on the Start screen as well as the color background, as you can see in Figure 3.6.

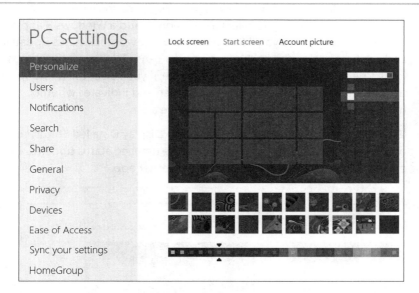

Figure 3.6   *Personalizing your Start screen*

 SHOW ME   Media 3.1—Personalizing Your Start Screen
Access this video file through your registered Web Edition at
my.safaribooksonline.com/9780789750518/media.

 **LET ME TRY IT**

Changing Your Lock Screen

You might have noticed that your system has a Lock screen that shows you a nice graphic and gives you the time. The Lock screen also shows you apps that run in the background and gives you quick status and notifications even though the screen is locked. To configure these settings you do the following:

1. From the Start screen (or Windows Desktop) bring up the Charms bar.

2. Select the Settings charm.

3. Select the Change PC Settings link at the bottom.

4. From the left-hand menu select the Personalize option and choose the Lock Screen link from the middle working pane.

5. As shown in Figure 3.7 you can select a preset picture that Microsoft has provided for you (there are several). Or you can click Browse, navigate to a photo of your choosing, and select that.

6. If you scroll down a bit from the image shown here you'll see a Lock Screen Apps section. If you select a plus sign to add a Windows 8 app to run in the background you'll find that it now shows quick status updates and notifications on the Lock screen. A user can select up to seven apps for the Windows 8 Lock screen. For example, if you select the Mail app a little Mail badge shows up on your Lock screen and indicates whether you have unread messages and how many there are.

7. Click the plus sign under Choose an App to Display Detailed Status. You can only choose one app that can provide more detailed status updates. The Calendar is a good choice for this, as is the Weather app.

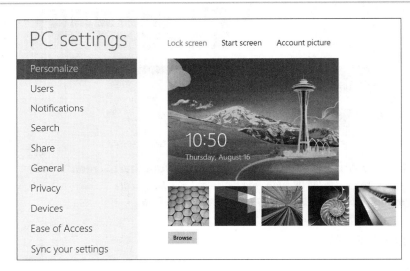

Figure 3.7 *Making Lock screen adjustments*

Although the Lock screen may be great for tablets, some may want to turn it off on their desktop systems. You can do this through the Local Group Policy Editor. To do this you go to the Start screen, type gpedit.msc, and press Enter. Navigate to Computer Configuration, Administrative Templates, Control Panel, and then Personalization. Double-click the entry Do Not Display the Lock Screen and then select Enabled. Click OK to close that window and then close the Local Group Policy Editor. The change takes effect immediately. As a result of this change you will no longer have a Lock screen when you boot or resume from sleep, for example, but will have the sign in screen.

SHOW ME   Media 3.2—Exploring Personalization Settings
Access this video file through your registered Web Edition at
my.safaribooksonline.com/9780789750518/media.

Tile Customizations

Your tiles (also known as *live* tiles) on the Start screen can be adjusted in many different ways. You might want to show administrative tools on the live tiles, or you might want to clear personal information off them. You might want to add new ones or move them around (as you learned in Chapter 2). All of this is possible within Windows 8. Let's review how you can work with various types of tiles.

 LET ME TRY IT

Change an Existing Live Tile

1. From the Start screen right-click or tap and hold an existing live tile.

2. When the App bar appears on the bottom of the screen, note the options you have available (see Figure 3.8). As you can see, with this particular tile you can choose to unpin it from the Start screen, uninstall the app, make the tile smaller, or turn off the "live" functionality of the tile.

3. You can also select a live tile and move it around to a better place on your Start screen.

Figure 3.8   *Making adjustments to live tiles*

Place Apps Where You Need Them

1. From the Start screen either slide your finger up from the bottom or right-click anywhere on the background space to reveal the App bar at the bottom. You see an All Apps icon. Select this option.

2. Note a variety of different types of applications are available including Metro style apps and standard applications (see Figure 3.9).

3. Right-click different apps to show you different options for their use and placement. In addition to the options you saw in Figure 3.8, you have the option to open the app in a window, run it as an administrator, or open the launch file location in File Explorer.

Figure 3.9   *Accessing apps and determining placement*

Adding Administrative Tools to Tiles

Administrative tools are a grouping of important tools that are helpful to network administrators, desktop administrators, and power users to help work with the deeper aspects of your OS. You can find these tools through the Control Panel, but if you work with them often, you might want an easy way to access them through the tiles on your Start screen.

1. From the Start screen bring up the Charms bar.

2. Select the Settings charm.

3. Select the Tiles option up toward the top.

4. Slide the slider option from No to Yes under Show Administrative Tools as shown in Figure 3.10.

You can also clear your personal information from tiles by selecting the Clear button.

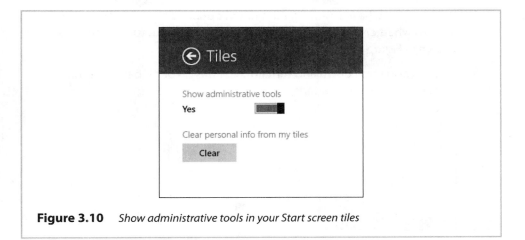

Figure 3.10 *Show administrative tools in your Start screen tiles*

Additional Personalization through PC Settings

There are certainly more settings you can adjust and configure to personalize your system and get it set up. For example, during the initial configuration process that I detailed at the start of this chapter you may have chosen the Express route and now you want to alter the express settings that were automatically chosen. Or maybe you want to peruse all the settings possible and determine on a case-by-case basis which may be worth altering.

It's important to note that there are PC settings options and then there are Control Panel options, which may include display settings for your Windows Desktop and so on. Before moving on to some of the more traditional personalization options within Windows 8 (that mimic many of the same settings found in Windows 7 Desktop personalization) let's review additional personalization through the PC settings options, some of which I discuss and demonstrate in greater detail in the chapters ahead.

Each of the following step-by-steps makes use of the PC Settings screen, which you can access by opening the Charms bar, selecting the Settings charm, and selecting the Change PC Settings link at the bottom of the bar.

Notifications

1. From the left-hand menu on the PC Settings screen, select the Notifications option.

2. At the top you have several configuration options that are on by default, such as whether to show app notifications, but you can turn these off (as shown in Figure 3.11).

3. You can also scroll down and turn notifications on or off based on specific apps that utilize notifications.

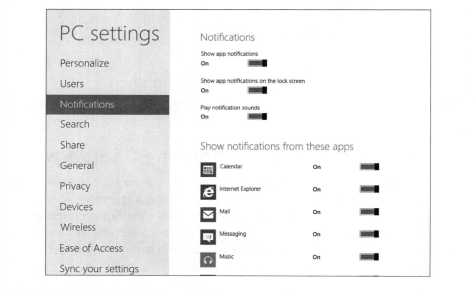

Figure 3.11   *Notification settings*

Search

1. From the left-hand menu on the PC Settings screen, select the Search option.

2. Similar to what you saw in Figure 3.11, at the top you have two configuration options that are on by default and can give you some control over how searches are ordered and saved.

3. You can also scroll down and change how specific apps use the search function.

Share

1. From the left-hand menu on the PC Settings screen, select the Share option (see Figure 3.12).

2. Here you can tweak how apps that can share data are listed and how often you share it.

3. You can also determine the number of items in the list up to 20 items, or choose Clear List.

4. Applications that are designed for sharing are listed as well and you can turn these on or off.

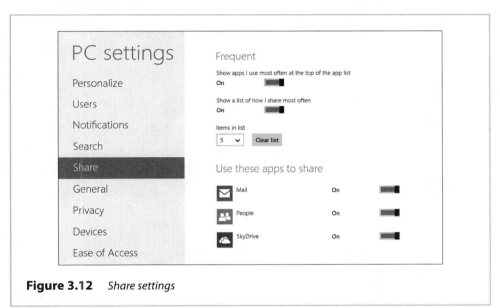

Figure 3.12   *Share settings*

General

1. From the left-hand menu on the PC Settings screen, select the General option (see Figure 3.13).

2. The Time setting allows you to configure your time zone although there are other ways to alter the time zone from the Windows Desktop options and/or Control Panel settings.

3. You can turn app switching on or off (and delete the history).

4. You can turn spelling options on or off (like autocorrect or highlight mis-spelled words).

5. You can add or change input methods, keyboard layouts, and languages.

6. In addition, you can find options to refresh your PC or recycle your PC (options to be discussed later).

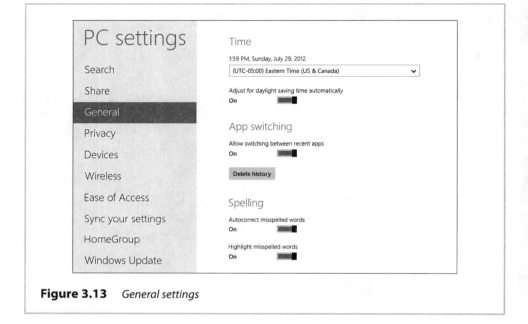

Figure 3.13   *General settings*

Privacy

1. From the left-hand menu on the PC Settings screen, select the Privacy option.

2. There are three privacy settings that determine whether apps can use your location, name, or picture, as well as whether to offer Microsoft anonymous information about your app-based browsing habits.

Devices

1. From the left-hand menu on the PC Settings screen, select the Devices option (see Figure 3.14).

2. You see a list of different devices that have been configured for your system; however, if you need to add a device you can click the Add a Device option at the top to search for devices that have been plugged in to your PC, for network devices, or for Bluetooth devices.

3. The Download Over Metered Connections is turned off by default. Metered connections are typically the sort of connection you use to connect to the Internet over a cellular network. As it says in Figure 3.14, this option is here to help prevent the extra charges some of these networks incur, which are often based on how much data you use. It's best to leave this option on the Off setting so that software related to connected devices doesn't make use of your metered Internet connection.

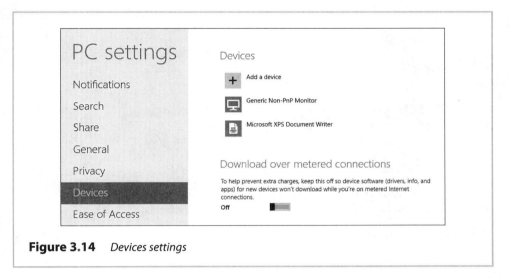

Figure 3.14 *Devices settings*

Ease of Access

1. From the left-hand menu on the PC Settings screen, select the Ease of Access option (see Figure 3.15).

2. These settings help persons with various difficulties to better make use of Windows. For example, you can turn on a higher contrast screen or make everything on the screen bigger to account for issues with your vision. You can also set how long notifications remain onscreen and change the size of the mouse cursor.

Caret navigation is a method of keyboard navigation that allows you to use keys on your keyboard (like Home, End, Page Up, Page Down, arrow keys, and Tab) to navigate through buttons, content, and text entry fields on web pages or on your OS itself.

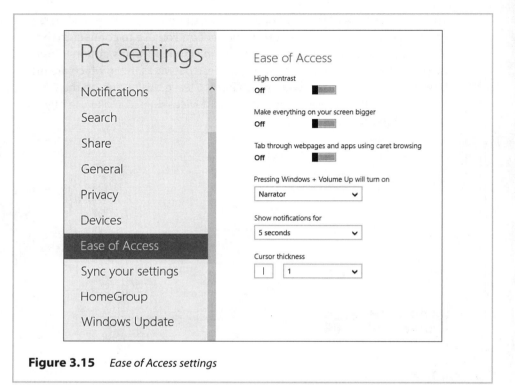

Figure 3.15   *Ease of Access settings*

Sync Your Settings

1. From the left-hand menu on the PC Settings screen, select the Sync Your Settings option.

2. At the top you can turn sync on or off. Then you can scroll down and turn on or off the settings for the following options:

   Personalize: Colors, background, Lock screen and your account picture

   Desktop Personalization: Themes, taskbar, high contrast, and more

   Passwords: Sign-in info for some apps, websites, networks, and HomeGroup

   Ease of Access: Narrator, Magnifier, and more

   Language Preferences: Keyboards, other input methods, display language, and more

   App Settings: Certain app settings and purchases made in an app

   Browser: Settings and info like history and favorites

   Other Windows Settings: File Explorer, mouse, and more

3. Sync over metered connections is another option, similar to the version of this control we covered in the "Devices" section, where you can choose whether to sync settings over metered connections (on/off) and choose to sync settings over metered connections even when roaming (on/off).

HomeGroup

1. From the left-hand menu on the PC Settings screen, select the HomeGroup option.

2. If there are no available HomeGroups on your network you can create one. If HomeGroups are available you can join them if you have the password.

> HomeGroups are covered in greater detail in Chapter 7 "Home Networking."

Windows Update

1. From the left-hand menu on the PC Settings screen, select the Windows Update option.

2. You can click the Check for Updates Now option to tell Windows to immediately look for updates to the Windows 8 operating system.

> To configure Windows Update settings you would go through the Control Panel itself.

Windows Desktop Personalization

The split personality of Windows 8 includes a split personalization settings issue. So far we have discussed the Start screen settings and the PC settings you can configure using the options provided through Settings on the Charms bar.

However, if we want to focus on the personalization of the Windows Desktop itself there are alternative methods for doing so that include accessing them through the Control Panel options, the taskbar settings, and so forth.

Accessing the Control Panel

The Control Panel is accessible in a couple of different ways. One way is by going to the Windows Desktop, accessing the Charms bar, selecting Settings, and then looking for the Control Panel shortcut link up at the top. Both this option and the Control Panel are shown in Figure 3.16.

Figure 3.16 *Accessing the Control Panel*

The Control Panel (discussed thoroughly throughout the book) can also be accessed from the Start screen by typing "Control Panel". It automatically comes up in the options for you to select.

Once you have the Control Panel up on the Windows Desktop you can view and adjust your computer's settings by Category or you can select the down arrow next to View By and choose either Large or Small icons.

Changing Display Settings

Your Display settings can be located through the Control Panel. You can also get to them quickly by working off the Screen Resolution settings, accessed off the desktop through a shortcut you can access by right-clicking the desktop and choosing Screen Resolution.

The Screen Resolution settings are easy to work with (see Figure 3.17). You can choose your display and resolution. You can click the Detect button to locate attached monitors/projectors. Click the Identify button to display a number for the display you are looking at. Using that information, you can choose the monitor and the display and resolution settings for that particular monitor (which is especially helpful in a multi-monitor situation).

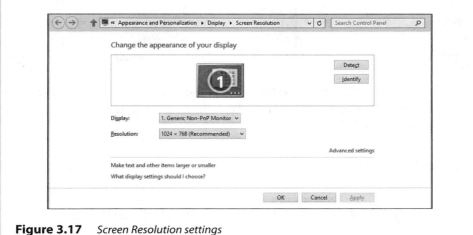

Figure 3.17   *Screen Resolution settings*

If you click the link Make Text and Other Items Larger or Smaller, you return to the Display settings (see Figure 3.18). (Or you can click the Display option in the address bar.) The Display screen is where you can choose Smaller, Medium, or Larger; each option provides a Preview of what that particular display looks like.

You can also select the Custom Sizing Options link to set custom text size options and change your text size to a size that suits your needs. You can select the Change Only the Text Size drop-down arrows to change the size (and add Bold) to the following options: Title Bars, Menus, Message Boxes, Palette Titles, Icons, and Tooltips.

You can also quickly select one of the links to the left to make other changes, such as calibrate the display's color.

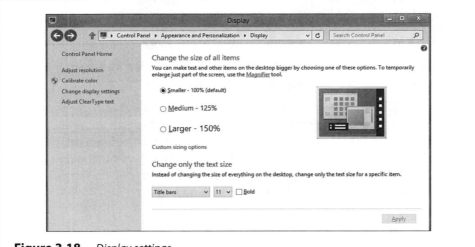

Figure 3.18   *Display settings*

One of the quirky aspects to the Display panel is that the Adjust Resolution link and the Change Display Settings link each returns you to the Screen Resolution options.

Clicking the Adjust ClearType Text link displays the ClearType Text Tuner, which you can use to turn ClearType on or off and then click through various steps of a wizard to refine your ClearText.

 **LET ME TRY IT**

Adjusting Your System to Work with Multiple Monitors

Using multiple monitors connected to a single system is an increasingly popular option in the computing world. You might, for example, need a little more screen real estate with your particular type of job or to operate more smoothly in your work or hobby. To control how Windows 8 treats your multi-monitor setup, follow these steps:

1. Connect both monitors to the computer and ensure your system recognizes both of them.

2. Right-click the desktop and choose Screen Resolution.

3. Both monitors should display in the preview window. Click Monitor 1.

4. Below the preview image, note the Display, Resolution, Orientation, and Multiple Displays settings.

5. Click Monitor 2. Note its settings as well (display, resolution, and so on).

6. Click the monitor you want to use as your main display. Make sure the Make This My Main Display check box is checked for this monitor.

7. If you want to duplicate the screen from your primary display onto your secondary display, select the Multiple Displays drop-down arrow and choose Duplicate Displays (which makes the second monitor a duplicate of the primary monitor). Otherwise, you will probably want to leave the default Extend These Displays option selected (which provides the extension of screen real estate you may be looking for).

8. If it's difficult for you to determine which monitor represents which number in the preview window, click the Identify button. Large numbers display on your monitors so that you can more easily discern which monitor is which.

9. You can also drag the monitor images at the top to tell Windows what the arrangement of display should be. Just select the monitor graphic and drag to see how you can manipulate these.

You can also pan wallpaper across multiple monitors or put a different wallpaper on each monitor. From the Desktop, just right-click anywhere on the background and choose Personalize to get to the configurations. The new feature here is the Span Picture Position choice at the bottom of the dialog. This lets you extend a single image across your multiple screens, as opposed to duplicating the same on each. You can still choose the repeated background, and whether to stretch, fit, fill, tile, or center the background image. To choose a different background for each display in the same Personalization/Desktop Background dialog, you right-click a background image's thumbnail, and a choice of your numbered monitors pops up (for example, Set for Monitor 1). Click the monitor on which you want the current image to display.

Altering Personalization Settings

As for Personalization settings Windows 8 supports different Themes, which combine a background color or image, a glass or window theme, a sound scheme, and a screen saver to form a unique theme style. You can package themes to share them with others.

Accessing Personalization settings can be done through the Control Panel by looking for the Personalization app. You can reach these settings by also going through the Control Panel using the Category view and choosing the Appearance and Personalization link. From there you can see all sorts of configuration options (shown in Figure 3.19). You can also right-click your Windows Desktop and choose Personalize. In addition you can go through the Charms bar: Select the Settings charm and then select the Personalization link, which takes you to the Personalization settings shown in Figure 3.20.

You can configure any type of theme you want. You can choose preconfigured ones or click the Get More Themes Online link. You can also alter desktop icons, mouse pointers, and so forth.

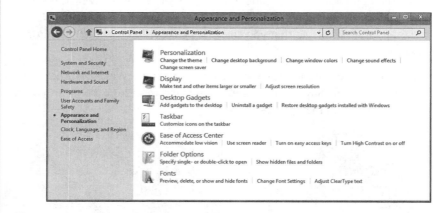

Figure 3.19   *Accessing Personalization settings*

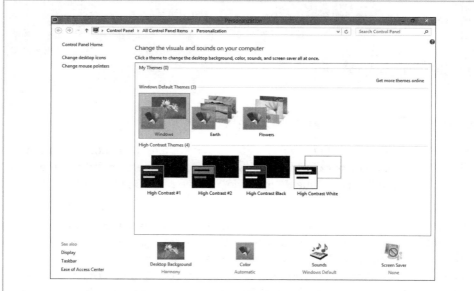

Figure 3.20   *Windows Desktop Personalization settings*

Adjusting Your Themes

When you are ready to add a little personality to your system, you typically want to start with the background.

1. Right-click your desktop and then select Personalize. You can now change the visuals and sounds of your operating system. You will also notice under the My Themes section that you can click Get More Themes Online to access more themes.

2. Note that you can select from among several preconfigured themes.

3. If you click each theme, the Desktop Background, Window Color, and Sounds settings (all listed below the list of themes) change to reflect your selection. When you click each setting, you can customize each theme.

4. Click your preferred theme and then close the Personalization box. You have now changed your desktop theme. You might have noticed the Screen Saver link and that, by default, no screen saver is selected. You learn how to customize a screen saver next.

 LET ME TRY IT

Customizing Your Screen Saver

There are a variety of different screen savers to choose from, and the following steps show you how you can adjust the one you are using:

1. Right-click your desktop and select Personalize.

2. At the bottom-right of the Personalization window, click the Screen Saver link to display the Screen Saver Settings dialog box (see Figure 3.21).

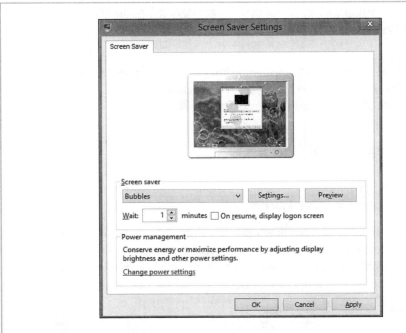

Figure 3.21   *Screen Saver settings*

3. In the Screen Saver area, click the down arrow to display the list of available screen savers.

4. For this example, choose Photos.

5. Click the Settings button to display the Photos Screen Saver Settings dialog box.

6. In this dialog box, click Browse to select a folder that contains the photos you want to use for your Screen Saver. You can also adjust the Slide Show Speed at which the photos change—Fast, Medium (the default), or Slow. Click the Shuffle Pictures box if you want to shuffle the photos.

7. After you choose your settings, click Save to save your changes and return to the Screen Saver Settings dialog box.

8. In the Screen Saver Settings dialog box, click Preview to see your screen saver in action. In the Wait box, you can set how many minutes to wait before your screen saver turns on. If you check the On Resume, Display Log on Screen box, you will be prompted for a username and password when Windows 8 comes out of the Screen Saver mode.

9. After you choose your settings, click OK to save the settings and close the dialog box. The Screen Saver Settings dialog box also provides you with Power Management options via the Change Power Settings link. Click this link to see your options. Power options are covered in greater detail in Chapter 10, "System Configuration Settings."

 SHOW ME   Media 3.3—Adjusting Your Background and Screen Saver
Access this video file through your registered Web Edition at
my.safaribooksonline.com/9780789750518/media.

 **LET ME TRY IT**

Configuring the Taskbar

To access the taskbar properties in Windows, simply right-click the taskbar and choose Properties. You can also locate the Taskbar item from within Control Panel. There is also a Notification Area Icons item that you can select from within Control Panel if you are looking at large or small icons rather than a category view.

You can learn about the differences between Control Panel icons and category views in Chapter 10.

Whatever manner you choose to access properties for your Start menu and taskbar, you will note three tabs on the window that appears: Taskbar, Jump Lists, and Toolbars.

Taskbar Tab

On the Taskbar tab, shown in Figure 3.22, you can select or deselect the following taskbar appearance options:

- Lock the Taskbar

- Auto-Hide the Taskbar

- Use Small Taskbar Buttons

You can also determine the Taskbar Location On Screen (Bottom, Left, Right, or Top). In most cases, users choose Bottom (the default setting).

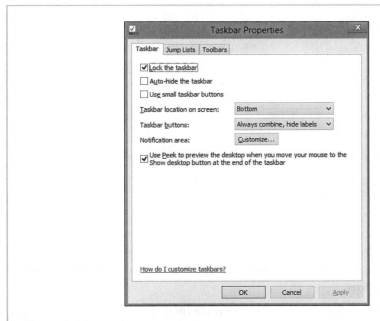

Figure 3.22 *Taskbar properties*

The Taskbar Buttons options allow you to determine how you want your applications and such to appear in the taskbar. A taskbar button is an icon that represents a program or document that you have opened. As you open more programs and documents, you create clutter on your taskbar. By using the Taskbar Buttons feature, you can choose to Always Combine, Hide Labels, Combine When Taskbar Is Full, or Never Combine.

The Taskbar tab also includes a Notification Area section (see Figure 3.23). Click the Customize button to display the Notification Area Icons dialog window, where you can select which icons and notifications appear in the Notification Area (which is also known as the notification tray or system tray). These options allow you to hide certain icons and notifications from your notification tray, which you may want to do if there are icons or notifications that you don't want or need to see. (This does not stop the programs behind these icons from running, however.)

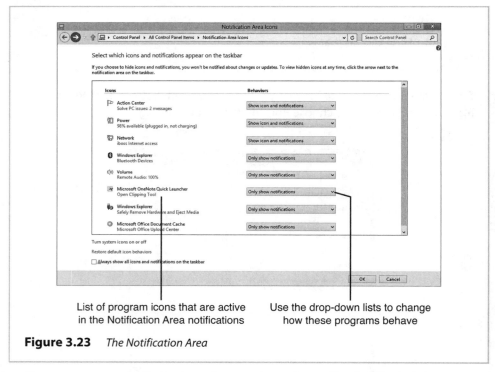

List of program icons that are active   Use the drop-down lists to change
in the Notification Area notifications   how these programs behave

Figure 3.23   *The Notification Area*

If you want to set the behaviors of system icons (items like the Clock, Volume control, Power options, and so on), click the Turn System Icons On or Off link near the bottom of the window.

There is also a check box you can use to turn on or off on the Taskbar tab that says Use Peek (previously called Aero Peek) to Preview the Desktop When You Move Your Mouse to the Show Desktop Button at the End of the Taskbar. This button used to be a little sliver that was easy to see but it isn't defined as an actual button any longer. Now, you just have to know it is there by hovering your mouse over the Show Desktop square, which makes other windows transparent.

 **LET ME TRY IT**

Adjusting the Notification Area

The following steps show you how to remove the Action Center icon from the Notification Area while still allowing notifications to continue to be shown from the Action Center.

1. Right-click the taskbar and select Properties to bring up the Taskbar Properties dialog box. The Taskbar tab displays by default.

2. On the Taskbar tab, in the Notification Area section, click the Customize button. A list of icons and their respective behaviors displays.

3. For the Action Center icon, click the Behaviors drop-down and choose Only Show Notifications.

4. Click OK.

With XP and Vista, the default behavior of the Notification Area (also known as the system tray) is for application icons to just jump into the tray until the point at which the icons grew to annoying proportions. Windows 7 (and now 8) prevents this by allowing only six (it was five in Windows 7) standard items (Action Center, Power, Network, Volume, Input Indicator, and Clock), all of which can be seen by clicking the Turn System Icons On Or Off link from the Notification Area settings. As you add new applications to the taskbar, their icons and notifications are hidden by default. If you want to show them, you have to adjust their respective notifications.

Jump Lists Tab

On the Jump Lists tab, shown in Figure 3.24, you can determine the number of recent items to display in jump lists (the default being 10 items).

There are also Privacy settings where you can select or deselect the options to Store Recently Opened Programs and/or Store and Display Recently Opened Items in Jump Lists.

Toolbars Tab

You have a few toolbars you can add to the taskbar from the Toolbars tab in the Taskbar Properties dialog (see Figure 3.25). You can add the Address toolbar, the Links toolbar, the Touch Keyboard toolbar, or the Desktop toolbar.

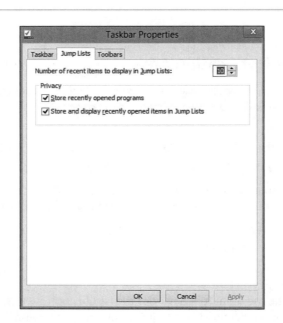

Figure 3.24   *The Jump Lists tab*

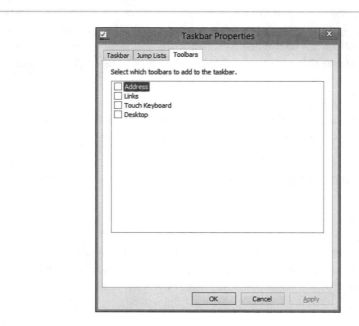

Figure 3.25   *The Toolbars tab*

 **LET ME TRY IT**

Adding the Address Bar to the Taskbar

There are toolbars you can add to your taskbar to help you personalize the bar.

1. Right-click the taskbar and select Properties to bring up the Taskbar Properties dialog box.

2. Click the Toolbars tab.

3. Select the Address check box and click OK. You now see an Address bar located on the taskbar.

There is a shorter way to get this done. Right-click the taskbar, go to Toolbars, and then click Address. You can use this same approach to add any toolbar you want to see on your taskbar.

Configuring Time Options

Typically, the Date and Time options are part of a discussion of the Control Panel because you find those settings there. However, your clock is part of your initial Desktop settings. And in Windows 8, you can take advantage of some cool options.

For example, you can actually set up multiple time zone clocks to be displayed for your personal or business needs.

To see the time and current calendar month, you can click the Time/Date option in your Notification Area. Click the Change Date and Time Settings link to display the Date and Time dialog box (see Figure 3.26).

This dialog box features the following tabs:

- **Date and Time**—Configure your Date, Time, and Time Zone settings, and more.

- **Additional Clocks**—Select the Show this Clock check box to display up to two additional time zones.

- **Internet Time**—Synchronize your system time with an Internet-based time server (typically already determined). You can click the Change Settings button to choose a different Internet time server.

Figure 3.26   *Date and Time dialog box*

 **LET ME TRY IT**

Adding an Additional Clock to the Notification Area

You might need or simply want to know at a glance what the time is in other parts of the world. Windows 8 allows you to add two additional clocks to your Notification Area.

1. Click the time and date on your taskbar to display a larger view of the calendar and clock.

2. Click the Change Date and Time Settings link. The Date and Time dialog box displays.

3. Click the Additional Clocks tab (see Figure 3.27).

4. Select the first Show this Clock check box so you can choose a time zone and a display name.

5. Click the Select Time Zone drop-down arrow and choose a time zone different from the one you already use.

6. In the Enter Display Name box, type a display name for the additional clock. Click OK.

7. Hover your mouse over the date and time on your taskbar, and you see the other time zones you have configured (see Figure 3.27).

Figure 3.27 *Multiple time zones*

This is a great tool for travelers who like to call home or for business employees who have offices and clients in other time zones.

 **LET ME TRY IT**

Change Desktop Icons

Maybe you like having the Recycle Bin on your Windows Desktop. Maybe you don't. Perhaps you prefer more icons. Whatever your preference you can alter the icons by performing the following:

1. From the Windows Desktop right-click and choose Personalize.

2. From the Personalization settings note the link to the left Change Desktop Icons. Select this link.

3. From the Desktop Icon Settings dialog, shown in Figure 3.28, you can turn additional icons on/off such as Computer, User's Files, Network, Recycle Bin, and Control Panel.

4. To alter the icon for various desktop icons, click the Change Icon button and choose additional graphics. To reset the default icons, click Restore Default.

5. The Allow Themes to Change Desktop Icons option is useful if you download and utilize a theme that has unique icons to go along with it.

Figure 3.28   *Desktop Icon Settings dialog*

 TELL ME MORE   Media 3.4—A Discussion of System Set-Up and Personalization in Windows 8

Access this audio recording through your registered Web Edition at
my.safaribooksonline.com/9780789750518/media.

In this chapter, we look at Mail, Photos, Videos, and Music. These built-in apps enhance the Windows 8 experience and are simple to learn.

4

Mail, Photos, Video, and Music

Using the Mail App

Our look at four key apps in the Windows 8 modern UI begins with an app that's as simple to use as its name implies—Mail. Mail allows you to access several different email accounts from one location. Since many people have multiple email accounts, the Mail app accommodates them by allowing for them to receive all their mail in one location.

The Mail app allows you to set up accounts from

- Hotmail.com
- Live.com
- MSN.com
- Exchange
- Office 365
- Outlook.com
- Google

 **LET ME TRY IT**

Setting Up a Mail Account

When you first start Mail, you are prompted to add your email from one of the account types listed in the previous section. With your login information for the account type in hand, here's how to do it:

The following steps show a typical sign in process using an Outlook.com account. Your steps may vary depending on the mail service you use.

1. On the Start screen click the Mail app to open it.

2. A screen appears requesting your existing email address. (You cannot use the Mail app unless you already have an existing email address.)

3. Enter the email address and password and then click Connect (see Figure 4.1).

4. Your account automatically loads showing your mail.

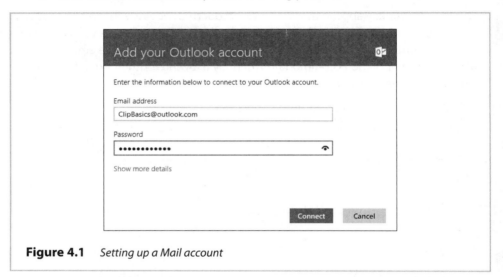

Figure 4.1 *Setting up a Mail account*

In most cases, a three pane view opens that represents the major working interface in Mail (see Figure 4.2).

To add additional mail accounts, just go to the Settings charm and select Accounts at the top. You have the opportunity to add more accounts just like you added the first one.

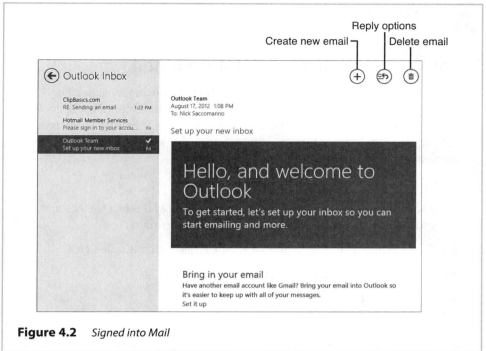

Figure 4.2   *Signed into Mail*

Here are the main areas in Mail:

- **Accounts pane**—Located on the left, this pane provides access to each account you have set up in Mail. Next to each account name appears the number of unread messages for that account.

- **Mailbox folder pane**—This shows the current folder in the selected email account.

- **Reading pane**—This shows the email message you have selected.

If your display is large enough, it shows all three panes simultaneously.

The Start screen uses live tiles to quickly update you with current information. The Mail application also uses a live tile that can be turned on or off. Keep in mind that it only shows information for new emails, so if you don't see any information at first, be patient. Once you get a new email it shows up on the Mail tile letting you preview some of the content before you actually open it.

 **LET ME TRY IT**

Sending, Replying, and Deleting Email

With your email account(s) loaded, you're ready to start using Mail. Reading your email is simple. Just select any email from the left pane and it appears in the Reading pane. The most commonly used actions for email are represented by three small buttons in the upper-right corner of the app (refer to Figure 4.2). Let's see how to send an email using the first button.

1. On the Start screen, open the Mail app.

2. If you have more than one email account, locate and select the account you want to send the email from on the Accounts pane.

3. Click the button that resembles a + sign. (This button is called New.)

4. Enter the email recipient's address in the To field.

5. Add a subject.

6. Add a message.

7. After your email is composed and ready to send, click the Send button in the right corner (see Figure 4.3).

That's it, your message is on its way!

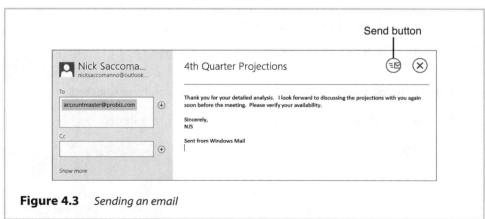

Figure 4.3 *Sending an email*

Don't be fooled by the seeming lack of commands. Showing the Mail app bar by right-clicking from within an email you are composing or swiping down from the top edge of the screen lets you pick from options like:

- Save Draft
- Attachments

- Font

- Bold, Italic, and Underline

- Text Color

- Emoticons

- And the More button at the end of the bar gives you the additional choices of adding a Bulleted list, Numbered list, Undo, or Redo commands.

Replying to an email follows the same steps as shown previously with the exception of step 3. Instead of clicking the New button, select the Respond button to the right of it that looks like an envelope with a curved arrow pointing to it (refer to Figure 4.2). This gives you three options:

- **Reply**—Use this to reply to the person who sent you the email.

- **Reply All**—Use this to reply to all email addresses the last email was sent to.

- **Forward**—Send the selected email to a different recipient from the one who sent it.

The last button in the trio looks like a trash can. Called Delete, this button lets you send any email you have to the Deleted items folder.

 **LET ME TRY IT**

Moving, Marking, or Pinning Mail to the Start Screen

From time to time you may want to move email around, say from your Junk folder to your Inbox. This process is easily accomplished as follows:

1. From the Start screen, open the Mail app.

2. Navigate to the email you want to move.

3. Right-click to bring up the app bar at the bottom.

4. Click Move.

5. Notice how the Mailbox folder pane and the Reading pane become washed out. From the Accounts pane on the left, select the folder where you want to move the email to.

6. The message has moved. To verify this, open the folder to double-check the move completed successfully.

Another option on the app bar is to mark an email as unread. You can follow almost all of the same steps provided here to do this except step 4. Instead, choose Mark Unread to show your selected email as unread. Notice also the number that appears to the right of your email folder in the Accounts pane when you do this. This number changes as you change the number of unread items in the folder.

You may also want to pin a particular email to the Start screen, which makes a specific email appear on the Start screen with a unique tile that resembles a moving envelope (see Figure 4.4).

Mail with a live tile update

Figure 4.4   *The Mail app with live tile updates*

Using Charms with Mail

Finally, while they may be easy to forget at first, charms open up powerful app-specific features. Here's a brief look at a few charms and how they can be used with the Mail app:

- **Search charm**—When you want to search your email, use the Search charm to quickly locate items.

- **Devices charm**—Use this to quickly print your emails from hardware connected to your device.

- **Settings charm:** Configure accounts, set permissions, and more from this charm.

 SHOW ME   Media 4.1—Using the Mail and People Apps
Access this video file through your registered Web Edition at
my.safaribooksonline.com/9780789750518/media.

Using the Photos App

Another new app, Photos, demonstrates the essence of the modern UI that Windows 8 brings to devices. Photos is not a location where you actually store pictures. Instead, it's a place where you go to view your photos from different sources. These sources can include anything from your computer to Internet locations like Facebook, SkyDrive, and Flickr. The ability to channel all these sources from one spot makes this a pretty handy app.

Built for showcasing your photos, this app has a gorgeous but simple look that belies what's going on under the hood. Open the Photos app by going to the Start screen and locating the Photos tile. The first thing you'll notice is the large tiles at the bottom, which represent the various sources where the app looks for your photos (see Figure 4.5).

Figure 4.5   *The Photos app*

 **LET ME TRY IT**

Showing a Picture from the Picture Library

If no photos show up in a photo source it means that source has no photos in it at this time, or your account with photos (like Facebook or Flickr) has not yet been set up in Photos. If you do have photos in it, you can open them quickly by following these steps:

The following exercise requires pictures to already be placed in your Pictures folder. If you have not done so already, locate a picture and use File Explorer to place it in the Pictures folder. Once this is completed, you can proceed with the following steps.

1. On the Start screen open the Photos app.

2. Select the Pictures Library tile.

3. Select the picture you want to look at.

4. To return to the Pictures library, left-click on the screen or press the Esc key on your keyboard.

5. An arrow with a circle around it appears in the upper-left corner of the screen. Left-click it to return to the Pictures library.

6. Left-click the arrow in the upper-left corner to return to the start of the Photos app.

One of the nice things about using a touch enabled device is how easy it is to navigate between pictures with just a quick swipe; or use the pinch command to turn a series of pictures into thumbnails for quick viewing. Mouse users will notice that subtle arrows appear on the screen edges letting you move forward or backward through pictures (see Figure 4.6). Keyboard users, you're not left out either. Use the left and right arrow commands on your keyboard to move through your collection.

Figure 4.6   *Navigating through pictures (notice the arrow on the right)*

Now that you know how to view your pictures, take a moment to set up your accounts if you have them with SkyDrive, Facebook, or Flickr. Pretty soon the pictures that you have uploaded and shown off to friends will be on display.

 **LET ME TRY IT**

Selecting a Background Photo

You may want to use a newly loaded picture as the background for the Lock screen, the App tile or the App background itself. The following steps show you how to do just that.

1. On the Start screen open the Photos app.
2. Select a location that contains the picture you want as the background.
3. Locate and select the picture.
4. Right-click the picture.
5. Choose Set as in the lower left on the bar (see Figure 4.7).
6. Select App Background.
7. A message appears saying "Setting App background...."
8. Navigate back to the start of the Photos app to see your new background.

Figure 4.7　*The Photos app bar*

 **LET ME TRY IT**

Displaying a Slide Show

Another feature of Photos is the ability to display your pictures automatically as a slide show. This too is easily done.

1. On the Start screen open the Photos app.

2. Select a location that contains the picture you want as the background.

3. Locate and right-click the picture from where you want the slide show to begin.

4. From the bar that appears at the bottom, select Slide Show (refer to Figure 4.7).

5. To end the slide show, right-click anywhere on the screen.

6. A back arrow appears in the upper-left corner of the screen. Left-click this to end the slide show.

Using Charms with Photos

The power of the Photos app becomes apparent when you also utilize charms to access your photos. Here's a brief look at some ways they can be used:

- **Search charm**—Use this charm to quickly find pics (see Figure 4.8).

- **Share charm**—An easy way to share your pictures. Just find a picture you want to share and then use the Share charm to bring up a sharing app like Mail.

- **Devices charm**—As in other apps, this charm lets you connect to hardware (such as printers or fax machines), enabling you to print or send a specific picture.

- **Settings charm**—Go here to configure app-specific settings. Select Options to see your choices. Also use this charm to locate Photos Help files.

Figure 4.8   *Using the Search charm to locate photos*

 SHOW ME   Media 4.2—Working with the Photos App
Access this video file through your registered Web Edition at
my.safaribooksonline.com/9780789750518/media.

Using the Xbox Video App

Clicking the Video tile starts the Xbox Video app, Windows 8's new and simple video player. If you're wondering what happened to Windows Media Player, you can rest easy. Windows 8 ships with Windows Media Player 12, which has the familiar style that has existed through several iterations of Media Player. Video is a brand new player that simplifies the process of playing videos. With large-sized controls and a simple interface, you'll be watching videos in it in no time.

Watching a Video

Just follow these steps to start watching a video.

The following steps show you how to play a video from within the Xbox Video app. To do this, make sure you first have placed a video in your Videos folder, which can be accessed through File Explorer. Once you have done that, you can proceed to the following steps.

1. On the Start screen left-click the red Video tile. This tile has a red triangle pointing right representing a Play symbol on it.

2. After the Videos app opens, play a video from the My Videos section by left-clicking on it.

3. Pause the video by left-clicking again on it.

4. Click the back arrow in the upper-left of the screen to return to Videos (see Figure 4.9).

Figure 4.9   *Playing a video using Xbox Video*

If you have used the Windows Phone video player you'll feel right at home with this player. Controls are easy to spot and intuitive (for some this is a welcome change compared to other Windows 8 apps). Of course, like other apps, some controls are hidden off the screen. To show these controls, right-click or swipe down from the top edge to show the control bar at the bottom of the app. There you have access to these simple controls:

- **Repeat**—Automatically plays the video over at the end

- **Previous**—Plays the last video

- **Play**—Plays the currently loaded video

- **Next**—Skips to the next video

- **Play To**—Allows the movie to be shared with devices such as an Xbox 360

PLAYING CONTENT FROM REMOVABLE MEDIA IN VIDEOS

With Windows 8's new focus on tablets many users will want to load up a storage card like an SD card or USB jump drive with videos or music and take their collection on the go. This idea is great since some tablets contain limited drive space. So popping in some removable media and playing a specific song or video is easy enough.

But what about if you want to add your collection on the removable media to your Windows 8 Video (or Music) Library? That's where the problems begin. Windows libraries do not permit non-hard drive based removable storage into the library. Try it and you get an error message from the Windows Libraries dialog box stating "This folder can't be included because it's on a removable device." Fortunately, there is a way to get around this, and it's not that hard. It involves creating a shortcut to the media on your drive.

1. On your Windows 8 device with the removable media inserted, make a shortcut to the media device on your desktop. Call it something obvious like MEDIA.

2. Move the shortcut to your C: drive and place it on the root of it. Now you have a shortcut to your media at C:\MEDIA.

3. Head over to the Videos Library located in File Explorer. Add a new library location and point to the shortcut you placed on the C drive, C:\MEDIA. Your media will now import into the Library.

Hopefully this is addressed in a Windows update or a service pack at some future time, but security features or other concerns might leave this in place as is. If that's the case, you'll need to use this workaround or a similar one to import your media card content into Windows Libraries for use in Windows 8 Xbox Video app or Music app.

Spotlight, Movies Store, and Television Store

The Spotlight, Movies Store, and Television Store enable Windows 8 users to acquire legal media content from a plethora of sources (see Figure 4.10). The two main sources are the Movies Store and the Television Store—while the Spotlight section features the best content from both. Naturally, the idea behind the app is that a user will buy or rent media from the Microsoft Marketplace through these channels.

Selecting from the Movies Store heading or the Television Store heading shows you expanded categories such as Featured or Genres. And for those on a budget, look in the Television Store for the heading Free TV (see Figure 4.11).

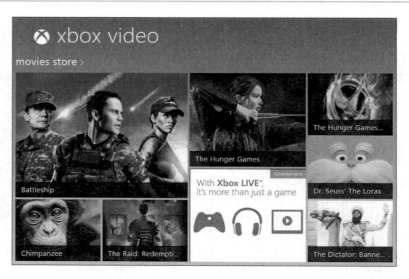

Figure 4.10   *The Movies Store*

These two entry points, Movies and Television, feature virtually the same navigation style and options (with the exception that Television offers some additional options regarding the format of shows spread across multiple seasons).

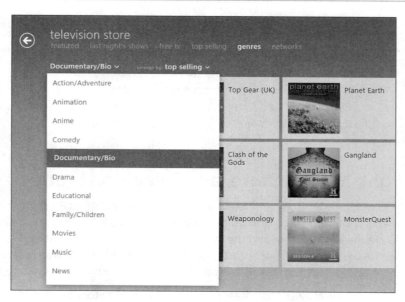

Figure 4.11   *Browsing the Television Store*

 **LET ME TRY IT**

Playing a Movie Trailer

To get started quickly, pick something from the Spotlight or Movies Store. For example, follow the steps below to play a movie trailer.

1. From the Start screen open the Videos tile by left-clicking it.

2. Use the scrollbar on the bottom (if necessary) to scroll to the Movies Store.

3. Select a movie that you want to see a trailer for and left-click the tile for that movie.

4. A miniature dialog opens. On the left side is an option that says Play Trailer; left-click this. (Not every movie in the marketplace contains a trailer. If you don't see this option, select another movie.)

5. The movie trailer begins playing.

Whether it's TV or movies you can complete a transaction right from within Windows 8 in the Videos app or on the website www.xbox.com.

To initiate the transaction simply attempt to buy or rent some content through the Xbox Video (or Music) app (see Figure 4.12). You are then presented with screens enabling you to purchase the content and complete the transaction.

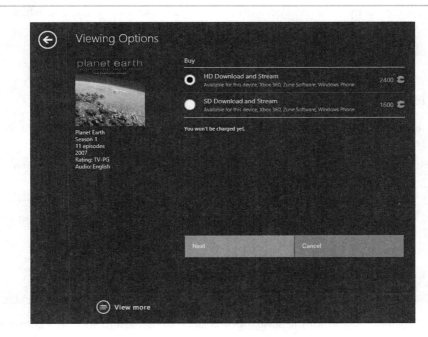

Figure 4.12   *Making a purchase within the Xbox Video app*

Using Charms with Xbox Video

Be sure and take advantage of a few powerful charms when you use the Video app. Here's a look at a few:

- **Search charm**—From here you can search the entire Microsoft Marketplace for video and TV content.

- **Share charm**—This charm makes it easy to share with others preview information and links to the Xbox marketplace about something you are watching.

- **Settings charm**—When you have questions about your account or want to configure preferences, head over to this charm.

 SHOW ME   Media 4.3—Exploring Xbox Video and Music
Access this video file through your registered Web Edition at
my.safaribooksonline.com/9780789750518/media.

Using the Xbox Music App

Similar in style and functionality to the Xbox Video app, the Xbox Music app brings to it the capability to access Microsoft's millions of songs in an easy-to-use format.

 **LET ME TRY IT**

Playing a Song

Just like the Xbox Video app, your on-board content is located on the left side of the app. Here's how to access it.

The following steps show you how to play a song from the Xbox Music app. To do this, make sure you first have placed a music file in your Music folder that can be accessed through File Explorer. Once you have done that, you can proceed to the following steps.

1. On the Start screen left-click the Music app.

2. After the app opens, play a song from the My Music section by left-clicking it.

3. To view controls for the song, right-click on the screen to show the controls (see Figure 4.13).

Figure 4.13   *Playing a song within the Xbox Music app*

If your device has hardware volume controls, you can adjust the volume easily with these. This feature comes in handy when you leave the Music app since a mini window with basic Volume, Play, and Pause controls opens when you touch the volume controls. So if your music is playing and you leave the Music app and head over to the desktop, you can use the hardware controls to bring up this menu and pause or change the song or volume without having to return to the Music app.

Accessing the New Releases and Popular Categories

Both the New Releases and Popular headings offer a genre search with the most popular styles displayed in categories on the left. Once you locate a song from one of the categories, a small window opens giving you extended options such as buying the album, previewing it, or Artist details.

As noted earlier, in the "Using the Xbox Video App" section, media content is delivered through the Microsoft Marketplace and uses the Microsoft Points currency. In addition, the Music app lets you listen to unlimited music using the Zune Music Pass. Either way, there is a lot to hear in the Xbox Music app (see Figure 4.14).

Figure 4.14   *Browsing the Xbox Music Store*

 TELL ME MORE   Media 4.4—A Discussion of Windows 8 Mail, Photos, Video, and Music Apps

Access this audio recording through your registered Web Edition at
my.safaribooksonline.com/9780789750518/media.

5

This chapter shows you how to get the most out of several Windows 8 features, such as the Store, SkyDrive, Weather, News, Reader, Maps, and more.

Additional Windows 8 Features

Windows Store

Going along with the recent trend to develop app stores, Microsoft has released the Windows Store as a fully integrated component in Windows 8. In this chapter's roundup of additional Windows 8 features, Windows Store ranks as the most important additional feature of all.

Every version of Windows has come with the capability for the user to install applications from a variety of sources: floppy disks, CDs, DVDs, Internet downloads, and more. This version of Windows continues that installation capability, but with the distinction that all apps that run off the Modern UI must come from the Windows Store.

By compelling developers to provide high-quality, virus-free apps that are distributed from a safe environment, the Windows Store quickly solves security, distribution, and installation issues in one fell swoop. Let's take a tour of the Windows Store.

 **LET ME TRY IT**

Navigating the Windows Store

1. On the Start screen, left-click the Store tile.

2. Using the scrollbar at the bottom, scroll through the different categories in the Windows Store (see Figure 5.1).

3. Locate a category that interests you and click the category heading.

4. After reviewing the apps, click the Back button in the upper left to return to the Windows Store main page.

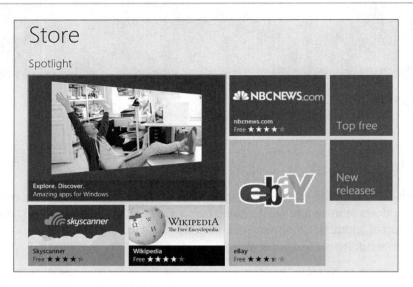

Figure 5.1   *The Windows Store Spotlight*

 **LET ME TRY IT**

Viewing Installed Apps

The app bar in the Windows Store gives you the chance to view all your apps or quickly return to the initial screen of the Windows Store app. Here's how to access the app bar to view your apps.

1. On the Start screen left-click the Store tile.

2. After the Windows Store opens right-click to show the app bar on top.

3. Click Your Apps to see a list of apps you have installed (see Figure 5.2).

4. Select an app by left-clicking it to bring up its various options, such as viewing details.

5. Deselect the app by left–clicking it again.

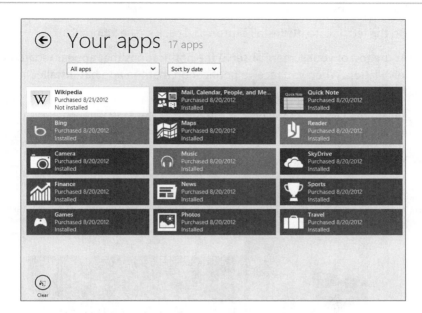

Figure 5.2   *Installed apps from the Windows Store*

Search the Windows Store

With its ever increasing collection of apps, you may want to know how you can search through the Windows Store for a specific app. There are actually a couple of ways to do this. On the one hand you can use the Search charm from the Windows Store app to locate apps. Just open the charm and start your search for an app in the search bar.

A faster way to perform the same search is to open the Windows Store and simply start typing the first few letters of the app you are looking for. Results start to appear onscreen before you finish typing the search!

 **LET ME TRY IT**

Installing an App

The whole process for installing Modern UI apps from the Windows Store is completely different from installing traditional Windows applications. To illustrate the difference and how this process works, let's install an app now.

1. On the Start screen click the Store app.

2. Locate an app you want to install and click it to select it.

3. On the left, locate the Install button and click it (see Figure 5.3).

4. At the top of your screen, observe the notifications that appear regarding installation. When you receive notification that the app has installed return to the Start screen.

5. Locate the last tile all the way to the right on the Start screen. This is the newly installed app.

6. Click it to open it.

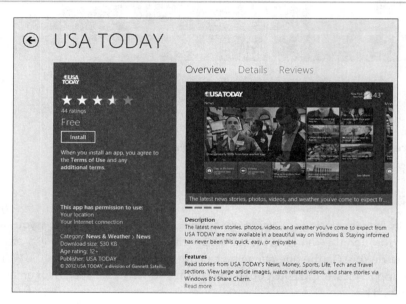

Figure 5.3   *Selecting an app from the Windows Store*

As you observe the process notice that there are no extra buttons to click, no installation options, no choices on settings for the application, or the like. Instead, it's a quick (in most cases) install that is unattended—just watch until it's done.

 **LET ME TRY IT**

Removing an App

The removal process of apps is similar in its unattended style, but this time, we don't even have to go into the Windows Store to do it!

1. On the Start screen locate an app that you want to remove and right-click it.

2. From the app bar at the bottom, select Uninstall.

3. A message appears indicating the app will be removed. Select Uninstall.

Easy in, easy out, that's how Modern UI apps come and go from the Windows Store.

> What about good old-fashioned desktop applications and the Windows Store? Actually, x86 applications (applications installed pre-Windows 8) are also available in the Windows Store. These are noted in the store as Desktop apps. The caveat here is that you must be running Windows 8 on an x86 device such as a traditional desktop or laptop computer and some tablets. Devices, mostly tablets, that run Windows RT cannot run these older style x86 apps.
>
> To see an example of a Desktop app in the Windows Store, look for a popular media app called Audials One 9. When you find it and go to install it, you are linked to a website where you can get the download for the application. Once launched, it opens the Desktop where you can complete the installation.

SkyDrive

SkyDrive is 7GB of free, secure, online storage that's integrated into Windows 8. Not a new feature, SkyDrive has existed in several iterations, but its current form is certainly the most ambitious. Tied to your Microsoft Account, the concept is that you can store various file types such as Microsoft Office documents, photos, videos, or any other types of files and quickly access or share them with others.

It's important to understand that there are various ways to access SkyDrive. For years, the most common way was to simply visit www.skydrive.com, log in, and work through a web browser to access your personal web files. It wasn't sexy or much fun, but it got the job done and, hey, it was free. Then in the spring of 2012 Microsoft released a desktop version of SkyDrive that integrated into Windows. This allowed you to access your SkyDrive content right through Windows Explorer, and it synchronized all your data automatically. With the capability to install this on multiple machines, this became a real hit in the tech community and at large. Enter Windows 8 and yet another way to access the SkyDrive was introduced, the SkyDrive app (see Figure 5.4). This app is the focus of this section.

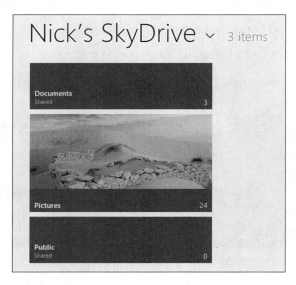

Figure 5.4   *The SkyDrive app*

The SkyDrive app lets you work with all of your data in the cloud without requiring you to download it locally. (Yes, you can download and upload files in the app, which we discuss later in this section.) The practicality of this manifests itself if you work between Windows 8 devices. Although your desktop might be able to fit all your SkyDrive data with ease, would your tablet also be able to hold this same data? How about your phone? By keeping it as a way to quickly work with your files in the cloud without downloading them, storage issues between devices is a non-issue.

Would you like to use both the SkyDrive Modern UI app and also have the SkyDrive Desktop app in Windows 8? Well then head over to the Windows Store and type in **skydrive**. In the search results locate the SkyDrive Desktop app. However before you install it take note; if your SkyDrive is full of data, you might just fill up your local drive. To get around this, consider purchasing a media card your device supports and set your SkyDrive folder to that instead of the local disk.

 **LET ME TRY IT**

Accessing Data on the SkyDrive

If you have not already worked with the SkyDrive, you may need a moment to get used to it. First, let's look at the default folders set up for you automatically and then add data to them.

The following exercise requires an Internet connection, Microsoft Account, and data such as a document, photo, or video.

1. On the Start screen left-click the tile that says SkyDrive.

2. Your SkyDrive opens. If a request for credentials appears, log in using your Microsoft Account to complete these steps.

3. Three tiles appear: Documents, Pictures, and Public (refer to Figure 5.4). Select Documents by left-clicking it.

4. Right click to show the app bar.

5. Select Upload.

6. Navigate to the location of the file you want to upload. Start by left-clicking the word Files.

7. Next, select the folder where the file is located.

8. Left-click the file you want to upload.

9. Left-click on Add to SkyDrive in the lower-left corner. After the upload completes, you find the file in your SkyDrive documents folder.

 **LET ME TRY IT**

Opening a Document Using the Word WebApp

One outstanding feature of SkyDrive is its capability to open and edit several Microsoft Office formats without having the actual application installed on your local computer. This is accomplished by using the free WebApp version of Microsoft Office integrated in the SkyDrive. Here's how to do it.

The following exercise requires a Word 2010 document to be available for upload to the SkyDrive.

1. From the Start screen open the SkyDrive.

2. Upload a Word 2010 document to the Documents folder.

3. Left-click to open the Word document.

4. Depending on your installed apps, you may be able to select from more than one way to open the document. Choose Internet Explorer.

5.   Your document appears in the browser (see Figure 5.5). If you want, select Edit in Browser from within Internet Explorer to actually edit the document online.

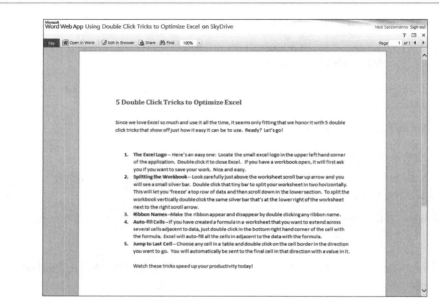

Figure 5.5   *Editing a Word 2010 document in the free Word WebApp accessed through SkyDrive*

Office WebApps offer a reduced feature set, but they are free. WebApps include Microsoft Word, Excel, PowerPoint, and OneNote.

Managing SkyDrive Files

After you start working with SkyDrive you may find it quickly filling up. For some, 7GB may represent just a portion of their music or video collection. Microsoft addresses this by providing additional tiers of paid storage. They are as follows:

-   Additional 25GB—$10.00 annually*

-   Additional 50GB—$25.00 annually*

-   Additional 100GB—$50.00 annually*

    *Cost may change over time

LET ME TRY IT

Viewing Your Space Utilization

If you want to know how much available space you have, follow these steps to see this graphically.

1. On the Start screen select the SkyDrive app.

2. When the SkyDrive app opens, go to the Settings charm.

3. Select Options.

4. Information regarding your space appears. Select Manage Storage to see more storage options including purchasing more storage.

Managing Your SkyDrive

No matter the size of your storage, you need to manage your data. Unfortunately the simple commands in the SkyDrive lend themselves to data consumption rather than robust file management. To access the simple commands, right-click (or if using a touch-based device, swipe down on the file) to show the app bar (see Figure 5.6). Here's a list of commands you see:

- **Clear Selection**—Deselect a file or (if multiple files selected) a group of files.

- **Download**—Download the selected file.

- **Delete**—Delete the selected file.

- **Refresh**—Refresh the SkyDrive to the latest synchronized point.

- **New Folder**—Create a new folder.

- **Upload**—Upload a file to the selected location.

- **Details**—Reset the icons of the folder to display file details.

- **Thumbnails**—Reset the icons of the folder to display file thumbnails.

- **Select All**—Select all files in the selected folder.

Figure 5.6 *The SkyDrive app bar*

 **LET ME TRY IT**

Sharing SkyDrive Files

One other feature to consider is sharing your SkyDrive files. Using the Share charm is an easy way to do this. Files that you share can be designated as read-only, or can allow editing capabilities through SkyDrive. Follow these steps to see how this can be done.

> Before the following steps can be completed, the SkyDrive needs to have a file already uploaded to it. Also a working Mail account is required.

1. On the Start screen, select the SkyDrive app.
2. Navigate to a file you want to share.
3. Right-click the file to select it.
4. With the file selected, open the Share charm.
5. Select Mail.
6. Add an email address, subject line, and a message if desired.
7. Click the Send button.

That's it! You've just shared a file from your SkyDrive account.

 SHOW ME   **Media 5.1—Utilizing the SkyDrive App**
Access this video file through your registered Web Edition at
my.safaribooksonline.com/9780789750518/media.

> When you share a file from SkyDrive, you are not actually sending a file, you are instead sending a link to the file. This link works as long as the file is not moved from or renamed on the SkyDrive. The same principle holds true for SkyDrive folders.
>
> In either case, use caution when sharing information. When distributed through an email, the secure link you provide to one party can be easily forwarded to others—perhaps many more than you intended.

Weather

The Weather app is a good example of how a well-designed Modern UI app can perform. When you first run the app, you are asked "Do you want to turn on location services and allow Weather to use your location?" You can choose to allow or block Weather. (Select block and you will see sample data.) Choose Allow to see regularly updated local weather in a beautiful layout (see Figure 5.7).

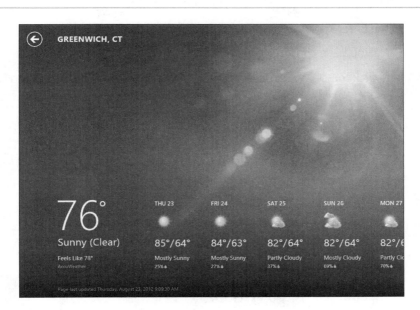

Figure 5.7 *The Weather app*

Categories you can scroll through in this app include

- Bing Weather
- Hourly Forecast
- Maps
- Historical Weather

Loading Multiple Locations to the Weather App

Sometimes you might want to see weather information for a location other than your default selection. The Weather app allows you to select multiple locations and view weather conditions for them. To see this in action, follow these steps.

The following exercise requires a working Internet connection.

1. From the Start screen open the Weather app.

2. Right-click to show the app bars on the top and bottom of the screen.

3. On the top app bar, select Places.

4. Click the dark gray tile with a + sign to load a different place.

5. In the Enter Location window type in the city.

6. Once you have chosen a city, click Add.

7. Left-click the city tile on the Places screen to load Weather information for this city (see Figure 5.8).

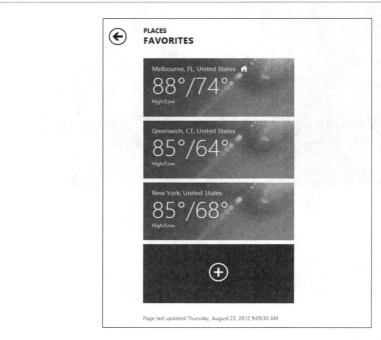

Figure 5.8   *Customized Weather locations*

Now scroll through the Weather app for information on your new location.

Pinning Multiple Weather Tiles to the Start Screen

You might find that you want to place a few different Weather tiles on the Start screen to see the weather for multiple locations at a glance. This is easily done.

1. From the Start screen open the Weather app.

2. Right-click to show the app bars.

3. Select Places.

4. If you have not already added the places you want to see weather information from on the Start screen, do so now.

5. Right-click to select a place you want to see on the Start screen.

6. Select Pin to Start.

7. The name of the tile with the city name is presented. If this is correct click Pin to Start (see Figure 5.9).

8. Repeat these steps for each tile you want to place on the Start screen.

Figure 5.9   *Multiple Weather tiles on the Start screen*

Using the News App

Like the Weather app, the News app has a similar design style that uses the full screen to present information. The result is news presented in a stunning app environment that's easy to access (see Figure 5.10). The default main sections of News are

- Bing Daily Top Story
- U.S.
- World
- Technology
- Business
- Entertainment
- Politics
- Sports

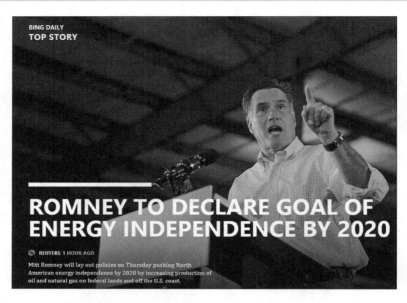

Figure 5.10   *The News app*

Scrolling through the News app quickly gets you to each section where multiple articles in each category are a tap or a click away. Each section heading has a small arrow to the right of it that allows you to expand the section's news offerings as well. Leave the News app and back on the Start screen the live tile also presents a small News tidbit for you to glance at.

 **LET ME TRY IT**

Customizing the News App

Where the News app really shines is its capability to let you customize both the news topics you are presented with and the sources where the News app pulls info from. First, let's customize what news topics are presented.

1. From the Start screen open the News app.

2. Right-click to show the app bar.

3. Select My News.

4. Left click on the + button in a gray box under the heading Add A Section.

5. Enter a news topic, such as Windows Phone 8 (see Figure 5.11).

6. Click Add. Repeat this to add more topics to My News.

Figure 5.11   *My News custom topics*

The My News section now contains your topic(s) culled from multiple news sources. But if you want to read news only from a specific news source such as BBC News, CNN, or *The New York Times*, then follow the preceding steps but instead of selecting My News in step 3, select Sources (see Figure 5.12). Choose from any of the news sources to get going or, as an added bonus after opening one of these sources, right-click (or swipe down from the top edge of the screen) to show the app bar and select Pin to Start to create a tile for the source on your Start screen.

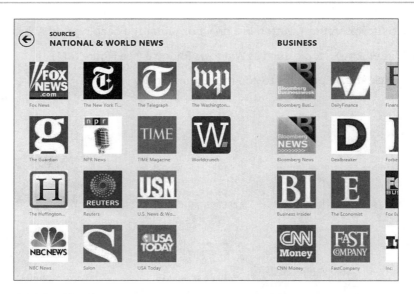

Figure 5.12   *Viewing news sources*

Additional Apps

Aside from the flagship apps that are part of the default Windows 8 configuration, several additional apps are worth noting as well. These integrated apps, such as Reader, Calendar, Maps, and Travel, enable you to read PDF files, view maps and directions, as well as access comprehensive travel information without having to install additional software. These apps extend the capability of Windows 8 without requiring you to install additional software. The first app in this section, Reader, offers a new feature to native Windows.

Reader

Ask anyone what the most popular document format is and many will respond PDF. Despite its widespread popularity, the PDF format has been largely ignored in previous versions of Windows. Often, one of the first installations people have made on a new Windows PC has been Adobe Acrobat reader or a similar PDF reader. To address this need, Windows 8 supplies a basic PDF reader, which is not surprisingly called Reader. Here's how to open it.

 **LET ME TRY IT**

Open a PDF with Reader

1. Choose a PDF file and open it. Reader automatically opens.

Or

1. From the Start Screen type **reader**.
2. The Reader app appears in the results. Select this to open Reader.

After you open a PDF file in Reader the full screen displays the document content. On a touch-enabled device, use the pinch commands to zoom in and out of the page.

Reader offers a basic feature set when you're working with PDF files. Tap or select text in a file to bring up a submenu with three features:

- **Highlight**—Allows you to mark up PDF files, which you can then save for later viewing

- **Add a Note**—Lets you fill a text box with notes that minimizes to a callout when not in use

- **Copy**—Copies the selection

You can view other PDF files by right-clicking the document (or swiping down from the top edge) and showing the Reader app bar. Commands, however, are limited. Reader lives up to its name by doing just that, letting you easily read PDF files (see Figure 5.13).

Zooming in or out of a PDF file in Reader is no problem, just use pinch gestures to accomplish this. With a mouse and keyboard, however, it's a little tricky. If you have a scroll wheel on your mouse, you can press the Ctrl button on your keyboard and use your scroll mouse to zoom in and out. Or accomplish the same results by holding the Ctrl button and using the + and – keys on your keyboard.

Calendar

With a simple layout and easy to use commands, Calendar accomplishes its task of letting you add appointments to a calendar. Offering a Day, Week, and Month view from the app bar, you can view your schedule how you like (see Figure 5.14).

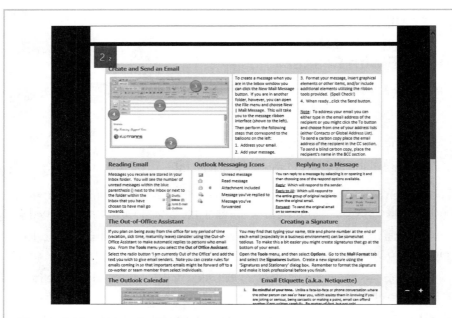

Figure 5.13   *Using the Reader app*

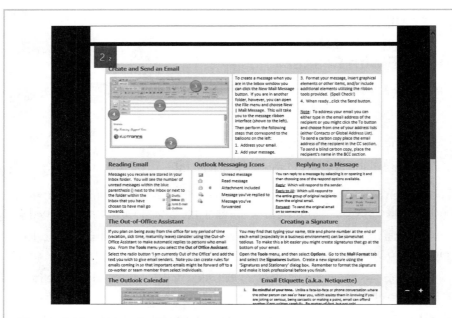

Figure 5.14   *Viewing the Calendar app bar*

 **LET ME TRY IT**

Adding an Appointment

The most common Calendar task, adding an appointment, takes just a few steps.

1. From the Start screen select the Calendar app.

2. Select a date to enter an appointment.

3. Add a Title to your appointment.

4. Fill out any other details as desired.

5. In the upper-right select the Save This Event button.

If you need to add more details to your appointment, select the Show More link to see more appointment options.

Notifications for your appointments show up on the Calendar tile on the Start screen and on the Lock screen. And just like other apps, your calendar content is synchronized with your other Windows 8 devices when you log in to them with your Microsoft Account. This is seamless and requires no configuration on your part—it just works.

Maps

Where would we be without an up-to-date map? Lost. Maybe that's why Windows 8 includes a feature that should be very popular on mobile devices—Maps.

When you first open Maps, you are asked whether Maps can use your location. Allow this and the app shares a bird's-eye view of your region on the map. Navigation is simple with touch gestures; just pinch in or out to zoom the map. Mouse users can left-click to show the plus and minus buttons on the left edge.

To move the screen in one-half increments press the Ctrl key and arrow in a direction.

Performing a search for a location is simple. Just use the Search charm from within Maps to bring up a location. Bring up the Maps app bar by right-clicking or swiping down from the top edge of the screen to utilize some commands like

- **Show Traffic**—Shows or hides traffic information on the map

- **Map Style**—Allows you to switch between Road view and Aerial view

- **My Location**—Centers the map on your location

- **Directions**—Creates highlighted directions to the locations of your choice while presenting written directions for this at the top of the app (see Figure 5.15).

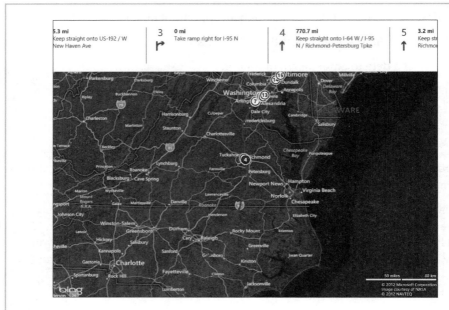

Figure 5.15   *Following directions in Maps*

Remember to use your charms while in the Maps app. For example, use the Share charm to email or send directions to someone. Or use the Devices charm to print the map directions you've just pulled up.

Travel

The Travel app (powered by Bing and Kayak.com) offers a multitude of travel-related selections. Explore, shop, or learn all from this one app. Travel contains access to so much data that it's easy to get lost looking at one beautiful place after another. Scroll through the app to see 360-degree panoramas of locations and selected magazine articles as well. After you're ready to dive in further, open the Travel app bar by right-clicking (or swiping from the top edge down) to see the following categories:

- **Home**—Returns to the start of the Travel app.

- **Destinations**—Explores the most popular regions in the world from here. To see selected geographical locations, select the down arrow next to the Region heading to show the locations by main areas.

- **Flights**—Offers a fast way to get pricing and book a flight from major airlines.

- **Hotels**—Like flights, you can get pricing and book a hotel room quickly and easily.

- **Best of Web**—Consider this one of the hidden gems of the Travel app. This section rounds out the Travel app with the following categories:

    - Explore

    - Plan a Trip

    - Tools

    - Budget Travel

    - Road Trips

    - Food and Wine

    - Tour and Cruises

    - Sustainable Travel

    - Family Travel

    - Frequent Travelers

 LET ME TRY IT

Locating a Travel Destination

With so many choices, where to begin? How about quickly finding information on a specific travel destination? This is easily done, as the following steps show.

1. From the Start screen select the Travel app.

2. From within the Travel app open the Search charm.

3. Type in your search and press Enter

4. Select a destination from the results.

The Travel app is a great way to explore the world from your Windows 8 device (see Figure 5.16).

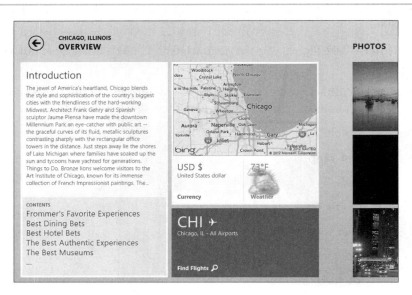

Figure 5.16   Exploring a destination in Travel

 SHOW ME   Media 5.2—An Overview of Windows Essentials 2012
Access this video file through your registered Web Edition at
my.safaribooksonline.com/9780789750518/media.

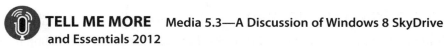 **TELL ME MORE**   Media 5.3—A Discussion of Windows 8 SkyDrive
and Essentials 2012
Access this audio recording through your registered Web Edition at
my.safaribooksonline.com/9780789750518/media.

With a sleek new design, Internet Explorer 10 bursts onto the scene in Windows 8 with not one, but two versions of the popular browser.

6

Internet Explorer 10

The Two Sides of Internet Explorer 10

One of the most popular features of Windows is its capability to browse the Internet. Windows 8 gives special attention to this in providing not one but two different browsers, a first for Windows.

Previous versions of Windows did offer a special mode to open Internet Explorer without add-ons, but this was still the same browser albeit with some features deactivated on launch.

Though both browsers are called Internet Explorer 10 and both are built off the same platform that offers expanded CSS3 support, hardware acceleration, and (in keeping with modern web standards) HTML 5 support, the user interfaces for each version are radically different and come in two styles:

- **Internet Explorer 10 app**—Located on the Start screen, this app is designed for touch-based devices first and sports a full-screen viewing mode. Quick and easy to use, it will become the default browser for many new users of Windows 8.

- **Desktop version of Internet Explorer**—Similar in style to Internet Explorer 9, this browser retains the look and feel of the previous versions of Explorer. Users who mainly work in the Desktop will find it remarkably easy to use.

Naturally there are some other differences between these applications that go beyond simple styling. A key distinction is that the Internet Explorer app does not support plug-ins while the Desktop version still retains plug-in support. A notable exception to this is the inclusion of the Flash plug-in, which has now been partially integrated into the Internet Explorer code itself.

Have you ever tried using a browser on a tablet running Windows XP, Vista, or 7? If so, you know how the browsing experience was—mediocre at best. Why was that the case? Simply, the pre-Windows 8 operating systems just were not built for touch commands. Sure, you could tap on a link, scroll up or down a page, or enter an address in the address bar, but the whole process was cumbersome. It was all too easy for your touch to be interpreted as something different, perhaps sending you to a different link or opening unwanted menu items.

Imagine the criticism Microsoft would have received had it retained this style of browser as the sole way to access the Internet. Rather than go this route and provide an inferior solution Microsoft took the unique two-pronged approach in providing two different browsing experiences. The result is the best of both worlds, a browser for your particular style of input. And instead of accommodating touch commands with elementary gestures, the Internet Explorer 10 app interface was built from the ground up with touch commands in mind.

Ultimately, the browser you choose to use depends on a variety of factors such as the device or computer you are using to run Windows 8, your method of input whether it be mouse and keyboard or touch commands or a combination of both. If you think you might lean toward the new Internet Explorer app, take a look at some of the commands and features mentioned in the next section. This will help you get the most out of using Windows 8.

Using the Internet Explorer 10 App

One of the high points of Windows 8 is the new full-screen Internet Explorer app. If you access this from a touch-enabled device, you'll be pleased to see that basic commands such as back and forth gestures, pinch to zoom, and the like are all there. As you peruse the browser, you'll likely notice the reduced number of commands that exist within the browser. You may find that this simplified approach to browsing is a welcome change from other browsers.

Now let's look at some specific features of the browser. We can start with looking at how to navigate to a web page.

 SHOW ME   Media 6.1—Using the IE 10 App
Access this video file through your registered Web Edition at
my.safaribooksonline.com/9780789750518/media.

 **LET ME TRY IT**

Opening a Web Page

1. On the Start screen select Internet Explorer.

2. On the black address bar at the bottom, click in it to select it.

3. Notice the current address is highlighted in blue. Type in the word **bing**.

4. Press Enter on your keyboard or press the white arrow in a circle to the right of the address bar to be taken to Microsoft's search engine (see Figure 6.1).

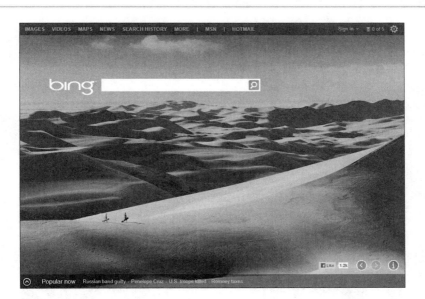

Figure 6.1   *Internet Explorer opened to www.Bing.com*

One of the first things you may notice about the browser is its full-screen look. This uncluttered view lets the web page stand out and minimizes distractions leading to a clean look. Of course this look may also cause an initial state of confusion. For example, where are the commands such as going back or forward in the browser? Not to worry, all these and more are hiding beneath the surface.

What has happened to the right-click? The answer to this question has to be one of the most disconcerting finds for power users running the Internet Explorer app. Instead of a host of menu options such as Search using copied text, Select All, View Source, Print, or Export to Microsoft Excel, the Explorer app provides few options if any when right-clicking on selected objects on a web page. Selecting text and right-clicking it simply gives you the option to copy it. Right-clicking a picture gives you a few more options but certainly not as many as you would think. As it turns out, all of these menu options still do exist, but only in the Desktop version of Explorer.

Let's show these features and more with a few quick commands.

LET ME TRY IT

Showing the Internet Explorer App Bars

1. On an open web page, right-click in the browser.

2. Notice the upper and lower app bars that appear simultaneously (see Figure 6.2).

Figure 6.2   *The Internet Explorer navigation and tab switcher bars*

The app bars (upper and lower) represent the key ways to navigate the browser. Let's examine the features on each one, starting with the upper bar called the switcher bar.

Using the Tab Switcher Bar

With a quick right-click or a swipe of your finger, the app bars of Internet Explorer appear onscreen and reveal shortcuts to quick commands. On the tab switcher bar (the upper bar), notice the current tab you have opened is represented by a small thumbnail tile in the left corner. Previous versions of Internet Explorer included the capability to have multiple web pages open at once, otherwise known as tabbed browsing. The Internet Explorer app continues this but executes it differently than other versions of the browser. Let's open multiple tabs in the browser.

LET ME TRY IT

Opening and Closing Multiple Tabs

1. Right-click to open the Internet Explorer app bars.

2. Click the + sign on the right side of the upper bar to open a new tab.

3. A blank website tab opens. At the bottom, type in the address bar where the curser is blinking the name of a website and press Enter on your keyboard.

4. After the web page opens, right-click on the web page. Notice in the upper bar the tabs you have opened appear as thumbnails (see Figure 6.3).

5. Click the first thumbnail tab at the top upper right to return to the first web page you opened.

6. After the web page opens, right-click on the web page. Select the X with a circle around it appearing on any of your thumbnailed tabs on the upper bar to close that specific tab.

Figure 6.3   *Multiple tabs open in Internet Explorer*

With your tabs neatly tucked away until you use them, your screen still shows the full browsing experience even if you have multiple tabs open.

If you intend to keep 40 or more tabs open at once, consider using the Desktop version of Internet Explorer 10 instead.

Using Tab Tools

A final button the upper app bar presents is called Tab Tools. This looks like a white circle with three dots in it and is located in the lower right of the upper app bar. The Tab Tools button launches two commands:

- **Close Tabs**—When selected, this command simply shuts all open tabs except the one opened onscreen. Use this to quickly close multiple tabs at once.

- **New InPrivate Tab**—This features lets you surf the Internet and not leave a trail behind. Keep in mind that this feature is only in effect while you have turned it on for a browsing window. Once you close the browser, it needs to be launched again for the next browsing session.

HOW INPRIVATE BROWSING WORKS

How different items are affected by InPrivate browsing:

Cookies—Kept in memory so pages work correctly, but cleared when you close the browser.

Temporary Internet files—Stored on disk so pages work correctly, but deleted when you close the browser.

Web page history—This information is not stored.

Form data and passwords—This information is not stored.

Anti-phishing cache—Temporary information is encrypted and stored so pages work correctly.

Address bar and search AutoComplete—This information is not stored.

Automatic Crash Restore (ACR)—ACR can restore when a tab crashes in a session, but if the whole window crashes, data is deleted and the window cannot be restored.

Document Object Model (DOM) storage—The DOM storage is a kind of "super cookie" web developers can use to retain information. Like regular cookies, they are not kept after the window is closed.

Source: http://windows.microsoft.com/en-US/windows-vista/What-is-InPrivate-Browsing

Using the Navigation Bar

With its contextual commands and hidden features the navigation bar (the lower bar) certainly has a lot going on. Because some of the commands are contextually based they may not all appear when you display the bar. For example, if you load only one web page, the back and forward buttons appear grayed out until you actually have a second web page to go back or forward to. Likewise an X appears near the address bar to indicate that you can stop a web page from loading. Once the web page fully loads, the X will be replaced by a curved arrow with a circle around it indicating you can reload the page. The use of these contextual commands simplifies the interface and makes only the commands you need accessible at any given time. Let's illustrate this with the back and forward buttons on the navigation bar.

 LET ME TRY IT

Using the Back and Forward Buttons

1. In the Internet Explorer app, right-click to show the navigation bar (see Figure 6.4).

2. If you have not already done so, open a web page.

3. Continue on to another web page from within that same tab.

4. After the web page loads, right-click to show the navigation bar again.

5. Select the back arrow to the left of the address bar to go back one page.

6. Once that page loads, select the forward arrow at the far right of the navigation bar to go forward.

> There is actually an easier way for mouse and keyboard users to get around Internet Explorer without using the navigation bar. Mouse users can simply move their mouse to the left or right edges of the screen until the back and forward buttons appear on the edges of the screen and then click these. Moving all the way to the right also shows a website scrollbar if available.
>
> Keyboard users will appreciate that familiar back and forward shortcuts still exist: Alt+Left Arrow to go back and Alt+Right Arrow to go forward. Up and down arrows on the keyboard let you scroll up and down a web page.

 SHOW ME   Media 6.2—Advanced IE 10 App
Access this video file through your registered Web Edition at
my.safaribooksonline.com/9780789750518/media.

Figure 6.4 *The navigation bar showing at the bottom of Internet Explorer*

Using the Pin and Page Tools Controls

The navigation bar also lets you accomplish other simple tasks. You'll note two other buttons on the navigation bar as well. They are

- **Pin to Start**—This button, which looks like a push pin, lets you place a short-cut to the current website you have opened onto your Start screen. Once you press this button, you have the opportunity to rename the shortcut before it lands on the Start screen.

- **Page Tools**—This button, which has a wrench icon, contains a small menu to three tools:

  - **Get App for This Site**—When you visit a website that offers a Windows 8 app the Page Tools wrench icon also includes a small + symbol, which tells you the Get App for This Site option is available. When you select it, you are automatically launched into the Windows Store and taken to the particular app. To see this in action visit www.Wordpress.com and look for the modified wrench with + sign on the navigation bar.

  - **Find on Page**—This actively searches the web page you are on for hits based on the search term you provide in the find bar. Previous and next buttons let you jump to other instances of the term on the web page.

  - **View on the Desktop**—Opens an instance of the specified web page in the Desktop version of Internet Explorer. This is useful when a website contains plug-ins and does not show properly in the Explorer app.

In practical day-to-day use, you may find yourself jumping between the Explorer browsers such as when you land on a site that plays videos or requires Java to play a game or some other add-on. Interestingly, Microsoft worked closely with Adobe to integrate Flash 11.3 into the Internet Explorer 10 code. This means that, techni-cally, Flash itself is not an add-on to the Internet Explorer 10 app; it's integrated right into it. Here's the catch: Due to performance, security, and battery issues, only a subset of Flash 11.3 is included.

In the real world this translates to some but not all Flash-enabled sites running in the Explorer app. If you reach a site that contains a version of Flash that is not included in the Explorer app, you may need to view that site in the Desktop version of Explorer to make it run right, which by the way has Flash 11.3 built right into it.

Using the Charms Bar Within Internet Explorer

From within the Internet Explorer app, the Charms bar extends the functionality of the application. The five charms that Internet Explorer 10 supports are Search, Share, Start, Devices, and Settings (see Figure 6.5). Here's a brief explanation of what each charm does in Internet Explorer.

- **Search**—The Search charm in Explorer executes the same system level search that works throughout Windows 8. When opened from Explorer, the search results are presented onscreen as you type.

- **Share**—Use this charm to open sharing apps like Mail or People to quickly share the website information you are viewing with other individuals.

- **Start**—Return to the Start screen with this charm.

- **Devices**—Relevant devices such as printers are shown enabling you to quickly process the document to a hardware device.

- **Settings**—This opens some specialized settings for the Internet Explorer app. Select Internet options to manage browsing history, permissions, Zoom, and encoding.

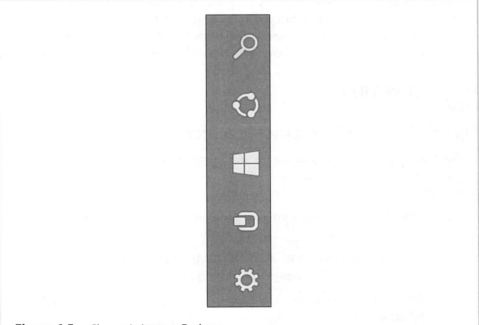

Figure 6.5   *Charms in Internet Explorer*

Bear in mind that the Charms bar does not show all of the same features as described for the Desktop version of Internet Explorer. Settings such as Internet options for that browser are still located within the Desktop version of the browser itself. Since we've brought up the Desktop version of Explorer, let's take a closer look at it right now.

Using the Desktop Version of Internet Explorer 10

As one of the longest tenured web browsers, Internet Explorer has enjoyed an evolutionary development for more than a decade. This tenth installment of the browser retains a familiar look while containing several new advancements. Let's begin our overview of the Internet Explorer Desktop browser by looking at browser tabs.

 SHOW ME   **Media 6.3—The IE 10 Desktop**
Access this video file through your registered Web Edition at
my.safaribooksonline.com/9780789750518/media.

Customizing Tabs

When browsing the Internet, it's easy to click on links that take us to new websites and open new web pages. Before you know it, you can have several web pages open, which can clutter the screen. Tabbed browsing gives you the opportunity to bring some order to your web viewing by allowing you to open multiple web pages.

 LET ME TRY IT

Open a New Tab in Internet Explorer

The following steps show you how to open new tabs in the browser. This allows you to quickly switch between several websites. Although this is simple to execute, it can be a powerful technique for viewing multiple web pages.

1. In the Desktop version of Internet Explorer, left-click your Internet Explorer icon on the taskbar.

2. Note your initial tab automatically loads your homepage. (or pages—if you have multiple home pages already configured).

3. Click the little tab outcropping located to the right of your existing tab. This opens a new tab (see Figure 6.6).

4. Press and hold the Ctrl button and then press the letter T to open another new tab.

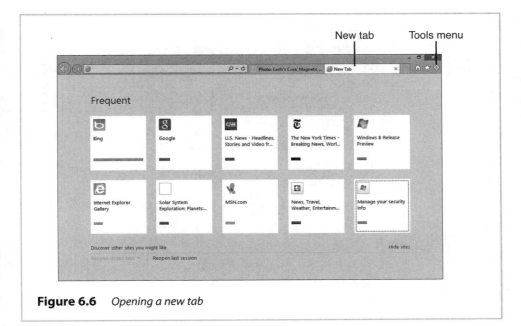

Figure 6.6   *Opening a new tab*

 **LET ME TRY IT**

Explore Tab Settings in Internet Explorer

You can adjust many of the settings for your tabs. To do this, locate the Tools gear in the upper right of the browser. Now follow these steps to access advanced tab settings in the Tabbed Browsing Settings dialog box.

1. In the Desktop version of Internet Explorer, click the Tools gear.

2. Select Internet options.

3. On the General tab, click the Tabs button (see Figure 6.7).

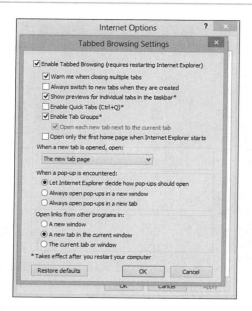

Figure 6.7   *Tabbed Browsing Settings*

Feel free to experiment with these setting in Explorer. The Tab settings allow you to reset this group of commands back to their default states, giving you the opportunity to see the original setup once again. This differs from the Reset button on the Advanced tab of Internet Options, which allows you to reset *all* Internet Explorer settings—not just the tabs.

4. Use the controls on this dialog box to control how tabs work. Some of the items you can change include the following:

   • Enable Tabbed Browsing

   • Warn Me When Closing Multiple Tabs

   • Always Switch to New Tabs When They are Created

   • Show Previews for Individual Tabs in the Taskbar

   • Open Only the First Home Page When Internet Explorer Starts

You can also determine how you want a new tab to be opened and how you want a link opened, so that when you click a hyperlink on a web page, it opens in a new window, opens a new tab of the current window, or the current tab of the current window—many options to work with.

Opening Multiple Pages on Browser Startup

 **LET ME TRY IT**

Configure Explorer to Open Multiple Tabs

After completing the following steps, you can have several different home pages open at the same time when you start your browser. In addition to saving time, it also ensures you are opening the correct URL every time.

1. In the Desktop version of Internet Explorer, click the Tools gear.

2. Select Internet options.

3. On the General tab, in the Home Page box, enter each web address you want to open when you start up IE. Each address should be on a separate line (see Figure 6.8).

You can also browse to a site you want to add to the home page list and then click the Use Current button on this dialog box to have IE place its address in the Home Page box.

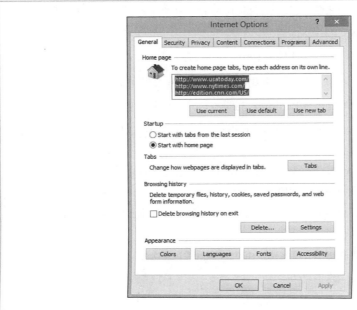

Figure 6.8 *Internet Options*

You may have noticed as you were working with the Tools menu that a new option appears, Add Site to Start Screen. As the name implies, this adds the current website to the Start screen. Also take note that even though this shortcut appears on the Start screen, the Desktop version of Explorer still opens when you select this tile.

Accelerators

The idea behind accelerators is to speed up routine tasks, allowing you to do in one (or a few) clicks what used to take several. Accelerator tasks include mapping locations, translation of words, and more.

For example, at times you might be reading an article in the news and want more information about the person in the article. That person might be a political figure, sports figure, or entertainer. An accelerator gives you faster access to more information on that individual.

 LET ME TRY IT

Adding an Accelerator to Internet Explorer

Follow these steps to add an accelerator to Explorer:

1. Open the Desktop version of Internet Explorer and select the Tools gear.

2. Choose manage add-ons.

3. In the left pane called Add-on Types select Accelerators.

4. In the bottom-left corner, click the Find More Accelerators link.

5. This opens the Internet Explorer Gallery (see Figure 6.9).

6. In the search pane on the upper right of the page type in **IMDB** and press Enter.

7. In the search results, locate Search on IMDB. To the right of that, click the orange button Add to Internet Explorer.

8. On the page that opens, again select the orange button Add to Internet Explorer.

9. This opens the Add Accelerator dialog box. Click the Add button.

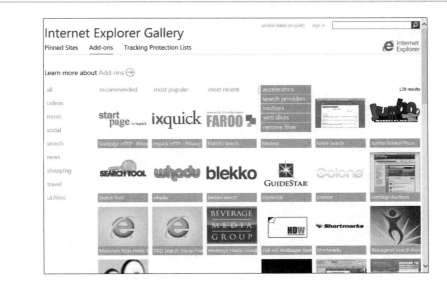

Figure 6.9 *The Internet Explorer Gallery*

Now you have successfully added an additional accelerator to the default collection that ships with Internet Explorer. To view how it works, navigate to a web page that contains some movie or celebrity information. Select a name and then right-click it. From the drop-down, you will notice a menu choice called All Accelerators along with a right arrow just waiting for you to move your mouse over it. When you do, you see the recently installed IMDB accelerator that was installed in this exercise. Click the IMDB accelerator to be launched to an IMDB web page with more content information for you.

Add-ons

What exactly are add-ons? The accelerators just covered in the previous section are one type. There's also ActiveX controls, browser extensions, browser helper objects or toolbars, and so forth. Sometimes we love certain add-ons, such as Flash players, because they expand IE's capability to give us more animated or interesting content. However, some add-ons can cause problems. They might also cause pop-ups or contain spyware.

Managing Add-ons in Explorer

The following steps show you how to take full control of your add-ons such as enabling or disabling specific add-ons if your browser is running slow or crashes unexpectedly. (This works great for troubleshooting problems in Internet Explorer.)

1. In the Desktop version of Internet Explorer, click the Tools gear.

2. Select Manage Add-ons. The Manage Add-ons dialog box appears (see Figure 6.10).

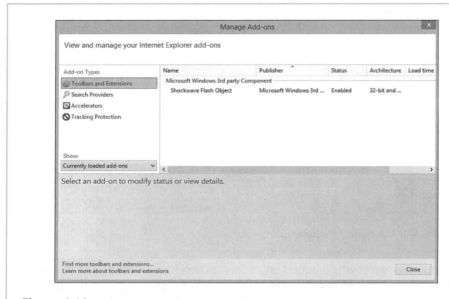

Figure 6.10   *The Manage Add-ons dialog box*

To see each add-on and its status, click each button on the left of the dialog box. You can configure these add-ons from this window. These buttons include the following:

-   Toolbars and Extensions

-   Search Providers

-   Accelerators

-   Tracking Protection

Pay attention to the Status column. This indicates whether the add-on is enabled or disabled. To change its status, right-click an item and then select from the menu to change whether it is enabled or disabled.

If an add-on you are looking for appears to be missing, you may need to view all add-ons to see it. You can easily do this from the Manage Add-ons dialog box and at the bottom of the left pane select the drop-down from which you can choose All Add-ons. Now you should see your "missing" add-on.

Compatibility View

Sometimes web developers need to redesign a site (in some cases requiring some necessary compatibility alterations for new browsers), but they haven't done it before a new browser is released. In those cases, you might go to a site and it won't look right or display data correctly. Internet Explorer 10 provides a Compatibility View feature, which is located to the right of the Address Bar. The button for Compatibility View automatically appears when you reach a page that is not compatible. Simply click this button to request Explorer to fix the page to display it in a way that works with the former coding. Explorer remembers your request the next time you visit the page, too.

Understanding Internet Explorer 10 Security Features

Internet Explorer has been around for a little more than a decade and has been riddled with so many security holes that over the past few years it has been losing ground to other browsers. With the release of Internet Explorer 9, Microsoft recaptured some of the market by matching the feature sets of newer browsers and also plugging the security holes. Internet Explorer certainly turned the security corner with Internet Explorer 9, and this continued commitment to security is shown clearly in Internet Explorer 10.

You find your security options in two locations. There is an entire Safety menu located on the Tools gear. You can also locate additional security settings by going to Internet Options on the Tools gear where you can locate items on the Security, Privacy, and Advanced tabs.

SmartScreen Filter

Protecting users from phishing is a combination of education and utilizing software technology. The scenario is simple. A user gets an email from a bank (possibly even what appears to be the user's own bank) or another merchant familiar to them (such as Amazon, eBay, or PayPal), asking for some information. If the user thinks the site is valid and doesn't know how to determine otherwise, he is at risk of providing information that might breach his financial or personal identity. The user provides his information and then the site redirects him to the real company site so that the user doesn't even know that they've been tricked.

These sites look so real sometimes that it can be difficult for users to know otherwise. The SmartScreen Filter helps by notifying your users if a site is suspicious. It can do this by comparing the site address that you type into your Address window to a list of known phishing sites. If you type a site that isn't on that list, but seems suspicious, it checks that site automatically, too. Sites are sent to a Microsoft server for confirmation. This provides up-to-the-minute security for users because these servers are updated constantly with new phishing sites. This global database is maintained by a list of providers as well as by user reports that come in from people who stumble upon sites that appear "phishy."

Turning on the SmartScreen Filter is not necessary because it's activated by default. You are notified while browsing the Internet if the software detects a known threatening website.

Like previous versions of Explorer you can disable this integrated protection, but why would you?

> The SmartScreen filter now has a spin-off that protects the entire Windows operating system called Windows SmartScreen. This is different from the Internet Explorer SmartScreen filter and has its own configuration settings in the Action Center. See Chapter 9, "Using Security Features in Windows 8," for more information about Windows SmartScreen.

Enhanced Protected Mode

Internet Explorer 10 also helps to protect us with a new Enhanced Protected Mode. Built off Protected Mode that was first introduced in IE7, this feature helps prevent malicious attackers from compromising your Windows 8 system. This mode better isolates your web tabs from those who would attack your system using rogue commands.

HOW PROTECTED MODE PROTECTS YOU

Here is a list of some of the new ways that Enhanced Protected Mode helps keep you safe:

Most PCs shipped in the last few years have 64-bit CPUs, and many have a 64-bit version of Windows installed. "64-bit" is usually thought of as a way to extend the amount of memory that a program on your computer can use: Because 64-bit processors use 64-bit memory addresses instead of 32-bit ones, a program can "address," or use, more memory if it's available.

A 32-bit number is large—it's a little more than 4 billion. A 64-bit address is a much larger number—roughly 18 pentillion and change (18,446,744,073,709,551,616). Not only does a 64-bit number let you address more memory, it also makes existing memory protection features such as ASLR (Address Space Layout Randomization) much more effective. Heap spray attacks, in which attackers plant malicious code at predictable locations, become much more difficult because it isn't practical to "fill up" a 64-bit address space—you'll run out of memory and disk space long before any sizable fraction of the address space is sprayed.

Source: http://blogs.msdn.com/b/ie/archive/2012/03/14/enhanced-protected-mode.aspx

 **LET ME TRY IT**

Enable Enhanced Protected Mode

To enable Enhanced Protected Mode for Internet Explorer 10, follow these simple steps:

1. In the Desktop version of Internet Explorer, click the Tools gear.

2. Select Internet Options.

3. Choose the Advanced tab.

4. Scroll down until you reach the Security heading.

5. Check the Enable Enhanced Protected Mode box (see Figure 6.11).

6. Click OK.

7. Restart your device to finalize the changes.

Figure 6.11 *Turning on Enhanced Protected Mode*

The Final Line of Defense

So, is that it? Are the security features listed in Figure 6.11 (and others included in Internet Explorer 10) all the protection a system needs when browsing the Internet? Not entirely.

Often, the bad guys who are trying to infect and take over computers adapt their methods over time. Despite all these precautions built in, often a simple social engineering attack can defeat even these sophisticated security technologies. The safest computing approach usually involves a combination of on-board security and then a well-educated user on the styles of attacks against your system. Internet Explorer 10 does its part well. Now it's up to users to also do their part in keeping Windows 8 secure.

 TELL ME MORE   Media 6.4—A Discussion of Internet Explorer 10

Access this audio recording through your registered Web Edition at
my.safaribooksonline.com/9780789750518/media.

This chapter delves into the home networking side to Windows 8 including HomeGroups and basic sharing and such to allow you to use Windows 8 in your home network environment or even small business environment.

7

Home Networking

An Introduction on Home Networking

Setting up a home network has never been astronomically difficult, but it's frustrating enough to novice users that they often give up or pay someone to come in and fix their networks. It's not the physical side that causes them pain. Walk into any store that sells computer equipment and you can pick up a wireless router or whatever else you need that will connect your home physically in a matter of minutes. But "sharing" your documents, printers, media, and so forth is a bit more challenging if you do not know how to do this (and even more challenging if you have a hodgepodge of system types—some systems running XP, Vista, or Windows 7).

With Windows 8, this pain point is addressed by HomeGroups, a feature that works only between systems running Windows 7 or 8. Obviously you can still network disparate systems together, but if you have an all-Windows 7 and 8 situation, the sharing is much easier to accomplish.

Connecting to a Network

It's typical these days for each home to have some form of incoming Internet connection. Often the cable company you work through or Internet Service Provider puts a box in your home that allows a single connection to be plugged into it. If you only have one computer that is an easy choice. However, in the modern world of multiple computers in a home, including wireless devices such as laptops, netbooks, tablets, and smartphones, more and more there is a need for your single home connection to serve multiple devices. It's becoming increasingly common for Internet Service Providers (ISPs) to provide a combination Wi-Fi router and modem to do the job of both in one box. When this is not the case, however, this is where the wireless router comes to the rescue.

Connecting to a Wireless Network

A wireless router is (usually) an under $50 purchase and may have four ports on the back for direct connectivity to a computer through an Ethernet cable. At the same time they may have single- or dual- (bunny ears) antennas that broadcast your network information through your home, although many modern wireless routers might not have any visible antenna.

Depending on the size and makeup of your home you may need an extender to have the signal available through your whole home.

Setting up your wireless router is not within the scope of this book; however, it is good to know how to do so. One thing we recommend when purchasing a wireless router is to see whether it also includes firewall and some form of parental control capabilities. One we personally like in this regard is Phantom Technologies iBoss Parental Control wireless router.

Sometimes your wireless router may offer access to your home (and neighbors) without any security enabled. This is your choice; however, it is recommended that you use a security setting on the router and set up a password.

 LET ME TRY IT

Choosing a Wireless Network

Once you have your router all set, devices can connect to it. With Windows 8 you connect to your router by performing the following steps:

1. From the Windows Desktop you should note an icon in the bottom right in the notification area that indicates you have a wireless adapter in your device. The icon may have a little star (see Figure 7.1), which indicates you have wireless networks available but are not connected to one. Select the wireless icon.

Wireless Internet access icon

Figure 7.1   *Wireless connection icon when not connected to network*

2. You may see several wireless networks to choose from. If they have a little security shield next to them this is a warning that these networks do not have a password associated with them and are open to the public. Select the wireless network you want to connect to. There is an option to Connect Automatically, which you can enable. Select the Connect button to connect to the network (see Figure 7.2).

Figure 7.2   *Making the connection automatic*

3. If the network is secured you are asked for a network security key (see Figure 7.3). Enter the password and click Next. Note that the security key might be on the router itself, or you might need to supply a password that was created when the router was set up.

4. You are asked whether you want to turn on sharing between PCs and connect to devices on this network. You can choose yes or no depending on whether you are on a home, work, or public network and how concerned you are about sharing.

5. You are shown as connected on the network list shown previously in Figure 7.2, and your icon in your notification tray shows that you're connected now.

Figure 7.3   *Putting in the network security key*

 SHOW ME   Media 7.1—Wireless Connection Settings
Access this video file through your registered Web Edition at
my.safaribooksonline.com/9780789750518/media.

 LET ME TRY IT

Advanced Wireless Connectivity

You may want to perform additional tasks with your wireless connection. The following steps show you how to accomplish this:

1. From the Windows Desktop select your wireless network connection icon in your notification tray.

2. Right-click on your connected network and note the following options (shown in Figure 7.4):

   Show Estimated Data Usage

   Set As Metered Connection

   Forget This Network

   Turn Sharing On or Off

   View Connection Properties

3. Each option presents a different focus. For example, if you want the system you are using to forget a connection that you have established in the past

you can click Forget This Network and will have to reconnect if you want to use it again in the future (meaning you will need to put the password in again).

Figure 7.4   *Advanced wireless options*

HomeGroups

As mentioned at the outset of this chapter a homegroup is a way to more easily share files and printers on your home network. You can share all sorts of things (and control what each computer on your network shares), such as pictures, music, videos, documents, and printers. They key is to create a HomeGroup and have others join it. If one already exists in your home all you have to do is join in and begin sharing.

 SHOW ME   Media 7.2—Working with HomeGroups
Access this video file through your registered Web Edition at
my.safaribooksonline.com/9780789750518/media.

Accessing HomeGroup Options

Everything you do to access and configure HomeGroup, as I'll show you in the following sections, is done from the HomeGroup settings window. You can access that window by following these steps:

   1.   From the Start screen, right-click the screen.

2. Click the All Apps button that appears on the lower-right corner of the screen.

3. Click Control Panel.

4. Click Network and Internet.

5. Click HomeGroup.

 **LET ME TRY IT**

Creating a HomeGroup

1. From the HomeGroup window, click Create a HomeGroup to launch the Create a HomeGroup Wizard.

2. Click Next and you can select what items will be available in your HomeGroup.

3. After making your selections click Next.

4. Your HomeGroup is created and you are provided a password. Take note of this password; it is provided by default. You can write it down and share it with others in the family so they can access shared items (so long as they have Windows 7 or 8 on their systems), or you can change the password to something you want.

5. Click Finish.

At this point you have successfully configured a HomeGroup. Notice that you now have more options in the Control Panel to manage your HomeGroup such as

- Change what you're sharing with the HomeGroup

- Allow all devices on this network such as TVs and game consoles to play my shared content

- View or Print HomeGroup Password

- Change the Password

- Leave the HomeGroup

After your HomeGroup is up and running, you can, at any time, revisit your settings in the Control Panel and make additional changes, such as adjustments to your media streaming options.

If you are having trouble creating a HomeGroup, make sure you check your version of Windows 8. Windows 7/8 Starter and Windows 7/8 Home Basic can *join* an existing HomeGroup but cannot start a HomeGroup. If you're having trouble connecting to a HomeGroup, verify your computer is actually connected to the correct network. If you have a wireless network connection, it can be easy to connect to the wrong network inadvertently and spin your wheels trying to solve a connectivity issue.

 **LET ME TRY IT**

Joining a HomeGroup

After a HomeGroup is up and running in your home, all the other systems need to join it. To do this, perform the following:

1. From the HomeGroup window, note whether a HomeGroup exists and is identified by your system. If so, click the Join Now option.

2. The Join a Homegroup Wizard appears. Click Next to proceed.

3. You can configure what you want to share with others when you join the HomeGroup (see Figure 7.5). You can select Shared or Unshared for Pictures, Videos, Music, Documents, and Printers & Devices. Then click Next.

4. You are asked for the password and then to verify it. Once complete, you have access to the homegroup settings (shown in Figure 7.6).

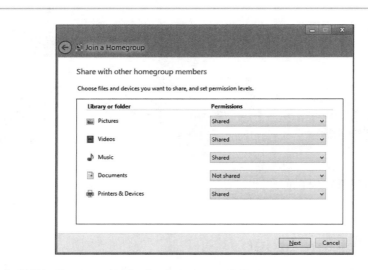

Figure 7.5 *Sharing with other homegroup members*

Figure 7.6 *Homegroup settings*

 **LET ME TRY IT**

Locating or Changing a HomeGroup Password

Follow these steps to retrieve your HomeGroup password. Once finished, you can print this password to save it for later reference or to distribute to others on your network.

1. From the HomeGroup window, click View or Print HomeGroup Password.

2. To print out the password, click Print this Page at the bottom right; otherwise, click Cancel (see Figure 7.7).

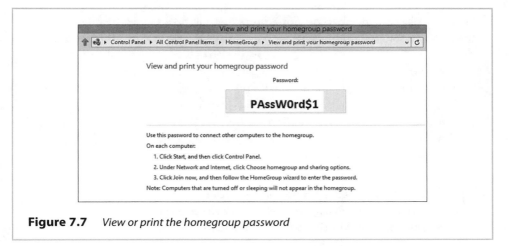

Figure 7.7 *View or print the homegroup password*

3. From the HomeGroup settings, if you want to change the password click Change the Password, which opens the Change Your Homegroup Password dialog box.

4. Verify that any current HomeGroup computers are on and not asleep or hibernating.

After you change the password, which will disconnect everyone from the homegroup, you need to go to each homegroup system and enter the new password.

5. Click Change the Password. You are prompted to accept the new password or change it.

6. Click Next.

7. Write down the password.

8. Click Finish.

One of the best parts to this is the use of Libraries. A folder such as Pictures is no longer a folder; it's a Library that can include multiple folders from multiple locations. You can control the addition of locations if you choose, but if Pictures is shared out, others can quickly view those new locations without finding a new way to connect to it. It all comes under the Library.

When it comes to sharing documents, the content is shared as read-only so that you do not have to fear items being changed without additional thought (although you can change this selectively, on a document basis, in File Explorer).

Some have asked why they cannot just create their own passwords right from the start. Apparently during the testing phase of Windows 7, the Windows development team discovered that users weren't aware they might be giving this password to others, so these users often used the same passwords they used to secure sensitive information. Rather than distribute this same password to others and potentially put their sensitive information at risk, users were given a starter password. This gave them the option of using this starter password or creating their own password. This practice has continued with Windows 8.

 SHOW ME   Media 7.3—Sharing Media
Access this video file through your registered Web Edition at
***my.safaribooksonline.com/9780789750518/media**.*

Sharing Additional Libraries with the HomeGroup

The following steps show you how to share items to your HomeGroup. In addition to adding these items to your shared library, you can also modify how they are accessed (such as view and edit).

1. On your Windows Desktop locate your Libraries using File Explorer.
2. Click on a folder you want to share, but do not open it.
3. In the top ribbon menu on the Share tab, click the drop-down arrow to the right of Share With.
4. Select HomeGroup (view and edit).
5. You might be asked for a confirmation of this. If so, click Yes.
6. This folder is now being shared as a library with view and edit (aka read/write) access to users in your HomeGroup.
7. If you want to see whether a library is being shared you can select it in File Explorer, and, with the Details pane view selected in the View tab, see whether a selected folder is shared by looking at the Shared With: field (see Figure 7.8).

Be advised that when you add libraries to the HomeGroup, those libraries need to be present and connected to be accessed. For example, you can add a folder on a removable external hard drive as a library to your HomeGroup, but it can only be accessed when the external hard drive is connected to your computer.

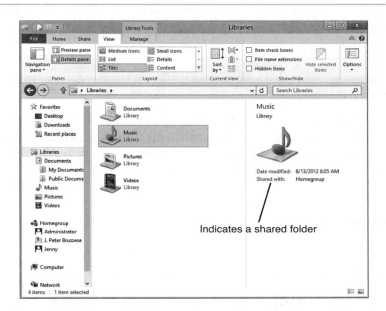

Indicates a shared folder

Figure 7.8 *Libraries are shown as "Shared with: Homegroup" after you share them.*

If you want to make a network resource part of your HomeGroup, the folder to add as a library needs to be indexed. If it isn't, a quick workaround is to make the folder available offline. This indexes the folder as it creates offline versions. You can include the folder in a library once you make it available offline. Keep in mind that these offline versions of the files in the folder will be copied to your hard drive. Make sure you have enough room on your local hard drive to accommodate the offline files that you have added to your library.

 **LET ME TRY IT**

Removing Libraries from the HomeGroup

The following exercise shows you how to select exactly which library you want to stop sharing with your HomeGroup.

1. On your Windows Desktop, locate your Libraries using File Explorer.

2. Click on a folder you want to stop sharing, but do not open it.

3. In the top menu, click the drop-down arrow on the Share ribbon, to the right of Share With.

4. Select Nobody.

The library is now removed from your HomeGroup. However, it is still accessible from the local computer.

Another interesting aspect of the HomeGroup approach is that it allows computers that are typically connected to a domain at work (such as a company laptop) to access a home network. You can join a HomeGroup and see the items in the home, but others will not be able to see back in to your system so your data is safe from prying eyes.

 **LET ME TRY IT**

Removing Your Computer from a HomeGroup

You can easily leave a HomeGroup. Follow these steps to accomplish this:

1. From the HomeGroup window, choose Leave the HomeGroup.

2. Click Leave the Homegroup.

3. Click Finish.

Troubleshooting Problems with HomeGroup

If you are having trouble with sharing in the HomeGroup, Windows 8 provides a HomeGroup troubleshooter to diagnose and locate potential problems (see Figure 7.9). By default, the troubleshooter is configured to apply repairs automatically. This is a nice feature that helps minimize support calls and lets the operating system self-heal.

 **LET ME TRY IT**

Using the HomeGroup Troubleshooter

The following steps show you how to identify issues with computers already connected to a HomeGroup:

These steps work only on computers already connected to a Homegroup.

1. From the Start screen right-click on the screen.

2. Click on the All Apps button that appears on the lower-right corner of the screen.

3. Click on Control Panel.

4. Click on Network and Internet.

5. Click on HomeGroup.

6. In the Other Homegroup Actions section, click Start the HomeGroup troubleshooter. The HomeGroup troubleshooter dialog box opens.

7. Click Next. The troubleshooter begins searching for problems and automatically fixes them (if possible).

8. Follow the wizard to complete the troubleshooter.

Public Folders and the HomeGroup

Public folder sharing (which is turned off by default) can be another easy way to share files and folders. Public folders are a quick and easy way to share a file without setting up an entire folder as a library. The weakness of Public folders, however, is that they do not restrict users to seeing only the files in the Public folder. Also, there isn't much in the way of permissions so anyone can modify a file in the Public folder. Generally, if it can be seen in the Public folders, it can be accessed. Still, if you want to share a file only temporarily with someone, Public folders are the way to go.

 **LET ME TRY IT**

Turning on Public Folder Sharing

After you complete the following steps, members of your network will be granted access to all items located in your Public folder. They will have full rights to all files in the Public folder.

1. From the Start screen right-click on the screen.

2. Click on the All Apps button that appears on the lower-right corner of the screen.

3. Click on Control Panel.

4. Click on Network and Internet.

5. Click on HomeGroup.

6. Click Change Advanced Sharing Settings.

7. Locate the Public Folder Sharing section under All Networks.

You have two different profiles with Public Folder sharing options. One is the Home/Work profile (which is most likely where you want to turn on this feature), and the other is the Public profile (which you typically want to keep locked down a bit more, so you may not want to enable it here).

8. Choose Turn On Sharing So Anyone with Network Access Can Read and Write Files in the Public Folders.

9. Click Save Changes.

10. A User Account Control (UAC) window might open. If so, click Yes.

The Network and Sharing Center

The Network and Sharing Center is your one-stop-shop for all your networking configuration controls, including adapters, sharing settings, and more.

The main panel, shown in Figure 7.9, displays information about existing network connections, and any resources the user can locate on the network. You have links at the bottom of the center for the following:

- **Set Up a New Connection or Network**—Set up a wireless, broadband, dial-up, ad hoc, or VPN connection; or set up a router or access point.

- **Troubleshoot Problems**—Diagnose and repair network problems or get troubleshooting information.

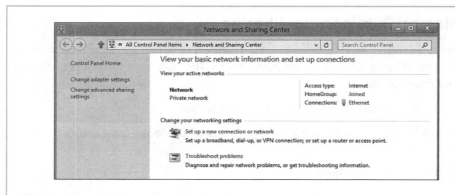

Figure 7.9   *The Network and Sharing Center*

With Windows Vista and Windows 7 the Network and Sharing Center had a mini network map. That has been removed in Windows 8.

On the left side of the screen, you can click links to Change Adapter Settings or Change Advanced Sharing Settings.

Of course, to connect on the network, you need to have installed a network adapter. These come in several forms, including network cards, USB wireless networks, or integrated network adapters built into your laptop or desktop. Fortunately, most modern network adapters are plug-and-play and get you immediately connected to the network after the cable or wireless connection is made.

If you have upgraded and suddenly disconnected from your network, there is a good chance your network drivers need to be updated. There are several ways to do this; one of these is from the aforementioned Change Adapter Settings link.

Here's a little conundrum: Your network adapter needs drivers to be updated so you can get on the Internet, but the only place to get these drivers *is* the Internet. The workaround for this could be a little tricky. The best answer is to download the drivers from another computer that can get on the Internet and then copy them to a portable USB key to install them on the computer that has the outdated drivers.

The next question is, "What type of network adapter do I have?" One way to find out is to look in Network Connections. Windows 8 might have recognized your network card but just might not have drivers for it. If you know you have a network adapter installed, you might have to consult with your computer manufacturer or take apart your computer to see the brand and model of your network card. If all this seems too difficult, buying an inexpensive plug-and-play USB network adapter is a low-priced alternative.

 **LET ME TRY IT**

Upgrade Your Network Adapter Driver

The following steps show you how to upgrade your network adapter drivers after you have downloaded them from the Internet or supplied a separate disc or USB drive that contains them:

1. Go to the Start screen.

2. Type **Control Panel**.

3. Select Network and Internet.

4. Click Network and Sharing Center.

5. In the left pane, click Change Adapter Settings (refer to Figure 7.9).

6. Point to the adapter you want to update, right-click, and select Properties.

7. If a UAC (User Account Control) window opens, click Yes.

8. Click the Configure button.

9. Select the Driver tab.

10. Click Update Driver.

11. If you have a disk or other location where you have updated network driver software, select Browse My Computer for Driver Software.

12. Type the location (or click Browse to locate the drivers) and click OK.

13. Click Next.

14. Windows searches the location for updated drivers. If it finds more than one choice, it presents you with all options. Pick the closest one to your specific hardware.

15. You might receive a notification that your drivers have not been digitally signed. Read the message carefully before proceeding. In many cases, the drivers will work. However, you have to decide whether to use them.

16. Upon successful completion and connection to the network, return to Network Connections to see an icon for your new connection.

When updating drivers, your hardware manufacturer might not yet have released drivers for Windows 8. If drivers for Windows 7 or Vista are available, install those instead. Often, drivers between the two systems are interchangeable. If and when Windows 8 drivers for your hardware are released, they most likely will be available as an optional download in Windows Update.

One newcomer to the Network and Sharing Center is View Your Active Networks, which is located just below the basic network map. Here you see all the networks you can connect to along with any to which you are currently connected.

Setting Up Your Network Location

You might have noticed each time you connect to a network for the first time a dialog box appears, asking you to select your network location. This feature was first introduced in Vista. The purpose of this dialog box is to automatically configure your firewall and security settings depending on your location. Here are the four network locations and an explanation for each one:

- **Home Network**—There are two instances when you choose this setting. One is for home networks and the other is when you know and trust the users and devices on the network. Because computers on a home network can belong to a HomeGroup, much greater access is allowed to available network resources. Network discovery is turned on for home networks, which allows you to see other computers and devices on the network and allows other network users to see your computer. This setting offers the easiest connectivity between computers and network devices.

- **Work Network**—Select Work Network if the network you are connected to is a small office or similar workplace network. You will be visible to other computers since network discovery (which allows you to see other computers and devices on a network and allows other network users to see your computer) is on by default. One restriction with this setting is that you cannot create or join a HomeGroup.

- **Public Network**—Choose Public Network for networks in public places (such as cafés, airports, or networks offering free Wi-Fi). This setting keeps your computer from being visible to other computers around you and is the most restrictive in terms of security and visibility. Use this setting on a public network to help protect your computer from any malicious software from the Internet. You cannot connect to a HomeGroup on public networks, and network discovery is turned off. Also consider using this option if you're connected directly to the Internet without using a router. A router serves as an additional layer of insulation from all Internet attacks. Without a router, your firewall needs to be set to a highly secure state. Also use Public Network if you have a mobile broadband connection. This also requires high security and firewall protection.

- **Domain**—If you see this setting, it is unchangeable and controlled by your network administrator.

When connecting to a secured network, the only requirement now is to enter the network security key (passphrase). If you are switching from Windows XP to Windows 8, this is a welcome change because you no longer have to specify the encryption type (WEP, WPA, or WPA2).

 **LET ME TRY IT**

Setting Up a New DSL Connection to the Internet

To complete the following steps, you need a broadband connection to the Internet along with the ISP-assigned username and password. Upon successful completion, you will have established a high-speed connection to the Internet.

1. Go to the Start screen.

2. Type **Control Panel**.

3. Click Network and Internet.

4. Select Network and Sharing Center.

5. Click Set up a New Connection or Network. This opens the Set Up a Connection or Network dialog box.

6. Click Connect to the Internet.

7. Click Next.

8. You are asked, "How do you want to connect?"

9. Select Broadband. The Connect to the Internet configuration screen opens.

10. Type your User Name and Password.

11. Select Remember This Password.

12. Click Connect to establish your new connection.

If you get your Internet service from a cable provider, you generally don't need to provide a username or password to connect to the Internet. You simply connect your hardware and it works.

 **LET ME TRY IT**

Network Access Through Computer

The following steps show you how to connect to another computer:

1. Go to the Start screen.

2. Type **Computer** and press Enter.

3. Note, at the top in the Computer ribbon you have several Network options including Access Media, Map Network Drive, and Add a Network Location (see Figure 7.10).

4. You can also see the various Network Locations you can connect to.

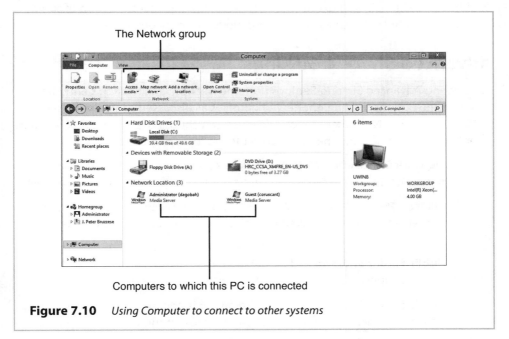

The Network group

Computers to which this PC is connected

Figure 7.10 *Using Computer to connect to other systems*

Utilizing the Network Connectivity Status Indicator (NCSI)

The NCSI is the little networking icon that sits in your Notification Area when viewing the Windows 8 desktop. It has four different states you can use to quickly see whether there is a connectivity problem.

It tells you either No Connectivity, where it has a little Red X, or Connectivity Problem, which has a little warning caution sign over it, or Local connectivity, which has only the computers, and then Internet Connectivity has the Globe on top of it indicating that you have access to the Internet.

Another enhancement to this icon is that it consolidates both wireless and wired network notification states into one icon. In the past, if you have a notebook computer and there is a network card built in and then also a wireless network card, you would have two network status icons, one of which might appear broken all the time because you don't usually have both plugged in and available.

With all your network connections tied to one icon, all you have to do to see the two separate connections is hover over the one icon, and you see the two distinct network connections listed there individually.

If your network is always on, you might not need the icon in the Notification Area, although it can help you to see whether there has been an interruption of some kind. For example, if you've accidentally dislodged a networking cable.

Advanced Sharing Settings

Selecting Advanced Sharing Settings from the Network and Sharing Center brings you to the options for different network profiles as discussed earlier in the section "Setting Up Your Network Location." Here you can choose the Home or Work profile or the Public profile. And then you can set the following options:

- **Network Discovery**—When Network Discovery is on, this computer sees other network computers and devices, and it is visible to other network computers.

- **File and Printer Sharing**—When File and Printer Sharing is on, files and printers that you have shared from this computer can be accessed by users on the network.

- **Public Folder Sharing**—When Public Folder Sharing is on, users on the network, including HomeGroup members, can access files in the Public folders.

- **Media Streaming**—When Media Streaming is on, users and devices on the network can access pictures, music, and videos on this computer. This computer can also find media on the network.

- **File Sharing Connections**—Windows 8 uses 128-bit encryption to help protect file-sharing connections. Some devices don't support 128-bit encryption and must use 40- or 56-bit encryption.

- **Password Protected Sharing**—When Password Protected Sharing is on, only a user who has a user account and a password on this computer can access shared files, printers attached to this computer, and the Public folders. To give other users access, you must turn off Password Protected Sharing.

One distinct setting between Private and Public settings is the HomeGroup connections setting (which you cannot use on the Public network side).

Media Streaming is one option that media lovers will get excited about. Enabling this option allows you to turn Windows 8 into a streaming media source for your network. By default, this feature is turned on, but you can customize it here in Advanced Sharing Settings. Click Choose Media Streaming Options to access these options.

There are a ton of possibilities with this:

- Listen to music on your Windows 8 machine from another computer on the other side of the house.

- View your videos on an Xbox 360 connected to the TV in a spare bedroom.

- Access your photo galleries stored on your Windows 8 machine on another computer.

Parents who are concerned with what content can be accessed are welcome to take control of this by clicking the Customize link. Here you can customize the content rating you will permit streamed to media programs and remote connections.

One other aspect of Media Streaming is that it runs independently of your file and print sharing security configuration. That means you can enable media streaming to multiple devices on the network without easing up the file and print sharing setup you have on the same machine.

Troubleshooting Network Problems

When you click the Troubleshoot Problems link off the Network and Sharing Center, this tool initially searches for troubleshooting packs and then presents them to you for both network and Internet options.

Troubleshooting packs are built to deal with common problems around specific topics such as printers, display, sound, networking, and so on. These packs contain a grouping of scripts to help detect a problem, resolve the problem, and then verify that the scripts actually did resolve the discovered problem.

 **LET ME TRY IT**

Accessing the Troubleshooting Packs

The new troubleshooting packs in Windows 8 are easy to locate and use. The following steps show you how to find them.

1. From the Start screen type **Control Panel**.

2. Click Control Panel.

3. Click Network and Internet (unless you have icons showing in Control Panel, in which case you can simply click the Troubleshoot link).

4. Click Network and Sharing Center.

5. Click the Troubleshoot Problems link, which opens the troubleshooting links to various packs (see Figure 7.11) including

- Internet Connections
- Shared Folders
- HomeGroup
- Network Adapter
- Incoming Connections
- Printer

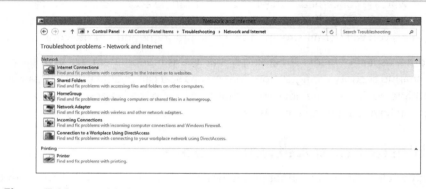

Figure 7.11   *Troubleshooting packs*

Selecting any one of the options provided opens a troubleshooting tool designed to specifically detect problems related to your choice. The benefit here is that you no longer need to search for every type of problem in the universe if your connection is giving you trouble—especially if you know that the problem is coming from the network adapter specifically or the Internet side of your network connection.

The network diagnostics automatically run a set of troubleshooting tools that analyzes all elements of the network or Internet item you've chosen and provides a systematic diagnosis of connectivity problems. It then automatically resolves the problems it finds or attempts to walk you through simple solutions.

Configuring Your TCP/IP Settings

There is a certain form of standardization in the networking world that allows our hardware to communicate with machines all over the world. Transmission Configuration Protocol/Internet Protocol (otherwise known as TCP/IP) serves as the prime communication language for our computers.

TCP/IP has evolved over the years. Windows 8 supports the latest version, IPv6. While this version supports more IP addresses than IPv4, the fundamentals of the IP stack have not changed. That's great news because that means there is little or no need for users to manually configure IP settings. For the vast majority of home users, changing TCP/IP settings is rarely—if ever—done.

Because you almost never have to configure TCP/IP settings these days, you might have forgotten some of the basics about them. Let's take a look at how to do it.

LET ME TRY IT

Opening Local Area Connection Properties

Follow these steps to see the settings for all the network adapters connected and recognized by the system.

1. From the Start screen type **Control Panel**.

2. Click Control Panel.

3. Click Network and Internet (unless you have icons showing in Control Panel, in which case you can simply click the Troubleshoot link).

4. Click Network and Sharing Center.

5. In the left pane, select Change Adapter Settings.

6. From an active network connection, right-click and choose Properties. (If a UAC window opens, click Yes.) This brings up the Local Area Connection Properties dialog box, shown in Figure 7.12.

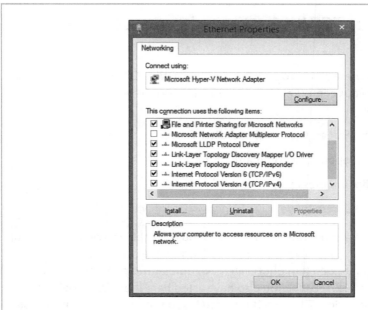

Figure 7.12   *The Local Area Connection Properties dialog box*

Dynamic Host Configuration Protocol (DHCP) is a critical part of most modern networks. Simply put, DHCP allows a computer (typically a server) or router (such as a wireless network router) to handle all the heavy lifting when it comes to creating and maintaining the network. A DHCP server provides the TCP/IP address to host devices on the network. The address is supplied in octet form (such as 192.168.0.1) and provided to devices on the network. Once DHCP is established and addresses are assigned, the network operates pretty much on its own. Windows 8 is set up out of the box to run in a DHCP environment.

There are occasions when some computers or devices might require what is called a static IP. This is a fixed address that never changes. This might be a requirement, for example, when connecting to certain network printers or copiers. Or port forwarding might be required on a certain machine. By and large, however, static IP addresses are seldom seen in mainstream home networks.

If you are asked to configure your TCP/IP settings, it's a good idea to know what your existing settings are. Then, if you have some trouble, you can restore those settings. A quick way to see your IP settings is to use the command prompt.

 **LET ME TRY IT**

Checking Your TCP/IP Settings from a Command Prompt

Upon completing these steps, you will be able to see the TCP/IP settings for all network adapters on your computer. This exercise accesses these settings through the command prompt.

1. From the Start Screen type **cmd** and press Enter.
2. A black screen opens to a command prompt.
3. Type **ipconfig** and press Enter.
4. Locate the IP address for your active network connection.

When working from a command prompt, you should be able to see the version of your IP address. (If not, you might need to scroll up on the command window to view all the IP information.) It might be an IPv4 address. The number appears in octet form (such as 192.168.0.3). You also have listed here the subnet, default gateway, and DNS information. This data is required if you ever need to establish a static IP.

The command prompt is another fast way to test your Internet connection when you have connectivity problems. For example, simply type **ping www.google.com** to send a ping request to Google. If it succeeds, you receive a reply with a status of the packet speed. If it fails, you receive a failure message, such as Ping Request Could Not Find Host.

If you need to change your TCP/IP address, first determine the type of address you have (IPv4, IPv6, or both). Once you know that, you can configure your new address.

 **LET ME TRY IT**

Changing a Network Adapter to Use a Static IPv4 Address

This exercise shows you how to change your IP settings from DHCP to static and how to insert an IPv4 address into your network adapter settings (see Figure 7.13). Keep in mind before attempting the following steps that you need to have the information you're changing to already on hand to complete them.

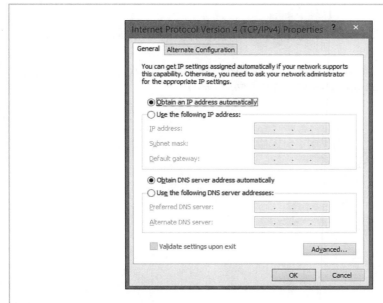

Figure 7.13   *Configuring a static IP address*

1. From the Start screen type **Control Panel**.

2. Click Control Panel.

3. Click Network and Internet (unless you have icons showing in Control Panel, in which case you can simply click the Troubleshoot link).

4. Click Network and Sharing Center.

5. In the left pane, click Change Adapter Settings.

6. From an active network connection, right-click and choose Properties. (If a UAC window opens, click Yes.) The Local Area Connection Properties dialog box appears.

7. Click the correct Internet Protocol Version (IPv4) and click Properties. The Internet Protocol Version Properties dialog box appears.

8. Select the Use the Following IPv*X* Address radio button.

9. In the IPv*X* Address box, type the new IP address.

10. Complete the information for Subnet Prefix Length box and the Default Gateway box, respectively.

11. Complete the information for the Preferred DNS Server box.

12. Click OK.

 TELL ME MORE   **Media 7.4—A Discussion of Home Networking in Windows 8**

Access this audio recording through your registered Web Edition at **my.safaribooksonline.com/9780789750518/media**.

8

This chapter delves into advanced networking features of Windows 8, showing advanced users how to get the most out of them.

Domain Networking

In this chapter, we discuss the more advanced networking features of Windows 8 and review modern network topology. This is content that you won't find applicable working on your typical small office or home network, but connecting computers together in a domain structure is standard in most mid- to large-sized organizations. This type of network is briefly examined, and you also learn how to connect to one.

Other aspects of Windows 8 networking explored in this chapter are HomeGroups, DirectAccess, BranchCache, AppLocker, Local Group Policy Settings, and remote connection applications already integrated within Windows 8.

Domain Networking

If you have ever worked in a corporate setting, you have probably used the keys Ctrl, Alt, Delete and then supplied a username and password to log on to the network or domain. Phrases such as domain, domain controller (DC), and Active Directory (AD) may not be familiar to you. However, these items are fundamental to securely sharing information and resources between computers on larger networks. One of the basic building blocks of an Active Directory structure is a domain. What is a domain?

A domain is a collection of computers joined together in a network under a single point of security administration. (Administration can also be delegated to groups of objects within a domain.) One or more of these computers must be running the Windows Server operating system (2003/2008) and be promoted to a domain controller. Once a server is promoted it runs Active Directory Services. We could write another whole book on what Active Directory is, does, and how to manage it, but as we are discussing networking with Windows 8, we will just mention one of the important roles Active Directory accomplishes. Active Directory authenticates users on a domain, which is to say it checks to see whether users are properly configured to gain access.

Before we dig deeper into that we first should mention that every computer on a network needs an IP address. An IP address is used to identify your computer on a network. It can be likened to your home address. If someone wants to send you a package he needs to know your address. The same is true when information or data needs to be sent to your computer. The IP address of your computer is needed to make sure the data is going to the right location.

How can you check to see what your IP address is? Follow these steps:

1. From the Start screen, right-click on the screen.

2. Click on the All Apps button that appears on the lower-right corner of the screen.

3. Click the Command Prompt tile.

4. Type **ipconfig** and press Enter.

5. Your IP address information appears (see Figure 8.1).

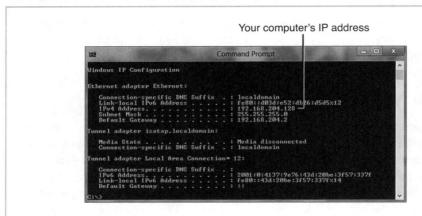

Figure 8.1 *Using ipconfig to determine your IP address*

Notice the series of numbers after IPv4 Address—this is your IP address. The Subnet Mask identifies what part of your address represents the network (or subnet) you are on and which part represents your computer on that network. The Default Gateway is the address of the router on your subnet; this is used if you need to communicate with a computer or device that is located on another subnet.

IPv6 is a new IP addressing scheme intended to replace IPv4. This is to alleviate the problem of running out of IP addresses with the IPv4 scheme. The IPv6 scheme allows for many more addresses. If IPv6 is used, ipconfig lists this information as well.

An IP address can be assigned to your computer in two different ways:

- **Dynamically**—When the computer powers up it looks for a DHCP server to get IP Address information (also gets some other information).

- **Statically**—You enter an IP address that has been provided to you.

A DHCP server could be a Windows server or an appliance or even a router that has DHCP capabilities. When your computer powers up it requests an IP address from the DHCP server. The DHCP server looks to see whether it has any available and if it does it assigns one to your computer for a specified period of time.

 LET ME TRY IT

Assigning an IP Address

Alternatively you could statically assign an IP address to your Windows 8 computer.

1. From the Start screen, right-click on the screen.

2. Click on the All Apps button that appears on the lower-right corner of the screen.

3. Click on Control Panel.

4. Click on Network and Internet.

5. Click on Network and Sharing Center.

6. Click on Change Adapter Settings in the left pane.

7. Right-click on your Ethernet Connection and select Properties.

8. Select Internet Protocol Version 4 (TCP/IPv4) in the list (see Figure 8.2).

9. While your selection is highlighted, click on Properties.

10. Click on the Use the Following IP Address radio button.

11. Now you can provide your IP Address, Subnet Mask, and Default Gateway.

12. Click OK and then click Close.

13. You can close out of any open windows.

 SHOW ME   Media 8.1—Configure TCP/IP Settings
Access this video file through your registered Web Edition at
my.safaribooksonline.com/9780789750518/media.

When assigning an IP address you will want to be sure you have valid information and that your IP address is unique on your subnet. In many larger companies IP addresses would be dynamically assigned to workstation computers and statically assigned to servers.

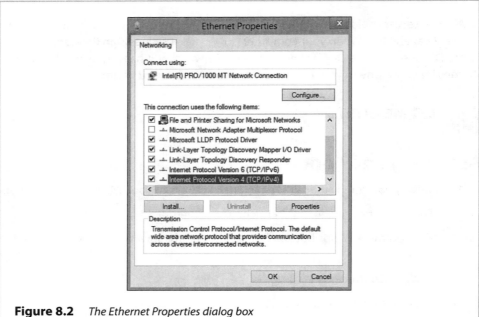

Figure 8.2   *The Ethernet Properties dialog box*

The Logon Process and Tokens

Remember the Ctrl, Alt, Delete we discussed earlier? This initiates the authentication process. When you supply your username and password and click OK, your credentials are sent to a domain controller and checked. If your username exists in the list, you have the correct password, and your account is not locked out or disabled, you gain access to the domain and are provided with a token. The token provided is based on your group membership. Now when you attempt to access a resource on the domain, such as a shared folder, your token is presented and checked to confirm the type of access you have to the object (Read, Modify, Full Control, and so on) or whether you even have permission to access the object at all.

A Discretionary Access Control List (DACL) is maintained on the objects themselves so that when a person/device/process attempts to access an object (shared file, printer, and so forth) the subject presents the token that includes groups the sub-ject is a member of. The object compares that token to the list. If any group or the user account has a Deny setting attached, the object is denied. Denied settings are kept at the top of the list so that denial is quickly determined.

Joining a Domain

You cannot just decide one day that you want to join a domain. You need to have a user account that has access on the domain and allows you to join computers to the domain. Additionally you need to be connected to the domain's network, either wired or wireless, and have an IP address that is within the scope of the domain's IP address ranges.

Once you have these items in place, the actual process for joining a domain is straightforward.

 LET ME TRY IT

Connecting to and Joining a Domain

Getting on the domain network requires authentication to the domain. The follow-ing steps show you how to accomplish this.

1. From the Start screen, right-click on the screen.

2. Click on the All Apps button that appears on the lower-right corner of the screen.

3. Click on Control Panel.

4. Choose System and Security.

5. Click System.

6. In the Computer Name, Domain and Workgroup Settings group, click the Change Settings link. (If a UAC window appears at this point, click Yes.)

7. The System Properties dialog box appears. Here you can see the current system properties. You can change the properties manually by clicking the Change button, or use a wizard by clicking the Network ID button.

8. Click the Network ID button. The Join a Domain or Workgroup dialog box appears (see Figure 8.3).

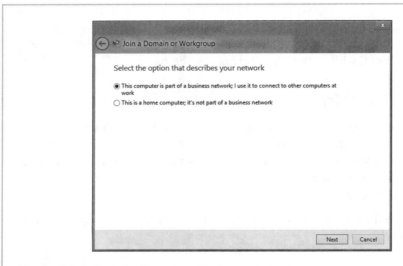

Figure 8.3   *The Join a Domain or Workgroup dialog box*

9. Select the type of network the computer will be a part of and click Next.

10. Select whether your company uses a domain or not and then click Next again.

11. Verify you have all the account information listed and click Next.

12. Type your User name, Password, and Domain name.

13. Click Next.

The wizard completes by attempting to connect you to the domain with the credentials you have provided. If you have done this correctly, your computer is added to the domain and represented as a computer object in Active Directory. Now any authenticated user can log in to the domain from your computer. This does not mean that they will automatically be able to change settings on your computer (only if they are given local access to these settings). You will notice on the logon screen you have an option to log on to the domain or to your local computer. The accounts used for these logons are different when logging on to your local computer authentication takes place on your local computer. When logging on to a domain, authentication takes place at the domain controller as discussed earlier.

Login flexibility is helpful to your network administrators. If a network administrator is troubleshooting a software issue on a certain computer, he doesn't have to carry all his software around each time he wants to solve a problem at a particular desktop. He can log in with his username and password to access all his technical resources, such as network drives and public drives containing software.

One thing to keep in mind when you join a domain is that there may be policies that apply to computer objects within the domain. So once you join you may find that you are unable to change some settings that were previously available to you, such as your Desktop and Date and Time settings just to mention a couple.

Domain-Joined Computers and HomeGroups

It has become common for us to use a laptop at work and then bring it home, so there may be a need to be a part of a domain at work and still be able to connect to shared files or media at home.

You can do this with Windows 8 because your domain joined laptop has the capability to detect and connect to a HomeGroup. Once connected to a HomeGroup you can access shared files or media on your home network. Other HomeGroup members are unable to access data on your work laptop, so business data remains secure.

That said, the capability to join a HomeGroup can be disabled by the domain administrator at will. So although you have the ability, you might not have the permission.

Creating a HomeGroup is covered in Chapter 7, "Home Networking," but after that's done, depending on your location, you can either connect to the domain your computer is a member of, or to the HomeGroup.

How does the computer know where you are? Network Location Awareness (NLA) is a feature by which the system can see whether you have changed network locations, and it can tag locations (with your help) as Home, Work, or Public. Windows 8 can switch profiles depending on which location you are using. Switching profiles affects your Windows firewall settings. When connected to a public network the firewall settings will be most restrictive.

Changing Advanced Sharing Settings

If your computer is joined to a domain, you probably won't be able to change the network location to Home or Work. It's still a good idea to configure your network options. This is easily done by changing your advanced sharing settings (see Figure 8.4).

Change sharing options for different network profiles

Windows creates a separate network profile for each network you use. You can choose specific options for each profile.

Private (current profile) ⌃

   Network discovery

      When network discovery is on, this computer can see other network computers and devices and is visible to other network computers.

        ⦿ Turn on network discovery
          ☑ Turn on automatic setup of network connected devices.
        ○ Turn off network discovery

   File and printer sharing

      When file and printer sharing is on, files and printers that you have shared from this computer can be accessed by people on the network.

        ⦿ Turn on file and printer sharing
        ○ Turn off file and printer sharing

   HomeGroup connections

      Typically, Windows manages the connections to other homegroup computers. But if you have the same user accounts and passwords on all of your computers, you can have HomeGroup use your account instead.

        ⦿ Allow Windows to manage homegroup connections (recommended)
        ○ Use user accounts and passwords to connect to other computers

Guest or Public ⌄

All Networks ⌄

🔧 Save changes   [Cancel]

Figure 8.4   *Advanced Sharing Settings*

 **LET ME TRY IT**

Manually Configuring Advanced Sharing Settings

The following steps show you how to configure several different sharing options. On completion, you will have customized how items are shared.

1. From the Start screen, right-click on the screen.

2. Click on the All Apps button that appears on the lower-right corner of the screen.

3. Click Control Panel.

4. Choose Network and Internet.

5. In the Network and Sharing Center group, click View Network Status and Tasks.

6. In the left pane, click Change Advanced Sharing Settings.

7. If not opened, click the Down arrows on the right to show your choices.

8. You may configure options in the following groups (you will see a description for each selection to guide you in your decisions):

   - Network Discovery

   - File and Printer Sharing

- Public Folder Sharing

- Media Streaming

- File Sharing Connections

- Password Protected Sharing

- HomeGroup Connections

9. After making your choices, click Save Changes.

10. If a UAC window appears, click Yes.

 SHOW ME   Media 8.2—Advanced Sharing Settings
Access this video file through your registered Web Edition at
my.safaribooksonline.com/9780789750518/media.

The Password Protected Sharing option is not available on domain networks. To use password-protected sharing, you must know the username and password of the other system for access.

The advantage of being joined to a domain is the connectivity to domain resources: other computers, printers, and so on. You may need to connect to other computers in the domain. This is not difficult; you just need to know the name or the IP address of the computer you want to access. We take a look at connecting to a remote computer later in this chapter. For now let's take a look at how we can determine our computer and domain name.

 LET ME TRY IT

Viewing Your Computer Name and Domain

The following steps show you how to view your computer name and the name of the domain it is joined to.

1. On the desktop, move your mouse over the right side of the taskbar (right side of the clock).

2. On the menu that appears on the right side of the screen, select Settings.

3. Click on PC Info.

4. The System page of the Control Panel opens.

5. In the Computer Name, Domain, and Workgroup Settings section, you see your computer name and if applicable your domain name.

Sharing files can be one of the best features of working in a domain environment. Most mid- to large-sized companies have a file server or other file sharing appliance connected to the domain. Administrators are able to manage security of the data based on your job role or in Active Directory group membership.

 **LET ME TRY IT**

Sharing a File as Read-Only with Someone Else on the Domain

You might want to share files on your local computer with others on the network. For this purpose, Windows 8 provides the Share With menu, which lets you share individual files and folders, and even entire libraries, with other people.

The following steps show you how to share files from your library with someone else on the same network.

1. From the Start screen, right-click on the screen.

2. Click on the All Apps button that appears on the lower-right corner of the screen.

3. Click on File Explorer.

4. Navigate to the file within your personal folder you want to share with another user on the domain.

5. Right-click the item you want to share and choose Share With.

6. Click Specific People. The File Sharing Wizard appears (see Figure 8.5).

7. Click the arrow next to the text box and choose the user you want to share the file with.

8. Click Add. The name appears in the list below the text box.

9. Verify that the Permission Level for this user is set to Read by clicking on the Down arrow to the right of Read.

10. Click Share.

11. If a UAC window opens, click Yes.

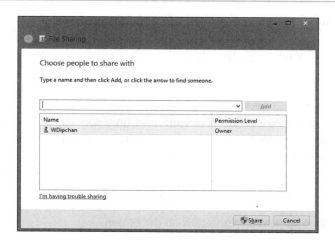

Figure 8.5 *The File Sharing Wizard*

12. You receive confirmation that the file has successfully been made available for sharing.

13. Click Email to send a link to this share to the user or copy the link, open an email client, paste the link into the body of the message, and then send it to the user.

14. Click Done.

If you are having trouble sharing an item, it could be due to one of the following factors:

- Only files from within your personal folder can be shared by default.

- If you don't see the Share With menu, you might be trying to share an item on a network or other unsupported location.

- If you're trying to share something in a Windows 8 Public folder, the Share With menu displays an Advanced Sharing Settings option. This option takes you to Control Panel, where you can turn Public folder sharing on or off.

 **LET ME TRY IT**

Using Advanced Sharing Settings to Share a Folder Outside Your File Library

Advanced file sharing lets you share more than just your libraries. If you choose, you can share the entire contents of your drive on a domain. For security reasons, this feature is turned off. If you feel you really must do this, use caution with whom you give permission to access it.

The following steps show you how to share files from outside your library with someone else on the same network.

1. From the Start screen right-click on the screen.

2. Click on the All Apps button that appears on the lower-right corner of the screen.

3. Click on File Explorer.

4. Navigate to the folder outside your library you want to share with another user on the domain.

5. Right-click the folder you want to share and choose Share With.

6. Click Advanced Sharing.

7. Select Advanced Sharing.

8. If a UAC prompt appears, click Yes or enter credentials to accept. The Advanced Sharing dialog box appears.

9. Select the Share This Folder check box.

10. Click Permissions.

11. Select Add (you can also remove users with the Remove button).

12. Choose a user or group to share your folder with.

13. Select the check boxes for the permissions you want to assign for that user or group.

14. Click OK.

15. Click OK again.

16. You have now created a share with share level permissions.

17. Click on the Security Tab to configure NTFS permissions.

18. Click on Add to add users.

19. With the user highlighted, click on level of permissions in the lower pane (notice you can specifically Deny access).

20. Once completed, click OK.

Now users on the domain that have been given permission to the share can navigate to the folder by going to Universal Naming Convention (UNC) path \\<yourcomputername>\<FolderShareName>.

Looking at DirectAccess and BranchCache

DirectAccess and BranchCache are features introduced in Windows 7 and also available in Windows 8. These features will not function unless these options have been configured on a server running Windows Server 2008 R2 or later on the network.

DirectAccess

With Windows 8 and Server 2008 R2, mobile users can access their corporate networks from any Internet connection without a Virtual Private Network (VPN) connection.

Typically, within a business network, users with mobile systems receive updates and policy changes only when they connect to the network. With DirectAccess, users do not even need to log in; as long as they have Internet access, the changes from IT can be applied.

This proves to be a real improvement for administrators in maintaining users on the go. Now, regardless of their location, administrators can be sure that even remote mobile users are guaranteed secure connections to their enterprise networks.

DirectAccess uses IPv6-over-IPsec for encrypted communications over the Internet and does not work with IPv4.

BranchCache

The name actually says what it does. Branch offices usually contain users who access data that might not be held locally (at the branch office). Using BranchCache, a user at a branch office can access various content that might be located at the main office. If, perhaps, another user at the branch attempts to access that same content, the second user can access that content faster because the content accessed by the first user can be cached on a local server.

You can set BranchCache to work in one of two modes:

- **Hosted Cache mode**—The server itself retains the cached files.

- **Distributed Cache mode**—Clients retain copies of the cached files. The server still ensures content is fresh, still maintains the latest version of files, and still maintains the permissions for accessing those files.

This type of feature requires various forms of security and some of the technologies in place include Secure Sockets Layer (SSL), Secure Message Block (SMB) Signing, and IPsec.

AppLocker

The greatest risk to any network comes from the inside, from users who have downloaded or installed unauthorized software and files that may contain viruses and malware. That is why AppLocker, shown in Figure 8.6, which is itself an update from the Software Restriction policies in Windows Vista, can really help to curtail those security risks.

AppLocker includes policy settings that can be configured to prevent unapproved software from running on a computer. These rules can be applied within Group Policy settings and can restrict all the way down to an application's version number.

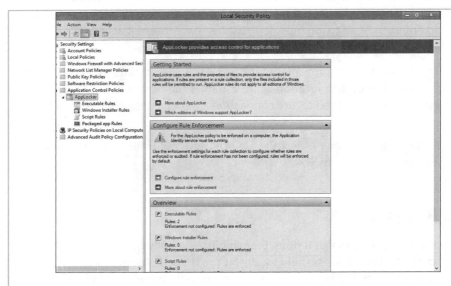

Figure 8.6   *AppLocker enables you to set policies on application usage*

Windows AppLocker contains several features:

- Audit-only mode
- Wizard to create multiple rules at one time
- Policy import or export
- Rule collection
- PowerShell support
- Custom error messages
- Rule scope can be configured for a specific user or group
- Default rule action deny

There are three types of rules:

- **Path rules**—Allow you to restrict program execution to a path (which works if all applications launch from the same paths).

- **Hash rules**—Use a cryptographic hash to ensure that the application is the right application—which works great so long as you don't have to constantly update the .exe file for the applications you use (because that changes the hash).

- **Publisher rules**—Use a digital signature from the publisher to identify the applications you approve.

 **LET ME TRY IT**

Open AppLocker to Configure Rules

The following steps show you how to access AppLocker, followed by an explanation of rule creation.

1. From the Start screen right-click on the screen.

2. Click on the All Apps button that appears on the lower-right corner of the screen.

3. Click Control Panel.

4. Choose System and Security.

5. Click Administrative Tools.

6. Double-click Local Security Policy.

7. If the UAC dialog box appears, click Yes.

8. In the console tree on the left pane, double-click Application Control Policies.

9. Double-click AppLocker and you will see rule containers.

A scenario where you might use AppLocker is if you wanted to create a rule to allow only those in the Finance department to execute certain financial applications.

You would begin by creating new rules. Right-click Executable Rules and begin with one of the following:

- **Create New Rule**—Launches a wizard that helps you create an AppLocker rule.

- **Automatically Generate Rules**—Automatically creates rules for all installed applications.

- **Create Default Rules**—Creates three rules that allow the execution of applications in both the Windows and Program Files folders.

AppLocker also has three enforcement modes:

- **Not Configured**—Rules and Group Policy Objects (GPOs) override this default setting.

- **Enforce Rules**—Enforces the configured rules.

- **Audit Only**—Allows you to preview which application is affected by a policy before enabling it. An event log records all data for review before enforcing a rule.

You can begin working with these features either through Group Policy settings or through the Local Security Policy on your desktop.

 **LET ME TRY IT**

Starting the Application Identity Service and Configuring AppLocker to Audit Rules

Auditing your rules first lets you check their effectiveness before applying them. For AppLocker to be enforced on a computer, the Application Identity service must be running.

The following steps show you how to start the Application Identity service. Next, you open AppLocker and configure it to audit rules.

1. From the Start screen right-click on the screen.

2. Click on the All Apps button that appears on the lower-right corner of the screen.

3. Select Run.

4. In the Run field, type **services.msc**.

5. If a UAC window opens, click Yes.

6. Right-click Application Identity.

7. Select Properties.

8. Using the drop-down arrow, change Startup Type to Automatic.

9. Click OK.

10. Right-click again on Application Identity.

11. Select Start.

12. Close the Services window.

13. From the Start screen, right-click on the screen.

14. Click on the All Apps button that appears on the lower-right corner of the screen.

15. Click Control Panel.

16. Choose System and Security.

17. Click Administrative Tools.

18. Double-click Local Security Policy.

19. If the UAC dialog box appears, click Yes.

20. In the console tree on the left pane, double-click Application Control Policies.

21. Double-click AppLocker.

22. In the right pane in the middle section, click the Configure Rule Enforcement link. The AppLocker properties dialog box opens.

23. On the Enforcement tab, in the Executable Rules section, select the Configured check box.

24. In the Executable Rules section, click the drop-down arrow next to Enforce Rules and choose Audit Only.

25. Click OK.

Using AppLocker's audit function allows you to see how applications would behave if your rules were enabled. It displays a list of all the files that will be enforced by the rule. As you examine this, you can spot any troubles that might crop up before deploying the rule.

Local Group Policy Settings

Local Group Policy settings have existed since the introduction of Windows 2000. From a network perspective, policies help administrators control groups of computers and users. But on a local level, you can still use a policy (the local policy) to control users who log on to that particular machine.

Vista included the Multiple Group Policy Objects feature, which provided for the use of more than one local policy. Multiple Group Policy Objects can be created to control the computer or users that log in. So, you can create a policy that affects an individual user or a policy that affects all standard users (called non-Administrators when configuring the policy). It is up to you.

To work with this feature, you need to access Local Group Policy settings, shown in Figure 8.7, from the Microsoft Management Console (MMC). When you add the GPOE snap-in, the Group Policy Wizard begins.

If you're experienced with using the gpedit.msc snap-in, know that this isn't the same as opening the policy with gpedit.msc (which opens the actual local policy itself). You are looking to configure a different policy here.

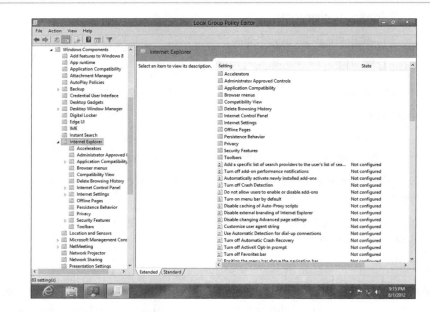

Figure 8.7   *Browsing through Internet Explorer policy options*

 **LET ME TRY IT**

Opening MMC and Saving the Local Group Policy Editor Snap-In

The following steps show you how to add the Local Group Policy editor snap-in to the Microsoft Management Console and save it. After this is completed, you can return to this saved configuration and open it directly.

1. From the Start screen, right click on the screen.

2. Click on the All Apps button that appears on the lower-right corner of the screen.

3. Select the Run tile.

4. Type **mmc** in the Run dialog box and click OK.

5. If the UAC dialog box appears, click Yes.

6. After the MMC dialog box appears, click File.

7. Choose Add/Remove Snap-In.

8. In the left pane, click Group Policy Object Editor.

9. Click the Add > button. This opens the Group Policy Wizard.

10. Local Computer is selected by default. Click Finish.

11. Click OK.

12. In the center pane, click Local Computer Policy.

13. In the top menu, click File and choose Save As.

14. Browse to a location where you can easily locate this file.

15. In the File Name box, type **Local Group Policy Editor.msc**.

16. Click Save.

From here you have the choice of setting policies for Computer Configuration or User Configuration. Past that, there are extensive choices to audit or to lock down the machine even further.

You might notice entries in your policy for your users that you never put there. This happens sometimes when you activate a security feature. For example, if you set up parental controls for a user, an individual user policy object is created behind the scenes. This policy then shows up in the policy editor even though you never explicitly added it here.

Creating a 90-Day Password Policy Using Local Security Policy Editor

The following steps show you how to create a 90-day password policy, which forces users to change their password every 90 days. Many companies force password changes to enhance the security of their network.

1. From the Start screen, right-click on the screen.

2. Click on the All Apps button that appears on the lower-right corner of the screen.

3. Click on Control Panel.

4. Click on System and Security.

5. Click on Administrative Tools.

6. Click Local Security Policy.

7. If a UAC window opens, click Yes.

8. Double-click Account Policies.

9. Double-click Password Policy.

10. Double-click Maximum Password Age in the right pane.

11. In the Local Security Setting tab, type **90** in the box.

12. Click Apply.

13. Click OK.

14. Close the Local Security Policy editor. Your changes have been made.

To use the Local Security Policy, you must be a member of the Administrators group on the local computer or you must have been delegated the appropriate authority to use it. If the computer is joined to a domain, members of the Domain Admins group will likely be able to perform this procedure.

Remote Desktop Connections

Accessing your computer or other computers remotely is increasing in demand as more and more users are working from home. Early on, PCAnywhere and now GoToMyPC.com have become major developers of this technology. Windows 8 brings us the latest Remote Desktop Connection Version 6.2 (see Figure 8.8).

Figure 8.8 *Remote Desktop Connection Version 6.2*

The Remote Desktop Connection client that comes with Windows 8 is equipped with new and enhanced features, including the Remote Desktop Protocol (RDP) version 8. The Remote Desktop Connection client includes the following features:

- Direct 2D and Direct 3D 10.1 application support
- True multimonitor support
- RDP Core Performance Improvements
- Multimedia enhancements
- Media Foundation support
- DirectShow support
- Low Latency audio playback support
- Bidirectional audio support

- A Detect Connection Quality Automatically setting under the Experience tab (see Figure 8.9)

- The ability to authenticate using Live ID and sync personal settings

Figure 8.9   *New features in Remote Desktop Connection include the Detect Connection Quality Automatically setting.*

 **LET ME TRY IT**

Opening Remote Desktop Connection

The following steps show you how to quickly open Remote Desktop Connection.

1. From the Start screen, right-click on the screen.

2. Click on the All Apps button that appears on the lower-right corner of the screen.

3. Click the Remote Desktop Connection tile. This opens the Remote Desktop Connection application.

4. In the lower left, click Show Options to view the following tabs:

    - General

    - Display

- Local Resources

- Programs

- Experience

- Advanced

Despite its simple interface, Remote Desktop Connection is a powerful tool. It simplifies your efforts to work on your laptop by giving you the ability to access all of your work-related programs, files, and network resources as though you were sitting in front of your computer at work.

 **LET ME TRY IT**

Configuring Remote Desktop Connection Permission on a Host Machine

Before you can begin working with Remote Desktop Connection, both the computer you sit at (client) and the computer you connect with (host) require some configuration. Microsoft has forced you to manually configure the program in an effort to provide a greater degree of security. Forcing manual configuration of the program—rather than enabling access by default—ensures unwanted guests do not have access to computers to do as they please.

The following steps show you how to modify the connection settings for Remote Desktop Connection (see Figure 8.10). After completing these steps, you will be ready to connect with another system.

1. From the Start screen, right-click on the screen.

2. Click on the All Apps button that appears on the lower-right corner of the screen.

3. Click Control Panel.

4. In the Control Panel group, click System and Security.

5. In the right pane, under System click Allow Remote Access.

6. The Remote tab of the System Properties dialog box opens (see Figure 8.10).

7. Select the second radio button, Allow Remote Connections to This Computer.

8. Click Select Users.

9. Add a username. (If you are an administrator of the machine, by default you will be able to connect.)

10. Click OK, and then click OK again.

Figure 8.10   *Modifying connection settings for Remote Desktop*

If you check the Allow Connections Only from Computers Running Remote Desktop with Network Level Authentication (Recommended) box only clients running RDP version 6.0 or later will be able to connect. RDP version 6.0 was introduced with Windows Vista. Windows XP Service pack 3 included RDP version 6.1, but you need to update the registry to take advantage of this function.

Network Level Authentication (NLA) requires a user to provide a username and password before establishing a session with the server. Older versions will establish a session and you will see the logon screen of the server. Allowing a session to the server before you authenticate uses resources on the server and could potentially be a risk for Denial of Service attacks.

To access a remote machine through Remote Desktop Connection, the machine needs to be out of sleep or hibernation mode. Make sure the settings for sleep and hibernation (if available) are set to Never.

 **LET ME TRY IT**

Connecting with Another Computer on the Same Network

With the system properly set up from the previous exercise, the following steps show you how to connect with another computer using Remote Desktop Connection.

1. From the Start screen, right-click on the screen.

2. Click on the All Apps button that appears on the lower-right corner of the screen.

3. Click Remote Desktop Connection. This opens the Remote Desktop Connection application.

4. In the Computer text box, type the computer name (or IP address, if you're on a local network).

5. In the User Name text box, type the username.

6. Click the Options button in the lower-left of the application. Select the Allow Me to Save Credentials check box.

7. Click Connect.

8. Log in with credentials.

9. On acceptance, you are logged in to the machine.

With the host computer properly configured, you can now access this computer from the client (provided you know the computer name or IP address).

RemoteApp and Desktop Connections

Windows 8 also features RemoteApp and Desktop Connections (see Figure 8.11), a new way to connect remotely to your computer. The focus here is on corporate networks. With this application, you can use access programs and desktops (remote computers and virtual computers) made available to you by your IT department.

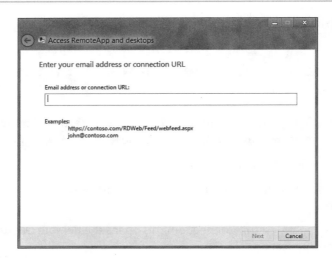

Figure 8.11 *Connect remotely with a URL through the new RemoteApp and Desktop Connections.*

When you're at home, you can access all the programs and computers that you normally would access only at work. By utilizing RemoteApp and Desktop Connections rather than Remote Desktop Connection or other means to connect, your network administrator can publish resources available for you to access and give you either a special file or URL to set up the connection. Then he can update these resources, which are then automatically passed on to you. With this type of connection, all of these resources are located in one easy-to-access folder on your computer. Using these resources is almost the same as if they were on your local network or on your computer.

 **LET ME TRY IT**

Starting RemoteApp and Desktop Connections Using a URL

The following steps show you how to use RemoteApp and Desktop Connections to connect your corporate network, assuming you have a corporate network configured to accept this type of connection.

1. From the Start screen, right-click on the screen.

2. Click on the All Apps button that appears on the lower-right corner of the screen.

3. Select Control Panel.

4. In the Search field, type **remote**.

5. In the Control Panel group, click RemoteApp and Desktop Connections.

6. In the left pane, click Access Remote Apps and Desktops. This opens the Access Remote Apps and Desktops dialog box.

7. In the Connection URL text box, type the web address provided by your administrator and click Next.

8. The Ready to Set Up the Connection dialog box opens.

9. Read the security warning provided and then click Next.

Adding Connection Resources opens and verifies the connection to start downloading the data.

 TELL ME MORE   Media 8.3—A Discussion of Domain Networking in Windows 8

Access this audio recording through your registered Web Edition at
my.safaribooksonline.com/9780789750518/media.

This chapter covers several security features integrated into Windows 8 and shows how to configure them.

9

Using Security Features in Windows 8

An Overview of New Security Features

One of the more compelling aspects of Windows 8 as an OS that should be deployed in both your home, small business, or the enterprise is the increase in security features, some of which can be demonstrated and are part of using Windows 8 and some of which operate under the hood.

One of the more controversial features to the new Windows release is called Secure Boot. The actual controversy doesn't have anything to do with the technology itself but with the drama surrounding Microsoft's mandates for its implementation on Intel and ARM systems. Essentially, it takes advantage of UEFI (Unified Extensible Firmware Interface), the modern-day replacement to the BIOS.

An ordinary BIOS cannot tell the difference between the legitimate boot loader and a rootkit. That's why Windows 8 systems ship with a certificate in the UEFI that analyzes the boot loader to ensure it is both the right one and is signed by Microsoft. If your system is infected with a rootkit, the UEFI won't boot. In other words, UEFI protects the pre-OS environment.

Secure Boot is the first part of what Microsoft calls the Trusted Boot process. The second part is a new security feature where Windows can protect the integrity of the kernel, system files, boot-critical drivers, and even the antimalware software (which is the first third-party piece to start up). As the system is booting, Windows 8 detects whether any of these elements have been tampered with and automatically restores the unmodified versions. I don't know why this wasn't implemented long ago, but I'm happy to see it now.

Another security capability available for systems using a Trusted Platform Module (TPM) is called Measured Boot. Microsoft has supported TPM for years, mainly for access and encryption management, but it is not widely adopted. It should be. As enhanced in Windows 8, this feature lets Windows measure every component from firmware through the boot drivers and stores these on the TPM on the system. This log is considered trusted (it is both spoof-and tamper-resistant), so the antimalware tool can use it to ensure the system is not running any malware. The antimalware tool can send this log to a remote system to have it evaluated, and the remote system may initiate corrective measures. Although this feature requires systems with the TPM built in, it brings greater security.

Along with the boot process enhancements to security, Microsoft focuses on every aspect of Windows 8 to ensure greater protection. For example, there are two new password types: a four-digit PIN and a picture password where you use a photo and set three gestures (on touchscreen devices) that ultimately comprise your "password."

Although you can choose your antimalware tool, Windows 8 comes with Microsoft's Windows Defender, beefed up to protect your system from all forms of malware. It uses Windows Update to update its malware signatures.

If you've played around with Internet Explorer, you know the Smart Screen filter protects your system from phishing attacks and harmful sites on the Internet. In IE9, Microsoft added a new feature called application reputation to help shield users from downloading applications that may be harmful. In Windows 7, Microsoft expanded the Smart Screen technology, URL reputation system, and file/application system to work across the entire OS—you're protected no matter what browsers you use. The version in Windows 8 is a bit stronger and there are ways to adjust it through the Action Center.

Microsoft has also enhanced security features such as BitLocker (which now supports drives that come encrypted from the manufacturer), AppLocker (which lets you control which applications can be run), and DirectAccess (which manages VPN connections).

The Action Center

The Action Center offers a quick access point for both security and maintenance aspects of your system. Security elements include the firewall, Windows Update, virus protection, spyware protection, and more. Maintenance elements include the new file history features, automatic maintenance features, and more.

Opening the Action Center

You can open the Action Center, shown in Figure 9.1, a few different ways:

- From the Start screen type **Action** and then select Settings from your Search pane, which shows you the Action Center option. Click Action Center to open it.

- From the Start screen type **Control Panel** and then open the Control Panel. From here you can select the Review Your Computer's Status option from under the System and Security category.

- From the Start screen type **Control Panel** and then open the Control Panel. From here if you change the View By settings to large or small icons you see the Action Center icon and can double-click that icon to open the Action Center.

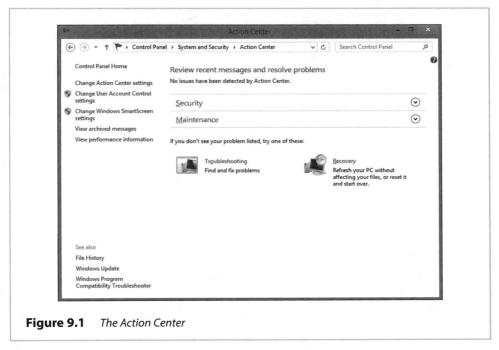

Figure 9.1   *The Action Center*

Security and Maintenance are the focal points of the Action Center. Once you open the initial screen, note the down arrows displayed in the Security and Maintenance sections. Click these arrows to see the state of the security and maintenance of your OS. Figure 9.2 shows the options listed in the Security group.

The Security group includes the following settings:

- Network Firewall
- Windows Update
- Virus Protection
- Spyware and Unwanted Software Protection
- Internet Security Settings
- User Account Control
- Windows SmartScreen
- Network Access Protection
- Windows Activation

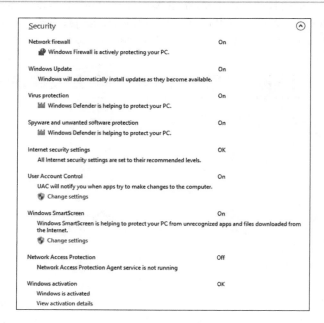

Figure 9.2   *The Security settings of the Action Center*

In the Maintenance section you can click the down arrow to reveal the status of the following settings:

- Check for Solutions to Problem Reports

- Automatic Maintenance

- HomeGroup

- File History

- Drive Status

- Device Software

 **LET ME TRY IT**

Change Action Center Settings

You can alter the settings to control what you see through the Action Center by performing the following steps:

1.   Open the Action Center.

2. Select the Change Action Center Settings link on the left-hand side (refer to Figure 9.1).

3. By default all the options are turned on; however, you can deselect and turn off both Security and Maintenance messages you feel are irrelevant by clearing the check box associated with that option (see Figure 9.3).

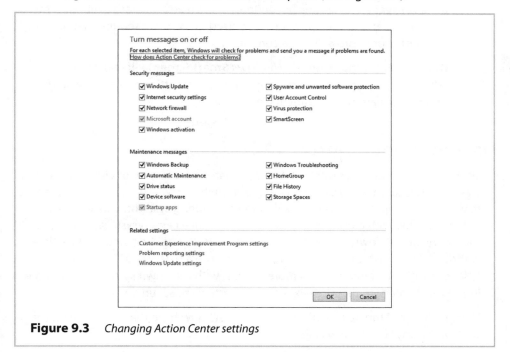

Figure 9.3 *Changing Action Center settings*

Windows SmartScreen

As mentioned earlier, one of the enhanced features in Windows 8 is the SmartScreen protection, which you can turn on or off through the Action Center as illustrated in Figure 9.3. There's more you can do with the Action Center, however, than just turn it on or off. The Change Windows SmartScreen Settings link on the left-hand panel of the Action Center allows you to leave it on, but customize how it works.

 SHOW ME   Media 9.1—Understanding Windows SmartScreen
Access this video file through your registered Web Edition at
my.safaribooksonline.com/9780789750518/media.

From the SmartScreen Settings page, you can choose how you want Windows to handle unrecognized apps by selecting one of the following options:

- **Get administrator approval before running an unrecognized app from the Internet (default and recommended option)**—If configured by an administrator, this setting will ensure standard users will need an administrator to provide credentials before the unrecognized app will run.

- **Warn before running an unrecognized app, but don't require administrator approval**—This setting, if configured by an administrator, will warn the standard user that the app is unrecognized but will not require that he gain administrator approval before continuing.

- **Don't do anything (turn off Windows SmartScreen)**—If chosen by an administrator (which is not recommended), this setting will make it so that there is no warning for unrecognized apps.

User Account Control (UAC)

User Account Control was dubbed the "most hated new feature of Vista" and yet that was likely because users weren't really sure what its purpose was. To truly appreciate it, you have to think about pre-Vista Windows operating systems. Usually users were either provided with administrative privileges to make certain system changes or they were locked down so that they couldn't even change their system clock time without an administrator's help. There needed to be a balance. UAC achieves that balance by giving standard users more abilities with their own systems without giving so much freedom that they expose their systems to security risks.

Here are a few of the abilities that standard users now have that they didn't have back in the days of Windows XP:

- View system clock and calendar

- Change time zone

- Install Wired Equivalent Privacy (WEP) to connect to secure wireless networks

- Change power management settings

- Add printers and other devices that have the required drivers installed on their computers or have been allowed by an administrator in Group Policy

- Install ActiveX Controls from sites approved by an administrator

- Create and configure a Virtual Private Network connection

- Install critical Windows Updates

- Change the desktop background and modify display settings

- Use Remote Desktop to connect to another computer

All users (including admins) run in a standard mode. This is what frustrated admins working with Vista, but we will get to that soon enough. Let's first consider how this benefits admins and users alike. With Windows 7 and 8, standard users now have more control over their systems, allowing them to do their work without having admin privileges and without bothering the administrator. In addition, standard users do not have the ability to do things that will hinder their machine or the network, so administrators have less to worry about. This not only prevents users from accidentally messing around with their systems or their networks, it prevents malware from sneaking into systems. If malware makes an attempt, a prompt appears and users cannot proceed without supplying credentials.

This process is called Administrative Approval Mode, and it treats all users as if they were standard users, requiring them to enter administrative credentials to proceed with operations that could potentially be used to harm the system. Even if you are an administrator, logged in already with your proper credentials, you still have to approve these actions, which can include installing a program or granting a running program access to the Internet.

When a user attempts to perform an operation that requires administrative credentials, a dialog appears, showing a little shield graphic next to the option and prompting the user for credentials. This has been called "over-the-shoulder" credentials because a user either knows the password for the admin or the admin can come over and type it for the user. Administrators can also disable this feature altogether; then the dialog box informs the user that she cannot perform the operation.

This sounds like a good thing, and it is a good thing. But it can be bothersome to an administrator. When an administrator logs into Vista and tries to access a resource that requires administrative credentials, the system still displays a dialog box that requires the admin to agree before moving forward. In a normal workday, a standard user might go the entire day without seeing one of these. But admins see bunches of these every day.

When this credential request is initiated you also see your screen darken—what Microsoft calls a Secure Desktop mode. When your computer is in this mode, only trusted processes running as SYSTEM continue running. This prevents malicious applications from manipulating the prompt for the UAC and can still achieve a spoofing attack on you. You might think you are clicking a UAC button but it is really a fake. So, this Secure Desktop mode is just as important as the credential requests.

One danger in getting too used to seeing these prompts is that you might just agree without reading what you're granting permission for. So, you should take a moment to make sure you requested the application that's asking for permission. In addition, you should make sure your antispyware and antivirus applications are up to date so that nothing accidentally gets through. Most antivirus applications include an auto-update feature for both the application and virus definitions.

Fortunately, you can control how UAC works without making extreme changes that are likely to compromise system security. There is a simple slider, shown in Figure 9.4, that you can use to select four different settings.

The slider options are found through the Action Center.

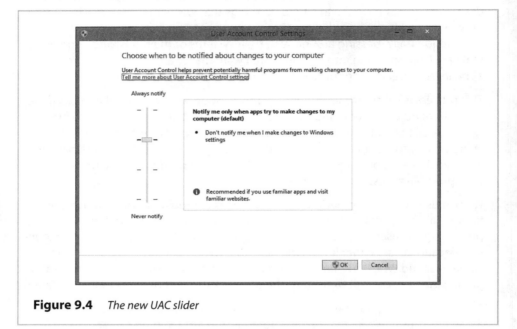

Figure 9.4   *The new UAC slider*

 **LET ME TRY IT**

Adjusting Your UAC Settings

Although I recommend that you leave UAC at its default setting, the following steps show you how to adjust the UAC settings. While many users opt to turn it off, this leaves your system more vulnerable to intrusion. Consider setting it to a low setting at first; you might find that a low setting works well without being intrusive.

1. Open the Action Center.

2. From the links pane on the left, click Change User Account Control Settings. Simply move the UAC slider to your preferred setting. There are four settings to choose from:

> Another way to adjust UAC settings is through the User Accounts link in Control Panel. You can select users and adjust their settings.

- **Always Notify Me When**—Apps try to install software or make changes to my computer and (when) I make changes to Windows settings. (Recommended if you routinely install new software and visit unfamiliar websites.)

- **Default—Notify Me Only When Apps Try to Make Changes to My Computer**—Don't notify me when I make changes to Windows settings. (Recommended if you use familiar apps and visit familiar websites.)

- **Notify Me Only When Apps Try to Make Changes to My Computer (Do Not Dim My Desktop)**—Don't notify me when I make changes to Windows settings. (Not recommended. Choose this only if it takes a long time to dim the desktop on your computer.)

- **Never Notify Me When**—Apps try to install software or make change to my computer or (when) I make changes to Windows settings. (Not recommended under any circumstances.)

Keep in mind the option to not dim the desktop is basically turning off the Secure Desktop mode. As you learned earlier in this chapter, this is important in the protection process.

UAC Within Your Network

User Account Control is certainly a positive solution for small offices, where you might not have a domain in place because you can create standard user accounts that allow users to log on to the system but don't allow them to make any major changes to the system if they don't have the correct credentials.

On an even higher level, UAC operates on a larger network level to protect computers in the enterprise. However, one concern is that administrators can be too easily tempted to give away their credentials in an effort to avoid the time-consuming task of providing the "over the shoulder" credentials that are needed.

If you have an application or device that requires administrative credentials and you don't want to constantly provide those for a user within your environment, you can use the Standard User Analyzer (SUA). It looks at the administrator credentials necessary for a standard user to run that particular application or hardware and then mitigates those permissions (loosens them up, so to speak) to allow that user to perform that particular operation without requiring the user to call upon the administrator to intervene.

For more information on the SUA, visit http://technet.microsoft.com/en-us/library/cc766193%28WS.10%29.aspx or watch a demo here: http://technet.microsoft.com/en-us/windows/standard-user-analyzer.aspx.

Windows Defender

Spyware, malicious or invasive software that installs itself onto your PC, typically along with some other program, can do any number of things to annoy you and slow your system. It can display pop-up ads, alter your Internet settings, and even use private information without permission. Windows Defender is Microsoft's answer to spyware (keyloggers, bots, rootkits, and so on) as well as viruses. It's a relatively simple tool (with an easy-to-use dashboard, as shown in Figure 9.5) you can use to perform an immediate scan of your system to look for the latest spyware or viruses and eliminate them from your system.

Figure 9.5   *Windows Defender*

Behind the simple dashboard of Windows Defender, the underlying engine constantly works in the background to protect you, even silently looking into ZIP files (or other archive file formats) for harmful software within them, even before you open the files (which is a huge benefit because many spyware/virus/malware creators use archive installers).

 **LET ME TRY IT**

Performing a Quick or Full Scan with Windows Defender

The following steps show you how to scan your computer for spyware that might be located in the most common file locations. The default settings should not be changed for this scan.

1. From the Start screen type **defender**.

2. Select the Windows Defender link that appears in the results.

3. Click the Scan Now button. By default, Quick Scan searches the most likely locations for any spyware and any apps that are currently running.

4. If you want to perform a Full scan of your system you can adjust the Scan Options and choose Full. A Full scan checks all the files on your hard disk.

 **LET ME TRY IT**

Performing a Custom Scan of Your Computer from the Windows Defender Console

Similar to the previous steps, the following steps show you how to select exactly what is scanned. With a Custom scan you check only the files and locations you prefer.

1. Open Windows Defender.

2. Under Scan Options select Custom Scan and then select the Scan Now button.

3. From the dialog window you can select the drives and folders you want to scan.

Some of us leave our systems on 24/7. If you don't, then you should know that Windows Defender is set up by default to scan your system at 2 a.m. each day. You might want to adjust this setting so it scans according to your computing schedule.

LET ME TRY IT

Checking for Windows Defender Definition Updates

Like all spyware protection software, Windows Defender is most effective after it has received the latest definition updates. The following steps show you how to download the latest updates.

1. Open Windows Defender.

2. Select the Update tab (shown in Figure 9.6).

3. Click the Update button.

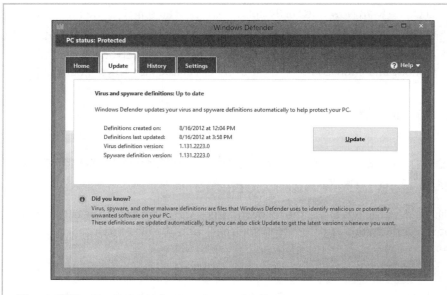

Figure 9.6   *The Update tab in Windows Defender*

LET ME TRY IT

Reviewing Windows Defender History

When Windows Defender detects items that are potentially harmful you are given the option to take actions. You can quarantine items (where items are prevented from running but not removed from your PC), allow them, or remove them. To see a list of items found and the actions you took, perform the following:

1. Open Windows Defender.

2. Select the History tab (see Figure 9.7).

3. Choose the View Details button to show the details.

4. Select one of the options (Quarantined Items, Allowed Items, or All Detected Items).

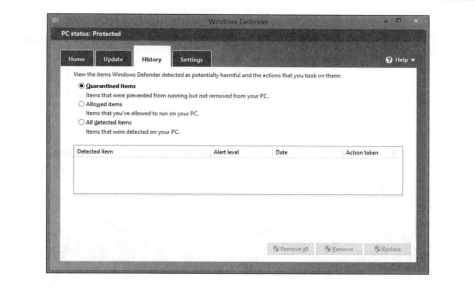

Figure 9.7   *The History tab in Windows Defender*

 **LET ME TRY IT**

Windows Defender Settings

Many stick to the default settings with Windows Defender; however, you may want to review these and make adjustments if you feel comfortable doing so and understand the purpose.

To view the Settings tab follow these steps:

1. Open Windows Defender.

2. Select the Settings tab. Note that there are seven options to choose from, including

- **Real-Time Protection**—Allow Windows Defender to protect you while you work. It can scan downloaded files and attachments as well as scan programs that run on the computer. You can turn this on or off. It is recommended you leave it on.

- **Excluded Files and Locations**—You can exclude certain files and locations to speed up your scan process; however, it leaves your computer less protected.

- **Excluded file types**—You can exclude file types from scans, which may speed up your scan process but can leave your computer less protected against the latest malware.

- **Excluded Processes**—You can exclude specific processes from scans, which (as noted above) may make your scan process faster but will leave your computer less protected. You should only exclude files with the extension .exe, .com, or .scr.

- **Advanced**—Here you can configure how scans are conducted, such as whether to scan the contents of archive files, scan removable drives, and more (see Figure 9.8).

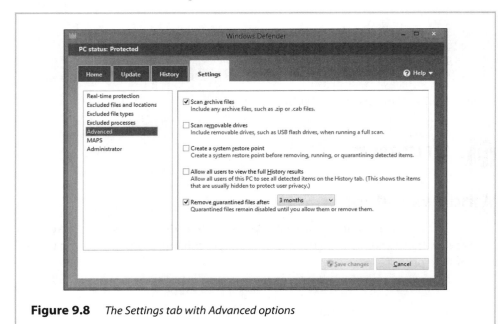

Figure 9.8   *The Settings tab with Advanced options*

- **MAPS**—MAPS stands for the Microsoft Active Protection Service, which was originally known as SpyNet. The purpose of this service is to have users automatically report back to Microsoft information about malware that has been detected. There are three options to choose:

- I Don't Want to Join MAPS

- Basic Membership (the default setting): which reports back basic information about the infection, such as where it came from, actions that you applied, and whether these were successful.

- Advanced Membership: In addition to basic information, choosing this option sends more detailed information about the malware and the location of the software, filenames, how it operates, and how it has impacted your PC.

- **Administrator**—Allows you to turn Windows Defender on or off.

3. When you're done making changes, click Save Changes to save your selections.

Windows Firewall

The Windows Firewall is meant to protect your system from hackers or malicious software gaining access to your system through the Internet or your network. It does this by breaking down your connectivity into two parts, a private network (home or work where you have a greater amount of trust) and a guest or public network (like a coffee shop with WiFi where you might not be as trusting).

Having the private network broken into home or work allows you to configure your HomeGroup network to allow persons within the same HomeGroup to easily share printers, libraries of files, pictures, music, videos, and so forth. (You can learn more about HomeGroup in Chapter 7, "Home Networking.")

Public networks (like an airport or a coffee shop) require a stricter level of protection. So rather than making changes on-the-fly, your system adjusts to the new network and is more protective based on the settings you put in place for public networks.

You can get to the Windows Firewall using any of the following methods:

- From the Start screen type **Firewall** and then under Settings choose the Windows Firewall link.

- From Control Panel categories you can select the System and Security option and then click Windows Firewall.

- From Control Panel items you can find the Firewall icon and access your settings in this way.

Initially you are shown basic status and information about your private and public networks, and you see whether you are connected to one or the other, as shown in Figure 9.9. From here you can access all the configuration aspects of the Windows Firewall.

Figure 9.9   *Windows Firewall*

 **LET ME TRY IT**

Turning On/Off Windows Firewall

The following steps show you how to turn on or off Windows Firewall. This can be done with little harm to computers not connected to the Internet. However, if your computer is connected to the Internet, you probably don't want to turn off Windows Firewall. If you need to allow a valid application through the firewall, you learn how to do this in the next section.

1. From the Windows Firewall settings, in the left pane, click Turn Windows Firewall On or Off.

2. Note the options available in addition to the Turn on Windows Firewall options (see Figure 9.10). These include

    - Block All Incoming Connections, Including Those in the List of Allowed Programs

    - Notify Me When Windows Firewall Blocks a New Program

    - Turn Off Windows Firewall (Not Recommended)

3. To the right of the red shields in both the private and public network settings, select the Turn Off Windows Firewall (Not Recommended) radio buttons to turn the Firewall off.

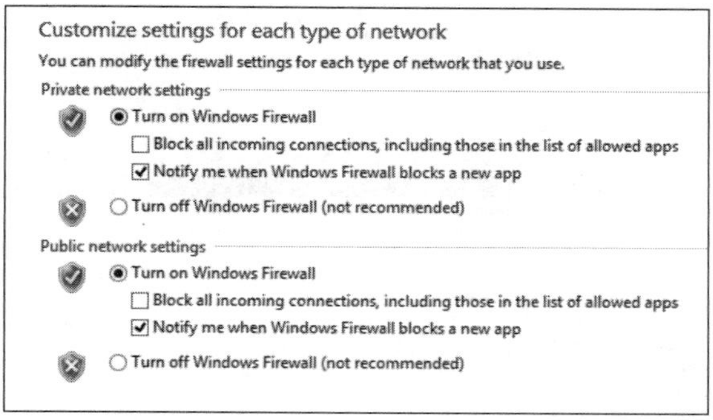

Customize settings for each type of network

You can modify the firewall settings for each type of network that you use.

Private network settings

◉ Turn on Windows Firewall

☐ Block all incoming connections, including those in the list of allowed apps

☑ Notify me when Windows Firewall blocks a new app

◯ Turn off Windows Firewall (not recommended)

Public network settings

◉ Turn on Windows Firewall

☐ Block all incoming connections, including those in the list of allowed apps

☑ Notify me when Windows Firewall blocks a new app

◯ Turn off Windows Firewall (not recommended)

Figure 9.10 *Windows Firewall Customize Settings*

If you are having trouble connecting to a network or resource, you might want to troubleshoot the problem by first turning off Windows Firewall temporarily. If you then succeed in connecting, it's safe to say that Windows Firewall was blocking the connection. You can then restore the firewall, letting the resource through as an exception.

 **LET ME TRY IT**

Allowing an App or Feature Through Windows Firewall

By allowing an app (formerly called programs) through Windows Firewall, you can keep the firewall turned on while letting a specific application through. The following steps show you how to do this.

1. Open the Windows Firewall.

2. In the left pane, click Allow an App or Feature Through Windows Firewall (see Figure 9.11). The Allowed Apps page appears.

3. Select the Name of the allowed app or feature from the list of apps available.

4. Select the Private and/or Public check box.

5. Click OK.

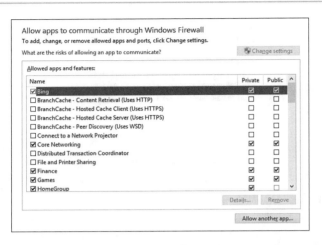

Figure 9.11   *Allowing apps through the Firewall*

If you need to add an app that isn't in the list already you can click the Allow Another App button.

Opening Windows Firewall with Advanced Security

In addition to the basic Firewall that comes with Windows 8, there is an advanced version as well (see Figure 9.12). To access the advanced Firewall you can perform either of the following:

- Open Windows Firewall and click the Advanced Settings link on the left side of the screen.

- From the Start screen type **Administrative** and go to the Administrative Tools. Then select Windows Firewall with Advanced Security.

The features on this page give you a tremendous amount of true control over your firewall settings—everything from creating rules for inbound and outbound connections to monitoring and much more.

You might also decide you want to open specific ports on your firewall. Ports are a lot like channels on your television. Your TV, for example, might have a single connection to the outside world, but by changing the channel you can go to news stations, movie channels—really hundreds of options. Your computer is similar in that it might be connected to the Internet but different ports allow for different access. For example, you have a port for sending email (Port 25), which uses a special protocol (Simple Mail Transfer Protocol or SMTP). You have a port for receiving email (Port 110 for the POP protocol). You have a port for your web browser to view web pages (Port 80 for the HTTP protocol), and so forth.

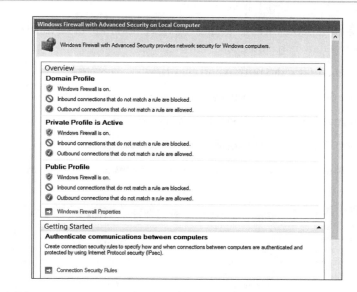

Figure 9.12 *Windows Firewall with Advanced Security*

From within the Firewall with Advanced Security you can see that profiles are used to help you, and this is especially helpful with systems that move. Desktops sit still, but laptops move. It's the moving aspect that makes them vulnerable to new situations, such as airport Wi-Fi connections or Starbucks hotspot locations. However, you can configure rules based on the following three profiles:

- **Domain Profile**—When your computer is connected to an Active Directory domain.

- **Private Profile Is Active**—When a computer is connected to a network that has a private gateway or router.

- **Public Profile**—When a computer is connected directly to the Internet or to a network that isn't considered private or domain.

 LET ME TRY IT

Open Local Ports in Windows Firewall

Certain software requires a single open port to function correctly. The following steps show you how to accomplish this.

1. Open the Windows Firewall.

2. In the left pane, click Advanced Settings. The Windows Firewall with Advanced Security on Local Computer page appears.

3. In the left pane, click Inbound Rules.

4. In the right pane, click New Rule. The New Inbound Rule Wizard dialog box appears (shown in Figure 9.13).

5. Select the Port radio button and click Next.

6. Choose Specific Local Ports, type the port number, and click Next.

7. Verify that Allow the Connection is selected and click Next.

8. Confirm that all three boxes are checked and click Next.

9. In the Name field, type **Custom Port Exception** and click Finish.

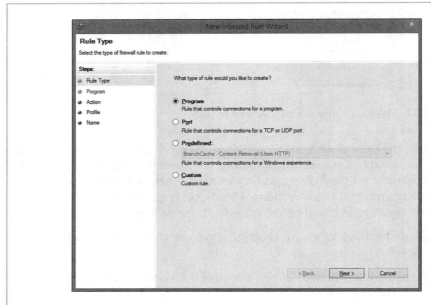

Figure 9.13   *New Inbound Rule Wizard*

You now see on the right pane (in the middle) the rule Custom Port Exception.

The firewall is Network-Aware in the sense that, based on the network (domain, private, or public), it can determine the settings necessary to protect the user for any given situation. But you are the one who needs to configure the policy that will be applied after the firewall determines your category network. Obviously, the more dangerous the situation (for example, a public Internet connection), the more strict the policy.

LET ME TRY IT

Restoring Windows Firewall Default Settings

The following steps show you how to restore the Windows Firewall settings to their default configuration. If you have made a lot of changes to your Firewall settings and just want to start from scratch, you'll find this a handy option. Just keep in mind that some software you have already installed and given access to the Internet might temporarily stop working, requiring you to re-grant it access.

1. Open Windows Firewall.

2. In the left pane, click Restore Defaults.

3. On the Restore Default Settings screen, click the Restore Defaults button. This displays the Restore Defaults Confirmation dialog box.

4. Click Yes. The firewall resets to the default settings and returns to the main Windows Firewall screen.

BitLocker Encryption

Typically, if you lose your laptop or if it's stolen, the data you're carrying will be fair game to anybody who now possesses your laptop. With BitLocker enabled, the entire drive is encrypted and a thief won't be able to switch out the drive and attempt to crack through the encryption. BitLocker uses Advanced Encryption Standard (AES) as its encryption algorithm with configurable key lengths of 128 or 256 bits. These options are configurable using Group Policy. (Note that BitLocker is only included with certain versions of Windows 8 such as Pro and Enterprise.)

One of the frustrations with earlier versions of BitLocker was that it was too complicated to configure once the OS was installed. You needed to make a BitLocker partition, and, if that wasn't done ahead of time, you had to jump through hoops by shrinking drives. Over time Microsoft developed better ways to manage all of this and created the BitLocker Drive Preparation Tool. That tool is built directly within Windows 8, so now you need only turn BitLocker on through Control Panel, System and Security, BitLocker Drive Encryption. The tool, shown in Figure 9.14, handles the rest.

For BitLocker to work, you must have one of the following:

- A laptop that has the Trusted Platform Module (TPM) chip version 1.2. The TPM chip is like a smartcard embedded into the motherboard. It has a predefined number of unsuccessful attempts configured so that a thief cannot force his way in.

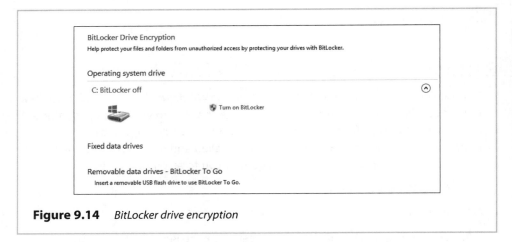

Figure 9.14   *BitLocker drive encryption*

- A USB storage device. Your system's BIOS must also be able to access USB devices prior to the boot-up of the OS. Just about any desktop or laptop system capable of running Windows 8 should be capable of booting from a USB drive.

 **LET ME TRY IT**

Setting Up BitLocker to Work on an Operating System

The following steps show you how to set up BitLocker encryption on a hard drive. You will be required to restart the computer, after which the drive will be encrypted. This process will take a while and will diminish performance until it's completed. Once it is done, you will receive a message stating that the process is complete.

1. From the Start screen type **Control Panel**.

2. Click Control Panel.

3. Select System and Security.

4. Click BitLocker Drive Encryption.

5. On your operating system drive letter, click Turn On BitLocker. If your computer meets the requirements to run BitLocker, it automatically prepares the hard drive for encryption and reboots the computer.

6. The BitLocker Setup Wizard continues the installation. Choose where to store the recovery key from the following locations: Save the Recovery Key to a USB Flash Drive, Save the Recovery Key to a File, or Print the Recovery Key.

7. Click Next.

8. Verify the Run BitLocker System Check is selected and click Continue.

BitLocker to Go

Where BitLocker encrypts your computer's hard drive, BitLocker to Go encrypts USB storage devices. You can then restrict those drives with a passphrase so that even your portable storage is protected.

Administrators can determine the passphrase length and complexity. By using policy settings, administrators can also require users to apply protection to a USB drive prior to writing to them in the first place. You can also use a smartcard to unlock a drive. In the event you forget the passphrase to unlock your drive or lose your smartcard, you are asked to create a recovery key (which can be saved to a file or printed) so that you can use the recovery key to access the drive.

 LET ME TRY IT

Setting Up BitLocker to Work on a Portable Drive

The following steps show you how to set up BitLocker on a portable drive. Upon completion of these steps, the drive will be encrypted.

1. From the Start screen type **Control Panel**.

2. Click Control Panel.

3. Select System and Security.

4. Click BitLocker Drive Encryption.

5. Select the removable drive you want to encrypt. This starts the BitLocker Drive Encryption Wizard.

6. Choose Use a Password to Unlock the Drive or choose Use My Smart Card to Unlock the Drive.

7. Click Next.

8. Choose where to store the recovery key from the following locations: Save the Recovery Key to a USB Flash Drive, Save the Recovery Key to a File, or Print the Recovery Key.

9. Click Next.

10. Click Start Encrypting.

The drive is now encrypted, after which it requires the key to access the data.

Windows XP SP3 and Windows Vista systems can read devices encrypted with BitLocker to Go. On other systems, the device, when plugged in, appears as a nonformatted device and you cannot access the data.

Password Protection and Account Settings

There are many different methods for logging in and accessing your Windows 8 desktop system. When working with a local account you can use some of Windows 8's new password protection types, which include normal passwords, picture passwords, and PINs.

Earlier in the book we reviewed the various PC settings. To locate these you go through your Charms bar, select the Settings link, and then select the Change PC Settings option.

From here you select the Users option and you see the different sign-in options for your account, if you are logged in with a local account (see Figure 9.15).

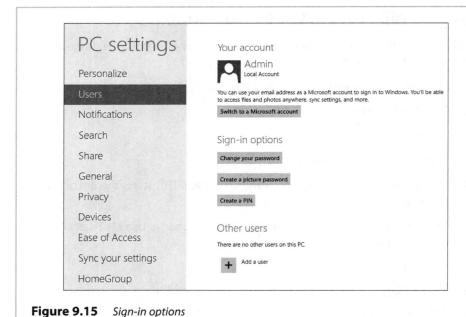

Figure 9.15   *Sign-in options*

So, one example is the PIN approach. If you select this you are asked to enter a four-digit PIN and confirm it, allowing you to log in using that PIN.

The Create a Picture Password option is another interesting new approach. First, you choose a picture and then you draw on the screen what you want as your password. Confirm your three drawing options and you are all set.

Now when you go to log in you have options (if you have set up both the PIN and the picture password) as you see in Figure 9.16.

Figure 9.16   *Logging in with new password protection*

Family Safety

You learn about Control Panel items and how to set up user accounts in the next chapter. However, being that this is a chapter on security, and certainly family safety is connected to that, we thought we would discuss this Control Panel item here.

Family Safety provides reports and control access to the Internet, games, apps, and more. You can manage these on the PC or through the Family Safety website accessed with Essentials.

Essentials is a suite of tools (including Family Safety) that can be found by visiting and downloading the tools at http://windows.microsoft.com/en-US/windows-live/essentials-home.

For starters, to use Family Safety options you have to have Standard user accounts (at least one). When you create the user account for a child in your home (or a young person visiting the library or a kiosk account, or however you plan on using this type of account) you are offering the ability to turn family safety on immediately over that account. If you choose to configure the settings at that time, wonderful. If not, you can always return through the Control Panel. Let's take a look at how you do that.

SHOW ME   Media 9.2—Working with Family Safety
Access this video file through your registered Web Edition at
my.safaribooksonline.com/9780789750518/media.

LET ME TRY IT

Turning On and Configuring Family Safety

On our system we have an Admin local account and a Child local account that we have created. We are going to configure family safety settings on the Child account. To configure the settings locally perform the following steps:

1. From the Start screen type **Control Panel**.

2. Click Control Panel. Change the view from categories to icons.

3. Select the Family Safety icon.

4. Select the Child account.

5. Turn Family Safety to On (enforce current settings), as shown in Figure 9.17.

6. You now have the ability to turn on and configure the following settings:

    *   Activity Reporting (On/Off)

    *   Web Filtering

    *   Time Limits

    *   Windows Store and Game Restrictions

    *   App Restrictions

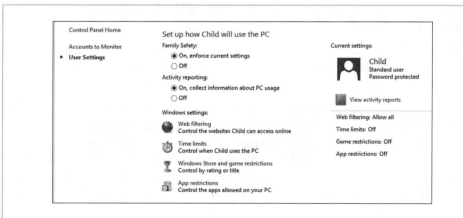

Figure 9.17   *Family Safety settings*

Web filtering is extensive and allows you to establish and enforce allow lists, allow or block online communication through IM and such, even prevent file downloads.

Each of the settings is interesting and powerful when you investigate a bit. For example, with Time Limits, you can determine how many hours a day a child can play as well as (or in addition to) configuring curfew for the child by establishing time ranges the child can use the PC.

Game restrictions allow you to allow or block games from the Windows Store or any game based on ratings or based on your own choices for the child account.

Applications, as well, can be restricted based on your selection.

The best part is that the whole thing is logged so you can turn on Activity Logging and check in on your children whenever you want. You can go one step further and manage it through Windows Essentials 2012 Family Safety application.

 TELL ME MORE   Media 9.3—A Discussion of Security in Windows 8: Thumbs Up or Thumbs Down?

Access this audio recording through your registered Web Edition at **my.safaribooksonline.com/9780789750518/media**.

This chapter introduces a number of Windows 8
system settings and how to best configure them.

10

System Configuration Settings

Windows 8 Should Work For You

We all want our interaction with technology to be as friendly as possible, thus the term "user friendly" is widely used in advertising new technology. However each of us may have different opinions on what and how features should work with Windows 8. Ultimately we bought a computer to accomplish something, maybe work, or maybe play. This chapter covers some configuration settings available to us that can make our work or play experience a more "user friendly" one.

First we need to know where to go to access the tools we need to fine-tune our Windows 8 operating system. The Control Panel is what we can call our toolbox. It is filled with tools or "items" that we can use.

You might be familiar with the Control Panel, as it has been an integral part of Windows since the beginning. Starting with Windows 95, however, we saw the Control Panel take on its modern form as a folder with shortcuts to applications (called *applets* in earlier versions of Control Panel).

You might recall as well that Control Panel had different views to work with: a Classic view that showed all your applet shortcuts and a default Home view that showed you categories of options.

In Windows 8, the Control Panel offers your items in a Category view to start with (see Figure 10.1). You can adjust the size of the icons by clicking the View By down arrow in the upper-right corner. Figure 10.2 shows Large Icons selected.

An alternative way to find Control Panel items is to search for them by name. If you have forgotten the name, simply type a letter or two of the name in the Search Control Panel field in the upper-right corner and Search returns a list of several items in the Control Panel—ideally what you're looking for.

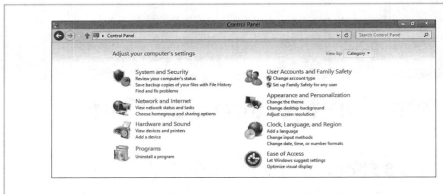

Figure 10.1   *Accessing the Control Panel using the Category view*

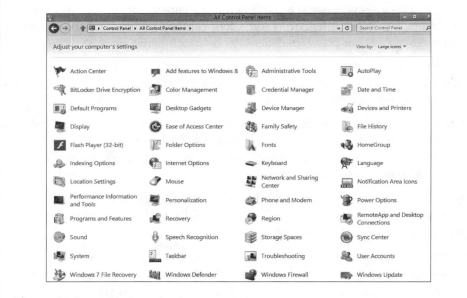

Figure 10.2   *Control Panel with Large Icon view*

Opening the Control Panel

How do you get to the Control Panel in Windows 8? There are a number of ways, as highlighted in Chapter 3, "System Setup and Personalization," so you can use the one you prefer or follow these steps:

1. From the Start screen right-click on the screen.

2. Click the All Apps button that appears on the lower-right corner of the screen.

3. Select Control Panel (you might need to scroll over to the right and find it under the Windows System heading).

Making Control Panel More Accessible

One thing you might want to do is have your Control Panel more readily accessible. You can have the Control Panel added as a tile on your Start screen or added to your desktop taskbar.

 LET ME TRY IT

Adding Control Panel to the Start Screen

Follow these steps to add the Control Panel as a tile on your Start screen:

1. From the Start screen right-click on the screen.

2. Click the All Apps button that appears on the lower-right corner of the screen.

3. Find the Control Panel under the Windows System heading.

4. Right-click Control Panel.

5. Select the Pin to Start option in the lower-left corner of your screen. (You will also see a Pin to Taskbar option; this adds the Control Panel to your desktop taskbar.)

6. Now once you return to your Start screen you see a Control Panel tile.

 LET ME TRY IT

Using Jump Lists with Control Panel

If you add the Control Panel to your taskbar it turns it into a jump list. Now when you right-click this icon on the taskbar, a jump list of recently used Control Panel items appears. This list dynamically changes depending on which Control Panel items you frequently access.

Let's say you do not want the whole Control Panel added to your Start screen, just one of the items that you use frequently. For example, you may want just the Administrative Tools to be added to your Start screen. While in the Control Panel, follow these steps:

1. Right-click Administrative Tools.

2. From the menu that appears select Pin to Start. (You also see a Create Shortcut selection; this adds a shortcut for the item on your desktop.)

3. Now when you return to your Start screen you see an Administrative Tools tile.

Using the Control Panel Items

If you are looking at Control Panel in Windows 8 and you are a former Windows XP user, you will note a lot of change. If you are a Vista or Windows 7 user, you will note some change, but not too much. Let's see how you can use some of these items to configure Windows 8 to work better for you.

Some of the items in the Control Panel are discussed in previous chapters or may be discussed later on. We do not focus on every item listed in this chapter, just some of the overall system settings that can make your experience with Windows 8 better.

The Action Center

As discussed in Chapter 9, "Using Security Features in Windows 8," the Action Center replaces the Security Center for XP and Vista users and was introduced in Windows 7 as the one-stop location for your security and maintenance dashboards. The Action Center is located in the System and Security category.

Administrative Tools

This is less of an item and more of a shortcut to Administrative Tools that you might need to use, such as Computer Management, Event Viewer, and Services (these are discussed in greater detail in Chapter 12, "Managing and Troubleshooting"). The Administrative Tools are located in the System and Security group.

AutoPlay

Use AutoPlay to change default settings for CDs, DVDs, and devices so that you can automatically (per your specifications) play music and movies, view pictures, and so forth.

This item gives you a single location, as shown in Figure 10.3, to determine the result you want when putting in different types of media. You can configure a DVD to automatically play within Windows Media Center or some other application. Or you can determine that pictures or audio files use specific options. Notice that you have more options than you did in Windows 7.

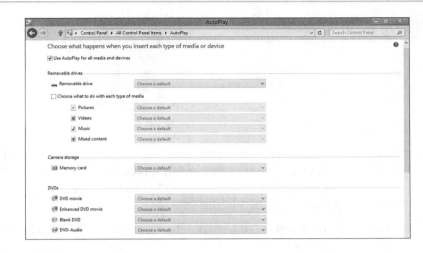

Figure 10.3   *The AutoPlay item*

 LET ME TRY IT

Modifying Your Picture, Video, and Audio AutoPlay Options

The following steps show you how to change the computer's behavior when you insert media such as CDs and DVDs.

1. From the Start screen right-click on the screen.

2. Click the All Apps button that appears on the lower-right corner of the screen.

3. Select Control Panel.

4. Choose Hardware and Sound.

5. Click AutoPlay.

6. Check the Choose What to do With Each Type of Media box. This enables the down arrows of your selections directly below this box.

7. In the Pictures media type, click the drop-down arrow and select a new action to take.

8. Select new actions to take for Video Files.

9. Select new actions to take for Music Files.

10. Select new actions to take for Mixed Content Files.

11. Click Save.

The AutoPlay options include settings for enhanced audio CDs or enhanced DVD movies. What are these? Well, sometimes artists include additional items on their CDs, like music videos and so forth. Basically these are CDs or DVDs that have different format types on them, requiring additional settings.

File History

This is Windows 8's integrated tool for backing up and restoring your files (see Figure 10.4). Windows 7 had an expanded and enhanced Backup and Restore application from previous versions of Windows. Windows 8 introduces File History, which gives you more functionality for backing up your files.

System recovery has been separated from this item and is under its own Control Panel item called Recovery. We discuss this further in Chapter 12.

Figure 10.4   *File History item*

Before you can do anything with File History you need to configure some space to copy your files to. You see the recommendation of adding an external drive to your PC and using this for your copied files. You also have the option to use a network location. Copying files to an external drive or network location certainly makes sense. If you were to make a copy of your files on your local drive, you would really be up the creek without a paddle if your drive crashed. Your original and historical files would be ruined.

 **LET ME TRY IT**

Saving File History to a Network Location

If you operate on a home or corporate network and want to save your File History to a network location, here's how you set that up:

1. From the Start screen right-click on the screen.

2. Click the All Apps button that appears on the lower-right corner of the screen.

3. Select Control Panel.

4. Click System and Security.

5. Click File History (notice that a quick search is done to see whether you have any external drives attached).

6. Click the Use Network Location link.

7. You are given the opportunity to choose from available drives or use a network location. If any external drives are attached, they show up in the list of available drives.

8. Click Add Network Location and the Select Folder dialog box opens (see Figure 10.5). Here you should be able to see other computers on your network. You can double-click on any of the computers and, as long as you have access, select a shared folder to copy your files to. (Interestingly you have the ability to select your local computer and save the files there.)

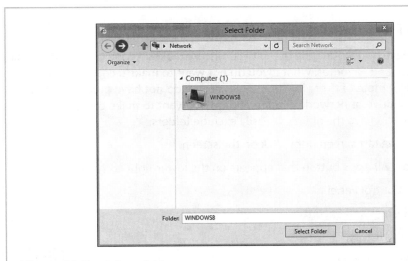

Figure 10.5   *Select a folder.*

9. Click Select Folder, and you see your network location added to the list of available drives.

10. With your new available network location highlighted, click on OK.

11. You see your network location under the Copy Files To area and see how much free space you have (see Figure 10.6).

12. Click the Turn On button, which is now enabled. You see that your files are being copied for the first time.

13. Once completed you can see when the last file copy took place and have the ability to run another backup at any time by clicking the Run Now link.

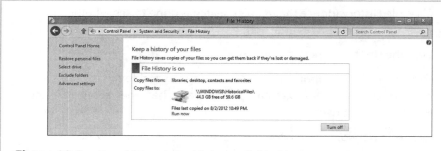

Figure 10.6 *Network location added to available drives*

 **LET ME TRY IT**

Excluding Folders from File History

You might have noticed that by default File History makes a copy of Libraries, Desktop, Contacts, and Favorites. What if you do not want to make a copy of all the contents of one or more of these locations? Maybe you do not have much space on your external drive or network location and do not want to make copies of unimportant files. You have the ability to easily exclude folders:

1. From the Start screen right-click on the screen.

2. Click the All Apps button that appears on the lower-right corner of the screen.

3. Select Control Panel.

4. Click System and Security.

5. Click File History.

6. Click Exclude Folders.

7. Click Add.

8. You now can browse your drives and select the folder that you want to exclude from File History copies. Once you have the folder selected click Select Folder.

9. The path to your excluded folder is now displayed in the Excluded Folders and Libraries box (see Figure 10.7).

10. Click Save Changes and exit out of the Control Panel.

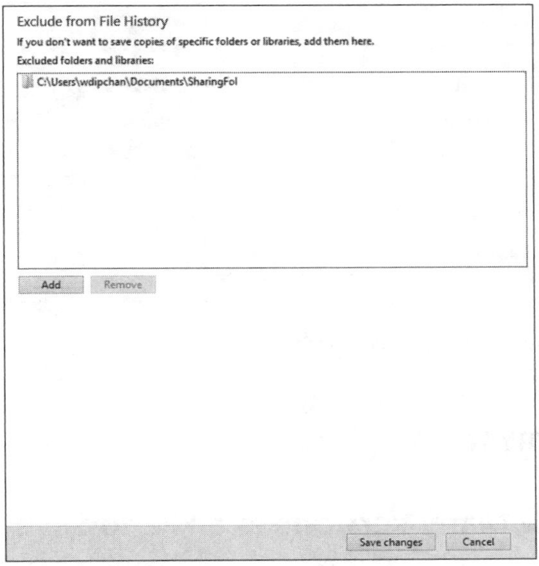

Figure 10.7   *Excluded folders and libraries*

Using File History's Advanced Features

With Windows 8 you have some, might I say, very cool advanced features with File History that enable you to configure your file copy strategy to best fit your needs and environment (see Figure 10.8). These options include

- **Save Copied Files**—Allows you to set how often your files are copied. After the initial run, each successive copy will be incremental. This means that only new or modified files will be saved.

- **Size of Offline Cache**—Configure how much of your disk will be used to copy files while disconnected from your external drive or shared network space. (Will sync up once connected.)

- **Keep Saved Versions**—This enables you to keep file versions for as long as you specify.

What are file versions? Basically every time you update a file and save it you create another version of the file. With File History you are able to keep versions of your files, which means if you accidentally save a file with incorrect data you can go back to the previous version, or even the version before that. You need to be careful and consider the amount of disk space you have available for your file copies. If you are constantly updating your files and have versioning set to Forever you can see how this fills up space quickly.

Figure 10.8   *File History Advanced Settings*

 LET ME TRY IT

Choosing How Many Versions of a File to Save

You might want to save versions of files for a maximum of three months (the final decision is really up to you). To do that, follow these steps:

1. From the Start screen right-click on the screen.

2. Click the All Apps button that appears on the lower-right corner of the screen.

3. Select Control Panel.

4. Click System and Security.

5. Click File History.

6. Click Advanced Settings.

7. Click the down arrow next to Keep Saved Versions.

8. Select 3 Months or your desired length of time from the drop-down menu.

9. Click Save Changes.

 LET ME TRY IT

Cleaning Up Old File Versions

If you decide to keep file versions Forever and find that your external drive or network location is running low on space, you can perform a cleanup of your file versions (this is not limited to only if you select Forever).

1. From the Start screen right-click on the screen.

2. Click the All Apps button that appears on the lower-right corner of the screen.

3. Select Control Panel.

4. Click System and Security.

5. Click File History.

6. Click Advanced Settings.

7. Under the drop-down box for Keep Saved Versions click the Clean Up Versions link.

8. In the File History Cleanup dialog box click the drop-down arrow and select desired amount of time (see Figure 10.9).

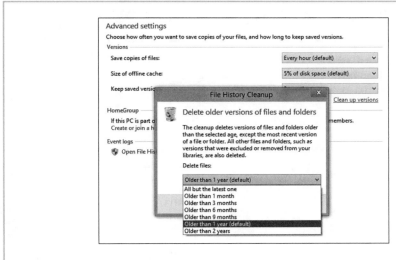

Figure 10.9   *File History Cleanup dialog box*

9. Click Clean Up. If no files meet the criteria selected you are notified. If there are files you see a completed successfully notification.

 **LET ME TRY IT**

Restoring File Versions

Now that you have a copy of your files, you can be confident that if you accidentally delete a file or if your data gets corrupted you can restore your files or even previous versions of your files. Restoring a file is straightforward.

1. From the Start screen right-click on the screen.

2. Click the All Apps button that appears on the lower-right corner of the screen.

3. Select Control Panel.

4. Click System and Security.

5. Click File History.

6. Click the Restore Personal Files link.

7. The Home – File History dialog box opens (see Figure 10.10). From here you can click the arrow at the bottom of the box to navigate to previous or next file versions if they are available. Each version is represented by the date the copy was made.

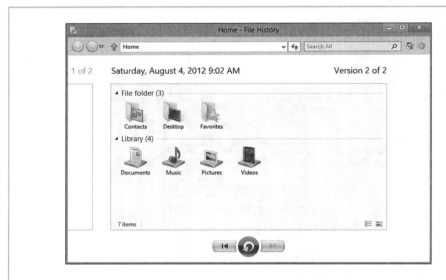

Figure 10.10   *File History dialog box*

8. Browse and select the file you want to restore.

9. Clicking on the center round button restores the file to its original location. If a file with the same name already exists in the original location you are presented with a Replace or Skip Files dialog box (see Figure 10.11). Within this box you have three selections:

   • **Replace the File in Destination**—Overwrites the file in the original location.

   • **Skip This File**—Does not restore the file.

- **Compare Info for Both Files**—Opens up a Conflict dialog box and allows you to choose which file(s) you want to restore and whether you want to keep the file in the original location. If you select both, the copied file has a number added to its name.

10. After your selections are made, click Continue.

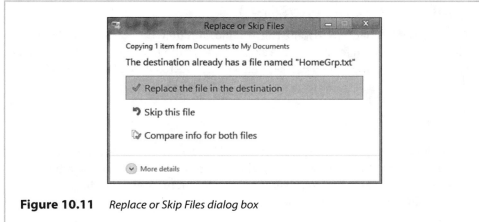

Figure 10.11   *Replace or Skip Files dialog box*

You do have some options when restoring a file. If you right-click on the file you want to restore you see the following options:

- **Preview**—Allows you to look at the file first to make sure this is the version you need restored (you can double-click the file to see a preview also then click the back arrow to return).

- **Restore**—Restores the file to its original location (same as clicking on the center round button).

- **Restore To**—Allows you to navigate to a different location to save the file. Once you select a different location the restore does not overwrite the existing file.

In each case once you perform the restore, the location that you restored the file to opens in a File Explorer window.

Another feature in Windows 8 that you can use to make an offline copy of your files is native .iso burning. This allows you to save files in .iso format as an image burned onto a CD/DVD. Disc images of backups can be saved as .iso files.

To open Windows Disc Image Burner, right-click any existing .iso file and choose Burn Disc Image. A simple dialog opens, letting you choose your disc burner drive. To start burning the disc image, click Burn.

SHOW ME   Media 10.1—Using File History
Access this video file through your registered Web Edition at
my.safaribooksonline.com/9780789750518/media.

BitLocker Drive Encryption

As discussed in Chapter 7, "Home Networking," this item helps you to configure BitLocker encryption for your entire system or with the new BitLocker to Go option to encrypt USB drives. The BitLocker item can be located in the System and Security group.

Color Management

The Color Management item was introduced in Windows Vista but was also available as a downloadable XP PowerToy. This tool is designed to establish a better screen-to-print match and to provide support for more reliable printing with today's powerful color devices (such as digital cameras and modern printers).

Keep in mind that whether you're working with the scanner, camera, computer, or printer, you are dealing with different devices that have different characteristics and capabilities with colors. Additionally, even software programs have different color capabilities. For example, the same picture opened by two different photo viewing applications might produce different results to the viewer.

Color Management maintains consistency between different devices and applications to produce a more uniform appearance. It's a tool that will mostly appeal to digital photographers who are serious hobbyists or experts in the field.

One of the simpler features of Color Management is calibrating the display.

 LET ME TRY IT

Using Color Management to Calibrate Your Display

The following steps take you through a wizard that helps calibrate your display colors. This requires you to adjust several onscreen sliders to set various color levels.

1. From the Start screen right-click on the screen.

2. Click the All Apps button that appears on the lower-right corner of the screen.

3. Select Control Panel.

4. In the Search field, type **color**.

5. Select Color Management.

6. Click the Advanced tab.

7. In the Display Calibration section, click the Calibrate Display button.

8. The Display Color calibration box opens. If you use multiple monitors, make sure you are viewing this box on the display you are attempting to calibrate. Click Next.

9. You will be presented with some instructions on using the Color Calibration tool. Click Next.

10. You now have an opportunity to adjust your brightness and contrast. If you want to skip the brightness setting you can click on Skip Brightness and Contrast Adjustment. Click Next.

11. An example of good and bad color brightness is displayed. Click Next.

12. Using the controls on your display, set the Brightness higher or lower until you can distinguish the suit from the shirt with the X that is barely visible. Click Next.

13. An example of good and bad contrast is displayed. Click Next.

14. Using the contrast control on your display, set the Contrast as high as possible without losing the ability to see the wrinkles and buttons on the shirt. Click Next.

15. You now have an opportunity to adjust RGB color balance control settings. You can choose to skip this setting by clicking on Skip Color Balance Adjustment. Click Next.

16. Using the controls on your display adjust the Color Balance, removing any color from the gray bars. Click Next.

17. Click Finish to save and start using your adjusted settings. Or click Cancel to revert back to original settings.

18. At the end of this dialog, a box is checked by default that initiates the ClearType Tuner that ensures text appears correctly. Leave the box checked or uncheck it (depending on your preference) and click Finish.

Credential Manager

This tool allows you to save your credentials (such as your usernames and passwords) for websites you log in to and other resources you connect to (such as other systems). These credentials are saved in the Windows Vault (see Figure 10.12). One of the coolest features here is that you have the ability to back up and/or restore the vault.

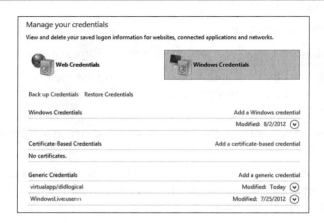

Figure 10.12   *The Credential Manager and the Windows Vault*

On first glance, this might look like you have the ability to use this feature for all of your website login information (Gmail, Twitter, Facebook, and so on). However, it works only with sites that can interact with Credential Manager and the Windows Vault.

 **LET ME TRY IT**

Adding Website Credentials to Windows Vault

The following steps take you into Credential Manager. To complete the steps, you need the name of a website that you want to add your credentials to along with the username and password required to log in to the website.

1. From the Start screen right-click on the screen.

2. Click the All Apps button that appears on the lower-right corner of the screen.

3. Select Control Panel.

4. Click User Accounts and Family Safety.

5. Click Credential Manager.

6. In the Windows Credentials section, click Add a Windows Credential.

7. In the Internet or Network Address box, type the address of the website or network location. Type your User Name and Password information. Click OK.

Your newly added credentials are listed. If you prefer, repeat this process with both Certificate-Based Credentials and Generic Credentials. When completed, click Back

Up Vault to choose a location to back up your stored logon credentials. Interestingly, instead of a Save button, you are asked to press Ctrl+Alt+Delete. This secures the Desktop during the save process and requires you to add a password to the backup file you are saving.

Date and Time

As mentioned in Chapter 3, this item is used to configure the date, time, and time zone for your system. However, it is the Additional Clocks feature that is really helpful. You can configure two additional clocks with their own time zones. When you hover your mouse over the time, you see the time in these other locations. The Date and Time item can be located in the Clock, Language and Region group.

Default Programs

This is a quick place to find your default program associations and file-to-program associations. For example, if you are tired of your MP3 files opening up with Media Player and you want them to open with WinAmp or some other player, you can make the changes here.

There are four options when you open up the Default Programs item.

- **Set Your Default Programs**—Need to choose between Firefox and Internet Explorer as your default browser? Here is where you can tell Windows 8 which one is your go-to application. The same is true for your email, contact management information, media files, and photos.

- **Associate a File Type or Protocol with a Program**—For an expanded view of all file types and protocols and their associated applications, you can select this option to ensure all your file types can be opened by the application you prefer.

- **Change AutoPlay Settings**—This option opens the AutoPlay item discussed previously in this chapter.

- **Set Program Access and Computer Defaults**—This is yet another way to specify which programs access certain information. You can choose the following: Computer Manufacturer (this appears only if a manufacturer established preconfigured settings), Microsoft Windows (for an all-Microsoft default world), Non-Microsoft (allows you to use only non-Microsoft programs; access to Microsoft programs is removed unless you select Custom), and Custom (for a mix and match of applications—it's the most logical choice for most of us, and that's why it's selected by default).

Changes made under the Set your Default Programs settings are unique per user. They won't affect other users on your computer. By contrast, the options you select for Set Program Access and Computer Defaults apply to all users on the system.

Devices and Printers

This feature shows you all the devices connected to your computer. Depending on the device, you can see items related to that device. For example, in Figure 10.13, you can see your Devices, Printers and Faxes, and any Unspecified items. By selecting the Microsoft XPS Document Writer, for example, it shows you some options in the Menu toolbar, such as See What's Printing, Print Server Properties, and more.

Figure 10.13   *Devices and Printers*

Device Stage

Where Devices and Printers really shines is in its interaction with Device Stage. This is a new way to interact with items you plug in to your computer, such as your phone, digital camera, printer, or portable media player. It works for USB devices and Bluetooth and Wi-Fi devices as well.

When you first plug in a device, instructions, called drivers, are loaded (if Windows 8 has them) that tell Windows how to access and use your device. If a driver isn't found, Windows 8 searches for the driver on the Windows Update website. Device Stage shows you all the applications, services, and information for a device. The manufacturer can create a device that supports Device Stage so that it appears on the taskbar with the correct image of the device and offers jump list displays for things you can do with the device.

This is a change from operating systems prior to Windows 7. With the older operating systems, you had to locate an application that went along with a device (such as a scanner). That meant clicking through various menus and applications to try to locate the feature you needed. If you didn't use the features for a while, it could digress into a lengthy search on how to perform a simple task. Now, with Device Stage, the device becomes the focus.

Because Device Manager features a device and all it can do, you now need only click on a device and all features associated with it appear front and center. The result is a far more logical approach to utilizing your hardware. Instead of searching for the scanner application, you can simply click Devices and Printers and locate the scanner. The entire experience makes Device Stage one of the most significant additions to the Windows operating system and quickly makes for a "must-have" feature.

 LET ME TRY IT

Using Device Stage to View a Device and Its Corresponding Jump List

The following steps show you how to access Device Stage. To view a device, you must have device hardware already attached to your computer.

1. From the Start screen right-click on the screen.

2. Click the All Apps button that appears on the lower-right corner of the screen.

3. Select Control Panel.

4. Click Hardware and Sound.

5. Click Devices and Printers.

6. Locate an enhanced device icon and double-click it. Device Stage items appear, including various menu items (depending on your device).

7. On the taskbar, right-click the device icon.

8. A jump list opens, showing available tasks you can perform with this device.

Display

These settings were discussed in Chapter 3, and they are accessible through both the Control Panel or by right-clicking your Desktop and choosing Screen Resolution. When using the Control Panel, the initial screen shows you ways to adjust the size of text and other items on your screen by using radio buttons (see Figure 10.14). On the left of the page, you will find links for the following options: Adjust Resolution, Calibrate Color, Change Display Settings, and Adjust ClearType Text.

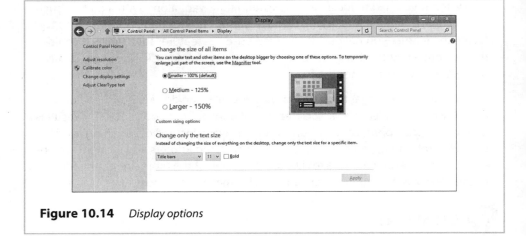

Figure 10.14   *Display options*

Ease of Access Center

Accessibility Options are included in Windows to enhance the functionality for users with limited vision, hearing, manual dexterity, or reasoning abilities. Microsoft has made some excellent efforts in these areas and we applaud their efforts.

When you open up the Ease of Access Center from the Control Panel, you immediately see several tools you can configure. You may notice one additional tool added since Windows 7 at the bottom of the Make Touch and Tablet Easier to Use list (see Figure 10.15). If you are not sure which tool is the right one, a special survey is available that might point you in the right direction from the start.

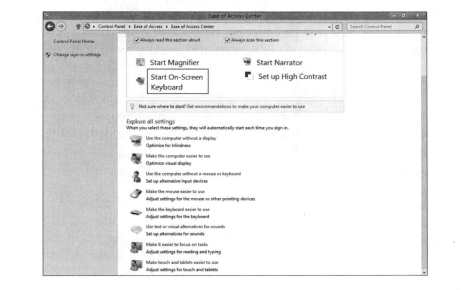

Figure 10.15   *The Ease of Access Center*

 LET ME TRY IT

Getting Recommendations to Make Your Computer Easier to Use

The following steps show you how to open the Ease of Access Center. You can choose from among several options to make your computer easier to use.

1. From the Start screen right-click on the screen.

2. Click the All Apps button that appears on the lower-right corner of the screen.

3. Select Control Panel.

4. Select Appearance and Personalization.

5. Click Ease of Access Center.

6. In the center of the page, in a yellow box, click the Get Recommendations to Make Your Computer Easier to Use link. The first page that appears is specific to Eyesight.

7. Read through the statements in each page and select each statement that applies to you. Click Next after each page, which progresses you to pages for Eyesight, Dexterity, Hearing, Speech, and Reasoning. If you want to go back to review or change any answers, click the blue arrow in the upper-left corner of any page.

8. When you have completed all five pages, click Done.

9. The Recommended Settings page opens, presenting you with customized choices based on your selections. Review the recommended settings and select the options you want to use.

10. Click Apply.

11. Click OK.

Some settings require you to log off and log on again to use them.

 SHOW ME   Media 10.2—Exploring the Ease of Access Center
Access this video file through your registered Web Edition at
my.safaribooksonline.com/9780789750518/media.

Enabling Other Ease of Access Tools

At the top of the Ease of Access Center page is the Quick Access to Common Tools feature, which provides you with access to Magnifier, Narrator, On-Screen Keyboard, and High Contrast tools. You can turn them on with a mouse click or you can hear the options read out loud to you (which occurs by default). You can press your spacebar to choose one of these options.

- **Magnifier**—Magnifier enlarges different parts of the screen. This comes in handy when you are viewing objects that are hard to see. It also allows you to see the whole screen more easily. Select from three modes:

  - **Full-Screen Mode**—With Full-Screen mode activated, your entire screen is magnified. Magnifier can follow the mouse pointer for you.

  - **Lens Mode**—When you select Lens mode, the area around the mouse pointer is magnified. Moving the mouse pointer causes the part of the screen that's magnified to move along with it.

  - **Docked Mode**—By choosing Docked mode, only a portion of the screen is magnified. Everything else on your display is normal size. This gives you control over which area of the screen is magnified.

- **Narrator**—Narrator is a simple application that reads aloud any text on the screen and requires that your speakers work. Several options are available, including changing the narrator's voice.

- **On-Screen Keyboard**—This lets you use the mouse to enter text onscreen. With the On-Screen Keyboard turned on, you can still use your traditional keyboard.

- **High Contrast**—This provides choices from several High Contrast Windows themes. A link here takes you to the Personalization menu, where you can select a High Contrast theme at the bottom of the page.

Located at the bottom of the Ease of Access Center is the Explore All Settings section. The options presented here help you utilize special tools to make Windows more accessible:

- **Use the Computer Without a Display**—This presents you with two main sections. The first, Hear Text Read Aloud, gives you an option to have Narrator open each time you log on.

- **Make the Computer Easier to See**—This feature optimizes your visual display so the computer is easier to see.

- **Use the Computer Without a Mouse or Keyboard**—This allows you to work with alternative input devices. One of these devices controls your computer through Speech Recognition.

- **Make the Mouse Easier to Use**—You can increase the size and contrast of the mouse pointer, helping you more easily see it onscreen. You can also use Mouse Keys, which is a way to use the numeric keypad to move the mouse around the screen.

- **Make the Keyboard Easier to Use**—You can turn on features such as Sticky Keys, which allows you to enter keyboard shortcuts (such as Ctrl+Alt+Del) one key at a time.

- **Use Text or Visual Alternatives for Sounds**—Turn on visual cues and visual warnings here.

- **Make it Easier to Focus on Tasks**—These options make it easier for you to type and manage windows, among other things.

- **Make Touch and Tablets Easier to Use**—Designed to make it easier to use touchscreens and tablets.

Folder Options

For the most part, the options available in Folder Options remain the same as those available in Windows 7. They include three tabs: General, View, and Search.

On the General tab, you can configure how you want to browse folders, and you can configure how you want to open items (using a single-click or using a double-click). Two check boxes in the Navigation Pane section are worth noting. By default, when you are working with Explorer, Windows 8 navigation shows you important items but not necessarily *all* of your items that you might be used to. If you select Show All Folders, you will see them all. You can also select Automatically Expand to Current Folder.

The View tab has a variety of options to choose from, and they are pretty straightforward. However, because many users do not know these options exist, we recommend that you scan through the options to gain a better understanding before you use them.

The Search tab has a few different groups of settings, such as What to Search, How to Search, and When Searching Non-Indexed Locations.

Fonts

Fonts displays all the fonts installed on the computer. In Windows 8 you can preview the fonts available by clicking the Preview button. Each thumbnail for the font shows three characters of the alphabet on the icon (see Figure 10.16). In addition, fonts of a combined set no longer take up different slots. They appear as one font that you can double-click to view other options.

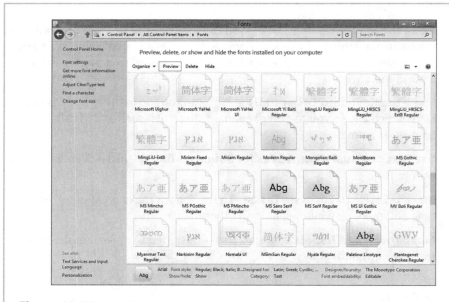

Figure 10.16   *Available fonts*

You can also toggle fonts on or off if you prefer (also known as hiding fonts). By default, Windows 8 hides fonts based on regional settings, but you can also manually hide them. The Font section is part of the Appearance and Personalization group.

A newer font to look for is Gabriola Regular. It is a beautiful script font and supports a variety of advanced OpenType functions.

HomeGroup

Discussed in detail in Chapter 7, the HomeGroup settings allow you to configure a smaller set of networked Windows 7/8 systems to share files (documents, pictures, music, videos) and printers as well as stream media to and from devices. The HomeGroup item can be accessed from the Network and Sharing Center.

Indexing Options

To speed up searches, Windows 8 has an indexing feature turned on by default. However, predefined locations are indexed by default, such as Internet Explorer History, Offline Files, Start menu, Users folder, and Windows Mail.

You can access Indexing Options in the Control Panel by typing **index** in the Search Control Panel box. When you click the Indexing Options item and then click the Modify button at the lower-left of the Indexing Options dialog, you can quickly add locations to the index. Keep in mind, however, that adding to the indexing increases the workload on Windows 8 in its effort to keep those areas up to date. But it makes for faster searches when you are looking for something that isn't on the standard index path.

Through Advanced Options you can also determine whether you want to index encrypted files, rebuild the index (if it is giving you problems), and find the location of the index file. You can also determine file types to include or exclude, among other options in the Advanced Options dialog box.

From time to time you are going to find that your index will crash, so to speak. If you find yourself in Outlook searching for an email that you know you have and you cannot get any results from your search or any search, you should rebuild the Index. It will take a few moments, but it will fix the problem.

Internet Options

The Internet Options group is located within Network and Internet on the Control Panel. Basically, these are your Internet Explorer10 settings—they aren't really your Internet Options. You can configure them from within IE by going to your Tools, Internet Options, or you can configure them here. Obviously, if you use another browser (such as Firefox or Safari), the vast majority of the settings you configure here will not apply on any other third-party browser, such as Firefox or Chrome.

Keyboard

To open the Keyboard item, simply type **keyboard** in the Search Control Panel box and then click Keyboard. Nothing new to report here. In the Keyboard Properties dialog that appears, use the Speed tab to configure the Character Repeat settings and the Cursor Blink Rate. Click the Hardware tab to access hardware information and properties.

Location and Other Sensors

To open the Location and Other Sensors item, simply type **location** in the Search Control Panel box and then click Location and Other Sensors. This is where you can configure the Windows-based sensors that can detect your location and the orientation of your system. So, essentially, Windows 8 supports both hardware and software sensors that can be designed for systems. Examples of hardware sensors are a GPS, a microphone, an accelerometer, or a motion detector. Software sensors might be based on information coming through the network or Internet.

One simple use for these types of features might be the support of ambient light sensors (ALS) so that the system automatically controls the brightness based on the available ambient brightness detected.

Mouse

The Mouse item is found in the Hardware and Sound group on the Control Panel. After you click Hardware and Sound, you see the Mouse link under the Devices and Printers group. Much like Keyboard, there is not much new to report. One item to take note of is ClickLock (which isn't new—it's been around since ME), which is located on the Buttons tab. If you have a hard time holding down the mouse button to move items and highlight text easily, ClickLock will help you. The other point to note is the fact that Windows 8 supports enhanced Wheel support. In the Mouse Properties dialog box, click the Wheel tab to configure Horizontal Scrolling.

Notification Area Icons

This option allows you to configure the settings for your Notification Area (also called the system tray) to show or hide certain icons or notifications. You can find Notification Area Icons by typing **notification** in the Control Panel Search box.

There are three settings for your icons:

- Show Icon and Notifications
- Hide Icon and Notifications
- Only Show Notifications

Family Safety

Family Safety can be accessed in the User Accounts and Family Safety group on the Control Panel. Family Safety provides you the ability to set times that users can use the computer and also gives you control over what games and programs other users can use.

 SHOW ME   Media 10.3—Working with Family Safety
Access this video file through your registered Web Edition at
my.safaribooksonline.com/9780789750518/media.

Performance Information and Tools

You can find the Performance Information and Tools item by typing **performance** in the Control Panel Search box. Discussed in greater detail in Chapter 11, "Performance and Monitoring Tools," this option takes you to your Windows Experience Index, where you can see an assessment of your system components on a scale of 1.0 to 9.9. You can also see links to all sorts of performance-oriented settings that can help improve the performance of your system, including adjusting visual effects, indexing options, power settings, and more.

Personalization

As discussed in Chapter 3, the Personalization settings can be accessed by the Control Panel and by right-clicking the Desktop and choosing Personalize. Here you can select a theme to quickly change the Desktop background, window color, sounds, and screen saver all at once. Or you can make changes to these items individually.

There are links that take you to other settings, such as Change Desktop Icons, Change Mouse Pointers, and Change Your Account Picture.

Power Options

These settings are always under scrutiny and constantly improving to meet the needs of a green IT effort. At home or in the office, reducing power usage is a good way to conserve battery life in portables and save on power spending. As shown in Figure 10.17, Windows provides several power plans to choose from.

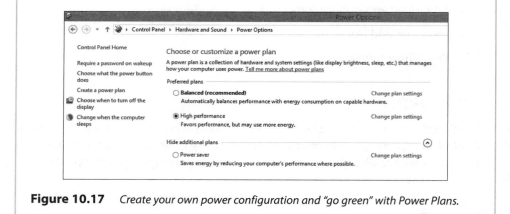

Figure 10.17   *Create your own power configuration and "go green" with Power Plans.*

The following power plans are designed to configure hardware and system settings to accommodate different power objectives:

- **Balanced**—This offers full performance when you need it and saves power during periods of inactivity. This is well suited for most configurations.

- **Power Saver**—This conserves power by reducing system performance and screen brightness. If you need to get the most out of a single laptop charge, this is the plan for you.

- **High Performance**—You need to click on the down arrow on Show Additional Plans to see the High Performance option. This increases the screen brightness and, in some cases, might increase the computer's performance.

If you are used to earlier power options, these power plans aren't new; they were formerly known as schemes. The difference is that now you can easily select one of three default options unless you want to get more involved.

You can configure the options in any one of those default plans or configure a personal plan that suits you. By selecting the initial link to edit settings, you will be selecting when to Turn Off the Display and when to Put the Computer to Sleep. If you select Change Advanced Power Settings, you are taken to a much more involved dialog with all sorts of options for password settings, when to turn off the hard disk, adapter settings, and much more.

LET ME TRY IT

Creating an Energy-Saving Plan in Power Options

The following steps show you how to create an energy-saving power plan. Laptop users have additional choices to select that are not shown here.

1. From the Start screen right-click on the screen.

2. Click the All Apps button that appears on the lower-right corner of the screen.

3. Select Control Panel.

4. Select Sound and Hardware.

5. Select Power Options.

6. In the left pane, click Create a Power Plan. This opens the Create a Power Plan page.

7. Select Power Saver.

8. In the Plan Name box, type **Reduced Energy Plan**.

9. Click Next.

10. On the Change Settings for the Plan page, there are two drop-down menus. From the Turn Off the Display drop-down, select 2 Minutes.

11. From the Put the Computer to Sleep drop-down, select 10 Minutes.

12. Click Create.

Your new reduced energy plan is now in effect.

To change the way the power buttons respond on your computer, in the left pane of the Power Options page, click Choose What the Power Buttons Do. When you press the Power button or Sleep button, you can have the computer shut down, sleep, hibernate, or do nothing at all. This page is also where you can configure your password protection on your Wakeup options.

Programs and Features

If you are coming to Windows 8 from XP, you might still be looking for the Add/Remove Programs item. In Vista, Microsoft replaced it with Programs and Features, which added the capability to Turn Windows Features On or Off (see Figure 10.18) in addition to uninstalling or making changes or repairs to installed applications.

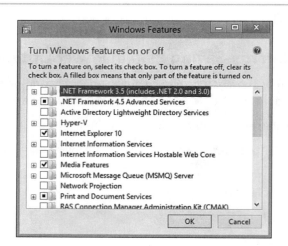

Figure 10.18   *Turning on Windows Features*

Some programs and features included with Windows 8 need to be turned on before they can be used. Certain other features are turned on by default, but you can turn them off if you don't use them.

In versions of Window prior to Vista, there was no "turn off" feature. Turning off a Windows feature (such as Internet Explorer 8 or Windows Media Player) meant uninstalling it completely from your computer. In Windows 8, turning off a Windows feature does not uninstall it, nor does it reduce the amount of hard disk space used by Windows. The features actually remain stored on your hard disk so you can "flip the switch" and turn them back on again. This applies only to Windows features, however; all other applications still require the traditional install/uninstall routine.

 **LET ME TRY IT**

Turning on Windows Scan Management

The following steps show you how to add extra Windows 8 features that were not installed by default—specifically, the Scan Management feature, which allows you to manage distributed scanners, scan processes, and scan servers. While performing this exercise, note the other options available to install.

1. From the Start screen right-click on the screen.

2. Click the All Apps button that appears on the lower-right corner of the screen.

3. Select Control Panel.

4. Select Programs.

5. In the Programs and Features group, click Turn Windows Features On or Off.

6. The Windows Features dialog box opens. Click the plus sign next to Print and Document Services.

7. Select the Scan Management check box.

8. Click OK to enable the Scan Management feature.

9. Click Close on confirmation that the feature is installed. The Scan Management feature is now enabled.

Recovery

A new location for your System Restore options, Recovery can be used to resolve many system problems by going back to a point in time where you can undo recent system changes and more. This is discussed in further detail in Chapter 12. You can find the Recovery item by typing **recovery** in the Control Panel Search box.

Region and Language

You can access Region and Language settings in the Clock, Language and Region group on the Control Panel. These Tools have been split into two different items, Region and Language.

- **Region**—We now have three tabs contained in this item.

  - **Formats**—Configure the default way your computer renders number, currency, date, and time. You can choose a specific format based on a country in the world and the options adjust accordingly. You can also choose to customize that format.

  - **Location**—This setting assists with some programs that provide local news and weather.

  - **Administrative**—Configure your international settings for your Welcome screen, System Accounts, and new User Accounts. Also set the default language for non-unicode programs.

- **Language**—Here you are able to add and remove languages to Windows 8 and move them up and down in priority (see Figure 10.19). By clicking on options at the right of the screen you see what your Display Language is and can add an input method. An input method involves changing the keyboard layout to support other keyboard layouts. You can read and edit documents in multiple languages by selecting the proper keyboard layout. You can even try different US keyboard layouts, such as the Dvorak keyboard, for improved typing speed. You can change the display language as well. The display language is the language used for wizards, dialog boxes, and menus.

Figure 10.19   *Change your language preferences*

RemoteApp and Desktop Connections

To find RemoteApp and Desktop Connections, type **remote** in the Control Panel Search box. As discussed in Chapter 8, "Domain Networking," this is a new Control Panel feature that you can use to access programs and/or desktops (remote computers or virtual systems) that have been made available by your network administrator. This feature is also connected with the new Windows Server 2008 R2 features for RemoteApp and Desktop Connections where RAD feeds provide a set of resources and these feeds are presented through this tool in Windows 8.

Sound

Customizing your sounds is a nice way to personalize your Windows 8 environment settings. The Sound group, found in Hardware and Sound, is where you can configure sound and recording options depending on the sound devices you have installed. The Playback, Recording, and Sounds tabs are the same as they were in Windows 7.

The Communications tab helps Windows to automatically adjust the volume of different sounds when you are using your PC to place or receive telephone calls. You can mute all other sounds, reduce the volume by 80 or 50 percent, or do nothing at all.

Speech Recognition

Speech Recognition has two primary functions:

- To allow you to control the computer by giving specific voice commands.

- To allow you to dictate text or have text read back to you in a Text-to-Speech (TTS) manner. The Speech Recognition tools provide you with the ability to train your computer to work with your voice or simply to train yourself to use the right commands to operate your computer.

Do you type fast? If not, pay attention to this section. For many, Speech Recognition works a whole lot faster than typing. If you're dictating, it gives you a chance to close your eyes and just talk to the computer, concentrating on your topic as the computer types every word you say. Later, when you have the main points down on the page, you can go back and correct any mistakes by using your keystrokes.

Before you start with Speech Recognition, your microphone has to be set up properly. In Control Panel, click Ease of Access Center and then choose Set Up Microphone. Complete this wizard to set up your microphone. If you have a choice between two microphone styles, go with a headset. This works much better with speech recognition and doesn't pick up as much background noise.

Once you have completed the setup, go straight to the Speech Tutorial. Here's why: The tutorials let you see how speech recognition works from all angles. Even better, you need to speak the commands to make it work. Meanwhile, as you get familiar with the commands, you not only learn the program, the program learns you. Speech Recognition begins to keep a voice profile on how you speak. Your accent, tone, pace, and style are "learned" by Speech Recognition. In fact, if someone else speaks into the microphone, the accuracy of Speech Recognition drastically declines. The system literally knows your voice.

Speech Recognition is available only in English, French, Spanish, German, Japanese, Simplified Chinese, and Traditional Chinese. You can change the language setting from the Advanced Speech options in the Control Panel.

Some users might want to set up their microphones and just jump right into Speech Recognition. The following Let Me Try It shows you a few things to do to get started right off the bat.

LET ME TRY IT

Using Speech Recognition

The following steps show you how to use only your voice to control your computer and dictate a paragraph to it. You need a computer microphone to complete this exercise.

1.   Make sure your microphone is plugged in and working correctly.

2.   From the Start screen right-click on the screen.

3.   Click the All Apps button that appears on the lower-right corner of the screen.

4.   Select Control Panel.

5.   Choose Ease of Access.

6.   In the Speech Recognition group, click Start Speech Recognition.

7.   Move the Speech Recognition bar to the top of your screen.

8.   Clearly speak "Start Listening" into your microphone. This turns on the Speech Recognition. The Speech Recognition readout says Listening.

9.   Say "Open WordPad." WordPad opens with the cursor blinking.

10.   Say "Watch the computer type when I speak."

11.   Say "Select Sentence." This highlights your entire sentence.

12.   Say "Bold." The sentence changes to boldface.

13.   Now dictate a paragraph to your computer and see how accurately it transcribes it.

In Windows 8, Speech Recognition allows users to interact with applications that are not specifically written with speech recognition in mind. If you are using a Microsoft product, such as Word, the tools work flawlessly (for a speech-to-text application, that is). If you are using other applications that are not compatible, a separate text box opens. You can speak into it and then insert the text to your application afterward.

Previous users of Speech Recognition find that the voice commands are largely—if not entirely—unchanged. And while the speech recognition was very good in Vista and Windows 7, Windows 8 seems to raise the bar a notch. For new users, print out the Speech Reference Card available in the Speech Recognition Group in Control Panel. From here you find simple commands to control your computer and commands to use during dictation.

If you still want even greater accuracy, select Train Your Computer to Better Understand You in the Speech Recognition group in Control Panel. This helps improve dictation accuracy.

During computer downtime, Speech Recognition can optionally review documents and email on your computer for commonly used words and phrases. This, too, can help improve recognition accuracy. A privacy statement is available online to help ease your Big Brother fears.

In the left pane of the Speech Recognition group, you can configure your recognition options by clicking the Advanced Speech Options link, which opens the Speech Properties dialog box. If more than one person uses Speech Recognition from the same user account, the Recognition Profiles area includes a New button you can click to add a new user's voice profile.

Sync Center

We are a synchronizing generation. We sync files and folders, digital cameras, email, cell phone apps and data, portable media players, camcorders, tablets, laptops, and so forth. With the Sync Center, you have a single item that helps you know how you're doing—how in-sync you really are.

Through the Sync Center you establish sync partnerships with devices you use and then you have a behind-the-scenes relationship with your device that allows the center to display information like a progress bar and a report of any problems or conflicts.

If you have a mobile device, a simple way to see the connection status without opening the Mobile Device Center is to open the Sync Center.

To open the Sync Center, open Control Panel, type **sync** in the Control Panel Search box, and click on the Sync Center that appears on the left of the screen. By design, the Sync Center has a simple layout. There are just a few links in the left pane and a main view window (see Figure 10.20).

- **View Sync Partnerships**—Sync your device, view recent sync activity, or change your sync settings.

- **View Sync Conflicts**—View any files that had conflicts during the sync process. If there are conflicts, you can resolve them one at a time as you view details for each conflict.

- **View Sync Results**—Review errors, warnings, and other sync information.

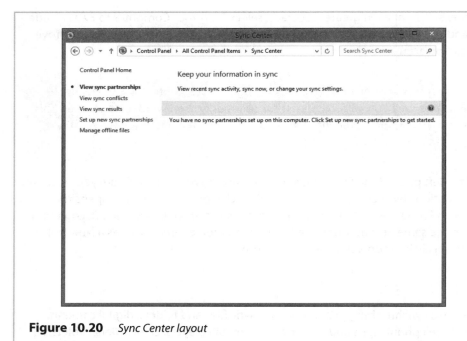

Figure 10.20   *Sync Center layout*

- **Set Up New Sync Partnerships**—Before you can sync with anything, you need to set up a new partnership for it.

- **Manage Offline Files**—This opens the Offline Files dialog box. Four tabs let you configure several options:

  - **General**—Disable offline files, open the Sync Center, or view your offline files.

  - **Disk Usage**—Provides a visual graphic of your available offline file space and temporary file space. Two options on this tab are changing your space limits and deleting temporary files.

  - **Encryption**—A simple Encrypt button lets you do just that to your offline files. If you are concerned with security, you might want to turn on encryption, which provides an additional level of access protection. If your computer is ever lost or stolen, encryption can safeguard files that contain sensitive or confidential information.

  - **Network**—Set the interval at which the Sync Center checks for a slow connection.

If EFS is available and you want to encrypt your offline files, be advised that you encrypt only the offline files stored on your computer; you don't encrypt the network versions of the files. Also, you do not need to decrypt an encrypted file or folder stored on your computer before using it. This is automatically done by Windows. The whole process is transparent to the user.

Another nice feature of Sync Center is that you can schedule your synchronization. So, for Offline Files, although you normally might sync, then go on a business trip, then re-sync (perhaps manually doing the syncs), you can use Sync Center to work on a schedule.

If you are wondering why you should use Offline Files, here are three reasons:

- You can keep working when the network goes down. With Offline Files, it doesn't matter if the network becomes unavailable. If this happens, Windows automatically opens offline copies of files stored locally and you can continue working. When the network returns, the offline files are synchronized back on the network.

- You can get the latest version of the network file. Just click to sync with your network folder and get the updated file.

- You can speed up work over slow connections. If your network has a slow connection, you can switch to working with offline copies of your network files. When you're done with the file, synchronize it with the network folder.

One issue that concerns some users when they're working with Offline Files is the synchronization process. The worry is that somehow, a file will not get updated correctly when it is modified offline, and, when the file is synchronized with the network, how will Windows know which version is correct? Simply put, if you are away from the network and have changed a file that someone has already changed on the network while you are gone, a sync conflict occurs when you are back on the network.

Windows prompts you that there is a conflict and asks you which version to keep. If you know in advance that the file you are working on will be updated before you get back on the network, rename the file so you can keep your work and merge it with the network version when you get back on the network.

System

The System item, discussed in greater detail in Chapter 8, shows you basic information about your system to begin with. It is more of a portal to other information.

For example, you can change settings regarding your computer name, domain, or workgroup settings. You can also access the Device Manager, Remote Settings, System Protection, and more Advanced System Settings. You can access the System item by clicking the System and Security group in Control Panel.

Taskbar and Start Menu

We discussed this item in great detail in Chapter 3. This item gives you control over the appearance and working behavior of the taskbar and Start menu. You can open the taskbar and Start menu from the Appearance and Personalization group in Control Panel.

User Accounts

On home systems or systems that do not connect to a domain you can use the User Accounts item to help you create new accounts and configure various aspects of those accounts.

If you are working on a system that is connected to a network domain, you will not be using this item because your user accounts are configured by an administrator for you. An exception to this would be if you wanted to configure local accounts on the system.

Windows 8 differs from past operating systems for user account creation. Two different types of accounts are available to you:

- **Microsoft Account**—This option requires you to provide an email account that is used for Microsoft services. When you sign in to Windows using a Microsoft account you will be able to

    - Download Apps from the Windows Store.

    - Get your online content (mail, calendar, photos) for your Microsoft apps automatically.

    - Sync settings online to make other Windows 8 computers associated with your Microsoft account look and feel the same. This includes browser settings such as favorites and history.

- **Local Account**—This type of account is used to log on to your local computer but will not have the extra features of a Microsoft account.

These accounts can be configured to be Standard or Administrator accounts.

LET ME TRY IT

Adding a Local User Account

The following steps show you how to add a user account in Windows 8. You are asked to create either a Microsoft account or a Local account.

1. From the Start screen right-click on the screen.

2. Click the All Apps button that appears on the lower-right corner of the screen.

3. Select Control Panel.

4. Click the User Accounts and Family Safety group.

5. Click User Accounts.

6. Click Manage Another Account.

7. Click Add a new user in PC settings. The PC settings page is now displayed.

8. Under the Other Users heading click Add a user.

9. If you plan to use a Microsoft account, enter the email address you use for that account. Here, we will add a Local Account.

10. Click Sign In without a Microsoft Account.

11. Select Local Account.

12. Fill in Username and Password information (see Figure 10.21).

13. Click Next.

14. Your account is created and you have an option to select the check box if the account is a child's account.

15. Click Finish.

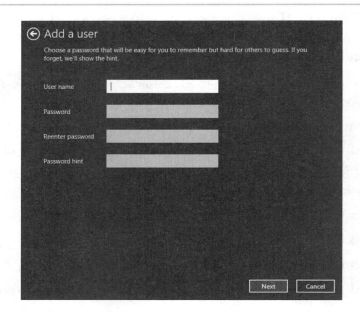

Figure 10.21   *Creating a new Local account*

Configuring an Account

After the account is created, you can configure a few options for it by clicking on the user on the Manage Accounts page:

- **Change the Account Name**—The name you type here appears on the Welcome screen and Start menu.

- **Change a Password**—In this dialog, you can change a password and password hint.

- **Set Up Family Safety**—This opens the Family Safety item, allowing you to customize the configuration of the account.

- **Change the Account Type**—Select between Standard User or Administrator accounts. You would want to limit the amount of users that have Administrator accounts, as these users will have full control of Windows 8.

- **Delete the Account**—Before deleting the account, you are prompted whether you want to save the user's personalized data (such as documents, favorites, music, pictures, and more).

 SHOW ME   Media 10.4—Managing Users

Access this video file through your registered Web Edition at
my.safaribooksonline.com/9780789750518/media.

Recovering Lost Passwords

From time to time a user might forget the password he uses to log on to Windows 8. Without the password, there is no logging on to the system—plain and simple. To ward off a potential problem, it's recommended that each password-protected user account create a password reset disk. Bear in mind, however, that the password reset disk needs to be created from the account requesting it, and you can only perform this on local accounts (you won't see the tool if you are logged in with a Microsoft account). This means if you've lost your password without having created a reset disk, you have no way of recovering the password.

 LET ME TRY IT

Creating a User Account Password Reset Disk

The following steps require you to log on to the account you want to create the password reset disk for. An optional USB drive can be used to save the password.

1. Log-on to the account you want to create a password reset disk for.

2. From the Start screen right-click on the screen.

3. Click the All Apps button that appears on the lower-right corner of the screen.

4. Select Control Panel.

5. Click the User Accounts and Family Safety group.

6. Click User Accounts.

7. In the left pane, click Create a Password Reset Disk. This opens the Forgotten Password Wizard. (If you intend to save this to a USB drive, insert that drive now.)

8. Click Next.

9. Select the location where you want to create the password key disk from the drop-down menu.

10. Click Next.

11. Type your account password in the text box.

12. Click Next. A progress indicator appears as the key is being saved.

13. When the indicator stops at 100%, click Next.

14. Click Finish. You can locate your key on the media you saved it to by finding the file userkey.psw.

Another quick way to reset your account password is to have someone who has an administrator account log on and manually replace your password. Then you can log on with the password they provide and change the password.

If you are an administrator doing this on behalf of a user, be careful; there is a potential risk involved. When you use an administrator account to reset a password for another user, that user loses access to his or her encrypted files, encrypted email messages, and stored passwords for websites or network resources.

This same risk does not apply if a user uses a password reset disk to reset her password.

 **LET ME TRY IT**

Deleting a User Account While Keeping the User's Files

From time to time, you might need to delete a user account. Like the other aspects of user accounts, this is easily done. The key to completing this is logging on with an administrator account.

The following steps show you how to delete a user account while keeping its data. On completion of the steps, the data is saved in a folder on the Desktop.

1. Log on to an administrator account.

2. From the Start screen right-click on the screen

3. Click the All Apps button that appears on the lower-right corner of the screen.

4. Select Control Panel.

5. Click the User Accounts and Family Safety group.

6. Click User Accounts.

7. Click Manage Another Account.

8. Select the account you want to delete by clicking on it.

9. Click Delete the Account.

10. You are asked to either Delete Files or Keep Files. Click the Keep Files button.

11. You are asked to confirm the deletion along with a message that the user's files will be saved in a folder placed on your Desktop. Click the Delete Account button.

12. Minimize the Manage Accounts page and locate the saved data in the folder Windows created on your Desktop.

Windows Defender

Discussed in great detail in Chapter 9, Windows Defender is a tool that provides protection from spyware and malware in real-time on your system. You can configure it to run quick scans or full scans either on a schedule or manually. Type **defender** in the Control Panel Search box to locate the Windows Defender application.

Windows Firewall

Also discussed in great detail in Chapter 9, Windows Firewall is a tool that helps to protect your system from unwanted access—access from both the outside world trying to come into your computer or from unauthorized applications that might be running on your system that you don't want to allow out from your computer. Type **firewall** in the Control Panel Search box to locate the Windows Firewall application.

Windows Mobile Device Center

PDA and smartphone users will find that they have an extra item in the Control Panel after installing their devices—the Windows Mobile Device Center. First introduced in Vista, the Windows Mobile Device Center is a replacement for all previous versions of ActiveSync.

SYNCING OLDER DEVICES

When Vista first burst onto the scene, users decried the lack of hardware compatibility for their legacy devices. In its first incarnation, Windows Mobile Device Center didn't help. Instead of having the ultimate operating system to synchronize with, many PDA users found they were unable to connect. Soon they were scurrying back to Windows XP, grumbling every step of the way. Subsequent releases of Windows Mobile Device Center have widely expanded the amount of devices able to connect and sync. However, if you have a very old PDA or smartphone, there's a good chance it might never connect. Here a few tips to try before you give up:

- If you are using a USB cable different from the OEM one provided by your manufacturer, be advised that despite looks, not all USB cables are created equal. I recently had to troubleshoot a device only to discover that both USB cables I tried to connect with (they work with every other USB device I have) were no good—only the OEM cable connected.

- Try searching through Internet forums to see what workarounds other users have used. Search through forums like www.brighthand.com with the keywords **Windows Mobile Device Center** and your device name (for example, Hp Ipaq 3735).

- If you find there is no support for your hardware, it might finally be time to upgrade that ancient relic.

There are two connection styles you can choose from when you first sync:

- Creating a Partnership

- Connecting Without Setting Up Your Device

With a partnership, Windows automatically synchronizes data from your device that you select. You can choose to sync contacts, calendar appointments, email, files, and more. Every time you plug in the device, the WMDC opens and syncs the data. This feature can be a lifesaver if the device's battery dies or you accidently delete data on your mobile device. Instead of losing the data permanently, it is "backed up" by being synchronized with your machine. Just plug it in, sync again, and your mobile data is restored.

 LET ME TRY IT

Setting Up a Partnership with Your Windows Mobile Device

The following steps show you how to create a partnership between your device and your computer. To complete this exercise, you need a smartphone or PDA running Windows Mobile.

1. Plug in your mobile device. Windows 8 finds new hardware and installs drivers for it.

2. After drivers are successfully installed, the WMDC starts. (If the WMDC does not start automatically, from the Control Panel, click Hardware and Sound. Click Windows Mobile Device Center.)

3. Look for a green check in the lower left along with the word Connected. (If you do not see this, unplug the device and turn it off. Reboot Windows 8. After Windows 8 has completely booted up, turn on the device and plug it back in. The Windows Mobile Device Center will auto start.)

4. On the right, click Set up your Device, and the Set up Windows Mobile Partnership dialog box opens.

5. Select which items you want to synchronize. (Note: Though it will be visible, you will be unable to select email unless you have already configured Outlook. A version of Outlook is provided with many mobile devices to utilize this feature.)

6. Click Next.

7. In the Device Name text box, type a name for your mobile device. This name shows up every time you open the WMDC.

8. Click Set Up. Windows establishes the partnership and attempts to sync the data. When completed, you see a date and time of the last sync under the word Connected.

After a partnership has been established, new options appear in the WMDC:

- **Programs and Services**—Here you find links to Add/Remove Programs, which opens a new dialog for installing or removing Windows Mobile applications. Also in Programs and Services are links to Microsoft resources, such as updates and help. The options here vary from one device to another depending on the manufacturer.

- **Pictures, Music, and Video**—Hover your mouse over this and an interactive window opens. Click the blue More button to reveal all your choices. The first link tells you how many media items exist on your device that have not been synchronized. Pictures/Video Import Settings brings up a dialog to fine-tune your import features, including giving you the ability to delete the item from the device after import. A third choice is to Add Media to your Device from Windows Media Player.

- **File Management**—Select this to browse the contents of your device. If your device has a storage card, it can be accessed from here.

- **Mobile Device Settings**—Clicking the More button opens up a bevy of links—Change Content Sync Settings, Manage a Partnership, Connection Settings, and more.

The other option you have when first synchronizing the device is Connecting Without Setting Up Your Device. This limits you to file sharing on the host system or using your device to share mobile broadband. This choice is a good option if you need to quickly connect to a machine to share data. For example, if you have a storage card on your mobile device, you can use it like a Jump Drive by plugging in your device to a host machine, starting WMDC, and selecting Connecting Without Setting Up Your Device. Once connected, the device shows up in Windows Explorer with access to your storage card.

Mobile broadband lets users tether a cell phone to a computer and access the Internet through the cell phone's network connection. To use this, you need a data card (SIM) and a mobile broadband data plan with a provider. This can be a great solution to get connected to the Internet in remote locations or areas that do not provide broadband service.

Windows Update

Windows Update is a way to connect to a Microsoft database that has drivers, patches, security fixes, and so forth to keep your OS installation up to date. Updates and software from Microsoft for Microsoft products are free as part of its maintenance and support services. If you choose not to configure Windows Update (see Figure 10.22), a large red shield tries to persuade you to turn it on, as do warnings in the Action Center.

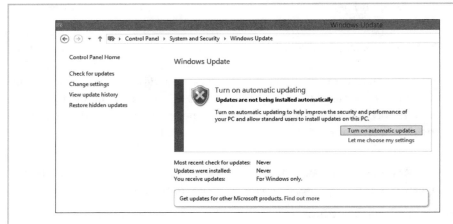

Figure 10.22   *The large red shield attempts to persuade you to turn on Windows Update*

If you share your computer with other users, every user gets the same update, regardless of who uses them. Users who are administrators by default can install updates. You can also allow users with Standard User accounts to have permission to install updates. This allows standard, non-administrator users to install updates manually.

For a home system, you can configure your Windows Update setting to connect to Microsoft and update your system or you can do it manually. If you are a network admin, consider using Group Policies to configure these settings for your workplace. And, if you have a large enough environment and a small enough network connection to the Internet, you might want to consider setting up a Windows Update Server. This goes out and downloads updates and then your network systems check in with the server and download from the internal system. It's a great way to ensure that all your systems are protected with the latest security patches and fixes.

With Windows Update, you configure your system to work on a schedule of your choosing (or none at all if you prefer to handle checking for updates manually, which is not recommended). What many disliked about Windows Updates in the past was that updates usually required reboots, and these reboots pushed a request box at you every 10 minutes until you complied with the request. Now you can choose longer periods of time (up to four hours) before that dialog box appears; the dialog simply is not as intrusive.

There are two different Windows Update classifications:

- **Important**—As the name suggests, these updates are important. They can improve security, privacy, and reliability. Generally, these updates should be installed when they are available and can be installed manually.

- **Optional**—These can include drivers for your hardware or new software enhancements from Microsoft (such as language packs).

Windows Update delivers the following different styles of updates:

- **Security Updates**—These contain fixes for product-specific, security-related vulnerabilities.

- **Critical Updates:** These are broadly released patches for specific critical but nonsecurity issues.

- **Services Packs**—Consider these as all of the above and more rolled up in one. Service Packs could also have a few requested design changes or features.

The status of Windows Update can appear in the Notification Area as a pop-up window letting you know updates are available and what their status is. For most users, leaving the settings on Install Updates Automatically works best. Advanced users might want to set their update configuration to either Download Updates But Let Me Choose Whether to Install Them or Check for Updates But Let Me Choose Whether to Download and Install Them.

 LET ME TRY IT

Configuring Windows Update to Download But Not Install Updates

The following steps show you how to configure how Windows Update behaves. Upon completion, updates are downloaded but not installed unless they are authorized by the user.

1. From the Start screen right-click on the screen.

2. Click the All Apps button that appears on the lower-right corner of the screen.

3. Select Control Panel.

4. Click System and Security.

5. Click Windows Update.

6. Click the Change Settings link.

7. From the Important Updates drop-down, select Download Updates But Let Me Choose Whether to Install Them.

8. Click OK.

Now when an update arrives, you can choose whether to install it. You are notified when updates arrive and can view and select which ones you want installed. Updates appear here as well for Microsoft Office applications and can include Office Service Packs, notifications, and more.

Every now and then, an update fails. This occurs for a variety of reasons. A couple of steps must take place for an update to happen. These range from scanning your machine for needed updates to downloading and then installing the update. Failure to complete any one of the steps causes an update failure. Before giving up, try to install the update manually.

To review installed updates, go to the left pane in Windows Update and click the View Update History link. Here you will find listed Name, Status, Importance, and Date Installed (or attempted install).

From time to time you might find your system doesn't react quite right after an update. Though rare, you might occasionally need to uninstall an update. The following Let Me Try It shows you how to do this.

 **LET ME TRY IT**

Viewing and Uninstalling an Update

The following steps show you how to view past Windows Update installations and then uninstall an update of your choice. This exercise requires you to have first connected to Windows Update and installed an update.

1. From the Start screen right-click on the screen.

2. Click on the All Apps button that appears on the lower-right corner of the screen.

3. Select Control Panel.

4. Click System and Security.

5. Click Windows Update.

6. In the lower-left of the page, click the Installed Updates link.

7. Click the update you want to remove.

8. From the top menu, click Uninstall. A dialog appears, asking you to confirm the uninstall.

9. Click Yes to uninstall the update.

In some cases, network users might be unable to remove an update. It might be that your computer is connected to a network where updates are managed by Group Policy. Or, if an update applies to a security-related area of the operating system, you might not be able to remove it. Get in touch with your system administrator or your IT department if you think an update that you can't remove is causing problems.

 TELL ME MORE   Media 10.5—A Discussion of System **Configuration Settings**
Access this audio recording through your registered Web Edition at
my.safaribooksonline.com/9780789750518/media.

This chapter examines Windows 8's on-board monitoring tools and shows you how to utilize them in day-to-day situations.

11

Performance and Monitoring Tools

Performance Information and Tools

What is one of the most annoying experiences you have with your computer? Undoubtedly most of you are thinking of the "Hourglass." Yes, when you click you expect an instant (or at least close to instant) result. How your computer performs is important, and a well-performing machine can save you valuable time and in some cases money.

This chapter looks at some of the things you can check when your computer is not performing as well as you want. We also cover items that you can use to proactively monitor your computer.

The Windows Experience Index (WEI) was first introduced in Vista. It returns largely unchanged in Windows 8 (see Figure 11.1) except for a few subtle refinements. The purpose of the WEI is to measure the capability of your computer's hardware and software configuration. After testing it out, the WEI expresses this measurement as a base score number. The higher the base score, the better.

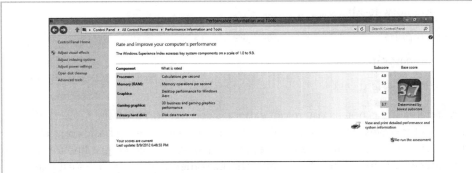

Figure 11.1   *The Windows Experience Index (WEI)*

 **LET ME TRY IT**

Running the Windows Experience Index Assessment

Before starting this exercise, shut down any applications running on your system. These could potentially slow system performance and return a lower score. The following steps show you how to run the Windows Experience Index assessment.

1. From the Start screen right-click on the screen.

2. Click the All Apps button that appears on the lower-right corner of the screen.

3. Select Control Panel.

4. In the Search box type **Performance**.

5. Click Performance Information and Tools.

6. In the lower right click Re-Run the Assessment. Your computer is now re-assessed, and you are provided with a base score rating.

Understanding the WEI Score

The base score rating is a number based on the five Subscore ratings for the following categories:

- Processor
- Memory (RAM)
- Graphics
- Gaming Graphics
- Primary Hard Disk

The final rating is not, as you might expect, a compilation of all the ratings. It's actually the lowest of the Subscore ratings. For someone using basic computer functions (such as surfing the Internet), a score of 4.0 would be just fine for them to use these basic functions. On the other hand, someone playing the latest hardware-intensive games would typically need a much higher score, perhaps 8.5 or above.

WEI scores range from 1.0 to 9.9. The high score was 5.9 in Vista, and 7.9 in Windows 7, so Windows 8's adjustment to 9.9 accounts for faster hardware since older operating systems were released.

Improving Your WEI Score

Can you get a higher base score on some components without upgrading your hardware? Yes. The improvement to your score won't be huge, but you can do a few things to make it better. Here are a couple suggestions to improve your computer's performance. Not all of these affect the base score, but they do contribute to improved performance overall:

- **Close all running applications**—Before running WEI, shut down as many applications as possible. These could have an impact on performance. If you really want to prepare the machine for the test, reboot it before running WEI. During the test, don't start or use applications.

- **Configure visual effects**—Changing how menus and windows display can have an effect on performance.

- **Adjust power settings**—These, too, can have an effect on your computer's speed. Select the High Performance option before running the test. If you are running this test on a laptop, make sure it is plugged in. Using a laptop with a battery draining down can cause some CPUs to enable a reduced power mode that slows the calculations in an effort to save energy. This can affect your Processor Subscore.

- **Clean up your hard drive**—This is always a good idea, and there are some good hard-drive cleaning tools in Windows 8, such as Disk Cleanup and Disk Defragmenter.

Conveniently you have easy access to the items you need to make these adjustments. On the left pane you see links to

- Adjust Visual Effects

- Adjust Indexing Options

- Adjust Power Settings

- Open Disk Cleanup

- Advanced Tools (discussed later in this chapter)

By knowing your base score, you can make better software purchasing decisions. The key is purchasing titles that are equal to or below your base score. For example, the hottest game on the market might require a high-performing graphics card. By understanding your Gaming Graphics Subscore, you can determine whether your machine can handle it. If your Gaming Graphics Subscore falls short yet you still want to try a game that requires a high-performing graphics card, your system might be sluggish or it might not run at all.

Seeing exactly how your hardware rates gives you a good feel for what needs to be upgraded next. In the never-ending upgrading world of computers, it's only a matter of time before a new component or two ends up on your shopping list.

 SHOW ME   Media 11.1—The Windows Experience Index
Access this video file through your registered Web Edition at
my.safaribooksonline.com/9780789750518/media.

Windows System Assessment Tool (WinSAT)

The Windows System Assessment Tool (WinSAT) is the behind-the-scenes application that creates your WEI.

For the most part, when you install an OS like XP, you get XP in all its glory, regardless of the box you are running it on. So, although the underlying parts might vary, the OS options should be the same, right? Or should they? Does it really make sense that two systems—one that is a $200 cheap-o box with cheesy hardware—should be put in the same position to handle the OS features of a $3,000 dream machine? Well, Windows 8 has a little underlying tool that helps to differentiate between the two, called WinSAT.

When you first install Windows 8, before the first login, WinSAT runs its testing process to see what your individual system can handle. It uses that information to determine which operating system features should be enabled or disabled by default. For example, if your system cannot handle some advanced features, the settings on your OS reduce to basic mode.

The WinSAT utility creates its output in the system directory: %systemroot%\Performance\WinSAT\DataStore. Each time you run WinSAT, a new XML file is generated in this folder with the date of the assessment stuck at the beginning of the filename—for example, 2012-01-01 12.00.00.000 Assessment (Formal).WinSAT.xml. There is also a file in this directory with the word *Initial* inside the bracketed part of the filename.

Advanced Tools

The Performance Information and Tools page includes an Advanced Tools link to the left. Clicking this option takes you to the Advanced Tools page (see Figure 11.2).

This page displays any performance issues you can address to improve performance as well as a variety of tools you can use to monitor or improve your performance. These tools include the following:

- **Clear All Windows Experience Index Scores and Re-Rate the System—** Forces a complete rerun of all Windows Experience Index tests.

Figure 11.2   *Advanced Tools for performance*

- **View Performance Details in Event Log**—Displays details of problems affecting Windows performance.

- **Open Performance Monitor**—Displays graphs of system performance and collects data logs.

- **Open Resource Monitor**—Displays real-time system resource usage and manages active services and applications.

- **Open Task Manager**—Displays information about the programs and processes currently running on your computer.

- **View Advanced System Details in System Information**—Displays details about the hardware and software components on your computer.

- **Adjust the Appearance and Performance of Windows**—Provides settings to change visual effects, processor and memory usage, and virtual memory.

- **Open Disk Defragmenter**—Displays the schedule used to automatically defragment your hard disk; you can modify this schedule to better suit your needs.

- **Generate a System Health Report**—Displays details about system health and performance.

The Reliability Monitor

What is your standard method for determining the reliability of your system? Most of us determine our system's reliability by how long it has been since it has blue screened on us or forced us to reboot. Unfortunately, that isn't the most "technically sound" way to assess reliability.

> In Vista, the Reliability Monitor was combined with the Performance Monitor that we discuss later in this chapter, in the section "Working with the Performance Monitor." These were split up in Windows 7 and remain that way in Windows 8, but the overall functionality within each is the same. They just look a little different (and have a few new features) because they have been restructured to work alone.

The main goal of the Reliability Monitor is to keep track of "reliability events," which have been defined as changes to your system that could alter the stability or other events that might indicate system instability (see Figure 11.3). Events monitored include

- Windows updates

- Software installs and uninstalls

- Device driver installs, updates, rollbacks, and uninstalls

- Application hangs and crashes

- Device drivers that fail to load or unload

- Disk and memory failures

- Windows failures, including boot failures, system crashes, and sleep failures

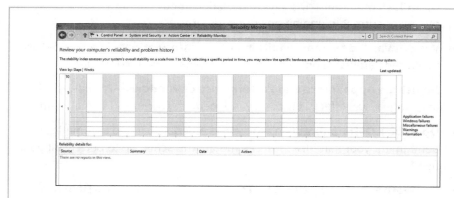

Figure 11.3   *Review your computer's reliability and problem history*

The Stability Index rating gives you a visual of how reliable your system performs over time. You are given an overall Stability Index score. Ten is perfection; one is the lowest. The Reliability Monitor retains up to a year's worth of data so you can really see how your system has been performing over time.

The Reliability Monitor displays a Stability Index rating 24 hours after installation and provides specific event information.

If you see a drop in stability, you can check the date the drop began and then see whether the decline was due to one of the following issues:

- Application failures

- Windows failures

- Miscellaneous failures

- Warnings

- Information

Because the main purpose of the Reliability Monitor is to display data, there is limited functionality. The menu at the bottom of the page allows you to save your history as an .xml file, view all problem reports, and check for solutions to all problems. Another option is to find solutions for individual events.

 SHOW ME Media 11.2—The Reliability Monitor
Access this video file through your registered Web Edition at
my.safaribooksonline.com/9780789750518/media.

 LET ME TRY IT

Using the Reliability Monitor to Check for a Solution to a Specific Application Problem

The following steps show you how to run the Reliability Monitor to check for a solution to an application failure. A connection to the Internet is required.

1. From the Start screen right-click on the screen.

2. Click the All Apps button that appears on the lower-right corner of the screen.

3. Select Control Panel.

4. In the search box type **reliability**.

5. Click View Reliability History. The Reliability Monitor opens.

6. Select an application failure from the Stability Index.

7. Click the Check for a Solution link. Problem reporting connects with the Windows Error Reporting service to locate and provide a solution.

The Resource Monitor

The Resource Monitor shows a real-time view of your system's CPU, Memory, Disk, and Network usage. As shown in Figure 11.4, you can select items in the CPU group to show those items in the graphs on the right. In addition, you can use the Resource Monitor to stop processes, start and stop services, analyze process dead-locks, view thread-wait chains, and identify processes-locking files.

 SHOW ME   Media 11.3—The Resource Monitor

Access this video file through your registered Web Edition at
my.safaribooksonline.com/9780789750518/media.

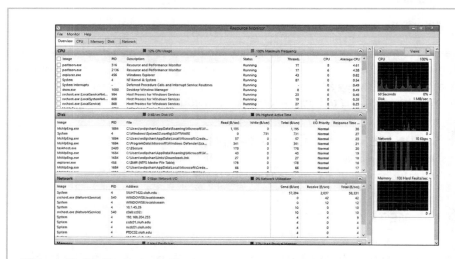

Figure 11.4   *The Resource Monitor*

 **LET ME TRY IT**

Open the Resource Monitor

The following steps show you how to open the Resource Monitor.

1. From the Start screen right click on the screen.

2. Click the All Apps button that appears on the lower-right corner of the screen.

3. Select Control Panel.

4. In the Search box type **Performance**.

5. Click Performance Information and Tools.

6. In left pane click Advanced Tools.

7. Select Open Resource Monitor and the Resource Monitor opens.

Understanding the Resource Monitor

When you first look at the Resource Monitor, you might not realize just how much data is available for analysis. There is a lot going on in the various tabs shown:

- **Overview**—This is the default tab shown the first time you start Resource Monitor. (On subsequent starts, Resource Monitor displays the last tab you viewed before closing it.) The center view pane displays four sections: CPU, Disk, Network, and Memory. Click the Down arrow to the right of each section to expand the section and display real-time stats.

- **CPU**—This tab contains four sections related to your processor: Processes, Services, Associated Handles, and Associated Modules.

- **Memory**—This tab shows a graphical display of your memory in use and includes a Processes tab.

- **Disk**—Click this tab to view processes with disk activity, disk activity, and storage sections.

- **Network**—Click this tab to view processes with network activity, network activity, TCP connections, and listening ports.

To the right, a view pane displays a graphical readout of CPU, Disk, Network, and Memory activity. This right pane changes as you click each tab to show a graphical representation of the data for that tab. For example, clicking the Memory tab changes the right pane to display Used Physical Memory, Commit Charge, and Hard Faults/Sec. Additionally, clicking the drop-down arrow at the top of the right pane allows you to customize the size of these graphs.

 **LET ME TRY IT**

Identifying the Network Address to Which a Process Is Connected

You need a working network connection to complete the following steps, which show you how to find a network address to which a process that might be using a large amount of resources on your computer is connected.

1. From the Start screen right click on the screen.

2. Click the All Apps button that appears on the lower-right corner of the screen.

3. Select Control Panel.

4. In the Search box type **Performance**.

5. Click Performance Information and Tools.

6. In the left pane click Advanced Tools.

7. Select Open Resource Monitor and the Resource Monitor opens.

8. Click the Network tab.

9. Find the process for which you want to see the network address it is con-
    nected to and select its check box. (If you don't recognize a process, select
    the System process.)

10. Click the TCP Connections title bar.

11. Examine the Remote Address to see which network address the process is
    connected to.

You might have noticed that when you select the process check box, it moves that
process to the top of the list. This enables you to focus on this particular process
rather than search for it as the list dynamically updates.

Another invaluable use for the Resource Monitor is the ability to view applications
that are not responding. You can view the wait chain of a process (see Figure 11.5)
and end processes that are preventing a program from working properly.

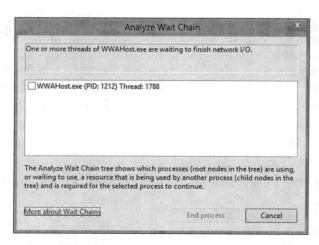

Figure 11.5   *Examining an unresponsive process wait chain*

LET ME TRY IT

Troubleshooting an Unresponsive Application Through the Resource Monitor

The following steps show you how to use the Resource Monitor to analyze applications. Before you begin, open a couple applications—such as Notepad and Paint—without saving them. Use these applications for analysis through Resource Monitor.

1. From the Start screen right click on the screen.

2. Click the All Apps button that appears on the lower-right corner of the screen.

3. Select Control Panel.

4. In the Search box type **Performance**.

5. Click Performance Information and Tools.

6. In the left pane click Advanced Tools.

7. Select Open Resource Monitor and the Resource Monitor opens.

8. Click the Overview tab.

9. Locate any process that is not responding, as noted by its blue appearance. Right-click the process and choose Analyze Wait Chain. The Analyze Wait Chain dialog box opens with a tree display organized by dependency.

10. Select a process and click the End Process button.

11. Repeat step 10 until the application responds.

Under normal circumstances, if you want to end an unresponsive application, you might use the Task Manager to end a task. Use caution when you use the Resource Monitor to end a task. You should use Resource Monitor to end a process only if you are unable to close the program by normal means. By ending an application process, the application associated with the process closes immediately and you lose any unsaved data. If you end a system process, it might result in system instability and data loss.

Working with the Performance Monitor

The Performance Monitor can show you performance data in either real time or from a log file. Data Collector Sets can be set to run immediately or on a schedule to collect and analyze specific aspects of your system.

Performance Monitor displays a visual representation of your system so you can inspect a variety of components, beyond what the Resource Monitor shows you (see Figure 11.6). Initially, you won't see more than the % Process Time. You can add more performance metrics (called *counters*) by pressing the + sign.

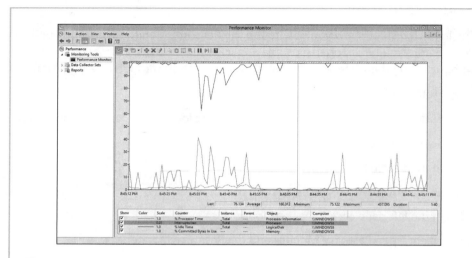

Figure 11.6   *Performance Monitor in real time*

When you first see the number of possible counters and instances, the task of choosing which items to monitor can seem overwhelming. There are roughly 100 different Performance objects for any given system (you can monitor the local system or a remote one). Each of those objects contains counters. (There are way too many counters to know them all.) Once you have all your counters set up, you can make changes to the way they are displayed. For example, you can change the line colors for each counter to make it easier to determine which line you are watching. You can change the format of the display to a graph, a histogram, or a report (numeric display).

Data Collector Sets allow you to use System-defined sets (there is one for System Diagnostics and one for System Performance) or User-defined sets (which is empty to start with; you literally have to create your own). You can also look at Event Trace Sessions and Startup Event Trace Sessions. Trace Sessions will log events to a file.

The goal is to use Data Collector Sets to collect the data and then the Report sections to view the data collected.

 **LET ME TRY IT**

Configuring the Performance Monitor to Display Results as a Web Page

The following steps show you how to open the Performance Monitor and configure it to save performance results for viewing in a web browser.

1. On the Start screen start typing **Perfmon** (no particular place on the screen).

2. A Search box appears with the Perfmon app on the left side. Press Enter and Perfmon opens.

3. Select Performance Monitor under Monitoring Tools in the left pane.

4. Right-click in the Performance Monitor display area and click Save Settings As.

5. Choose where you want to save the file.

6. Type a name for the HTML file.

7. Click OK.

8. Navigate to the saved HTML file and open it. It displays captured performance information in your browser.

As an admin, you would find it both time-consuming and monotonous to have to physically be at every computer to run Performance Monitor. Fortunately, network administrators or those with administrator rights can now remotely gain access to this feature and connect.

 LET ME TRY IT

Connecting to a Remote Computer with Performance Monitor

The following steps show you how to connect Performance Monitor to another computer on the network. To complete these steps, you need a working network connection and a connection to another computer on the network.

1. On the Start screen start typing **Perfmon** (no particular place on the screen).

2. A Search box appears with the Perfmon app on the left side. Press Enter and Perfmon opens.

3. Select Performance in the left pane (top of the tree).

4. On the top menu, click Action and then select Connect to Another Computer.

5. If you know the name of the computer you want to monitor, type that name; if you don't know the name, click Browse to locate it.

6. Click OK.

 LET ME TRY IT

Comparing the Performance of Two Computers

You may want to compare specific counters on separate computers. You can do this by adding counters from different computers within the same Performance Monitor window. The following steps add two counters (% Committed Bytes in Use) from separate computers to the same Performance Monitor instance.

1. On the Start screen start typing **Perfmon** (no particular place on the screen).

2. A Search box appears with the Perfmon app on the left side. Press Enter and Perfmon opens.

3. Click Performance Monitor under Monitoring Tools in the left pane.

4. Right-click in the lower pane and select Remove All Counters. You now have a clean slate, no counters.

5. Click the plus sign to add a counter. This opens the Add Counter dialog box.

6. In the Select Counters from Computer box you can type the name of the remote computer with \\ preceding the name. You now establish a connection to the remote computer.

7. Find Memory in the list of counters and expand by clicking on the down arrow to the right.

8. Select % Committed Bytes in Use to highlight the selection.

9. Click the Add button and your selection moves to the right Added Counters pane.

10. Now you can put another computer name in the Select Counters From Computer box (you can use your local computer if desired). You establish a connection with this computer.

11. Repeat steps 7-9.

12. You now have both counters (same counter from different computers) in the right Added Counters pane.

13. Click OK and you have real-time monitoring of Memory % Committed Bytes in Use on two computers.

> There are two requirements to viewing performance counters from a remote computer. First, the Performance Logs and Alerts firewall exception must be enabled on the remote computer. Second, users in the Performance Log Users group must also be listed in the Event Log Readers group on the remote computer.

 LET ME TRY IT

Creating Data Collector Sets from Performance Monitor

The following steps show you how to use Performance Monitor to collect data. You have the opportunity to configure settings to complete this task.

1. On the Start screen start typing **Perfmon** (no particular place on the screen).

2. A Search box appears with the Perfmon app on the left side. Press Enter and Perfmon opens.

3. Expand Data Collector Sets in the left pane.

4. Right-click User Defined.

5. Select New and then Data Collector Set. The New Data Collector Set Wizard opens (see Figure 11.7).

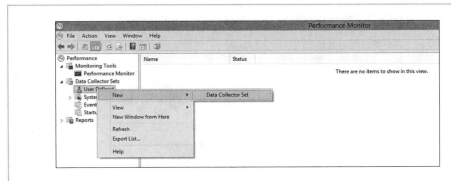

Figure 11.7 *Creating a new Data Collector Set*

6. Type a Name for this data set and choose whether you want to Create from a Template (preconfigured settings) or Create Manually. Select Create Manually and click Next.

7. Choose what kind of data you want to collect. The Create Data Logs radio button is selected by default. Select the Performance Counters check box and click Next.

8. Choose the Performance Counters you want. Click the Add button.

9. The dialog box that opens should look familiar. Choose which counters you want to add and from what computer (as we did earlier in this chapter). Let's expand Processor Information and then select %Processor Performance to highlight this selection.

10. Click Add to move your selection to the Added Counters pane.

11. Click OK and you see your counter added to the Performance Counters box.

12. You have the option here to also configure how often this counter gets checked and logged. By using the Sample Interval and Units boxes you set how often this counter will be checked. Leave the default settings for now and click Next.

13. Choose where you want to save your data collection file. Click Browse to choose a location, type the path in the Root Directory field, or just leave the default path. (%SYSTEMROOT% is an alias for the location of your operating system files, usually c:\windows.) Once you have entered your path click Next.

14. You can configure the Data Collector Set to run as a different user if needed, and you can choose what to do once you finish the wizard. Your options are

    - Open the Properties for This Data Collector Set

    - Start This Data Collector Set Now

    - Save and Close

15. Leave the default Save and Close selected and click Finish.

After you click Finish and return to the Windows Performance Monitor, there are a few things you can do with this saved data (as you learn in the following section).

Editing the Properties of a Created Data Collector Set

The following steps build on the previous steps and show you how to modify the properties of a Data Collector Set.

1. On the Start screen start typing **Perfmon** (no particular place on the screen).

2. A Search box appears with the Perfmon app on the left side. Press Enter and Perfmon opens.

3. Expand Data Collector Sets in the left pane.

4. Right-click the data collection set for which you want to modify the properties and choose Properties.

5. After completing your modifications, click OK.

To start the Data Collector Set immediately, right-click it and choose Start.

After you have set up your data collectors, you can save the data in the form of logs that you can review later if necessary to help troubleshoot performance issues.

Not all log files are created equal. If you create a log file in Windows 8, it is not backward compatible with earlier versions of Windows prior to Windows 7. However, log files created in earlier versions are viewable in Windows 8.

 LET ME TRY IT

Setting Up a Log Schedule for a Data Collector Set

The following steps show you how to create a log schedule for a Data Collector set.

1. On the Start screen start typing **Perfmon** (no particular place on the screen).

2. A Search box appears with the Perfmon app on the left side. Press Enter and Perfmon opens.

3. Expand Data Collector Sets in the left pane.

4. Click on User Defined.

5. In the console pane, right-click the name of the Data Collector Set that you want to schedule and choose Properties.

6. Click the Schedule tab and click Add.

7. Using the drop-down arrows, configure the Beginning Date, Expiration Date, and the Start Time (under Launch).

8. Click OK.

9. Click the Stop Condition tab.

10. Select the Overall Duration check box.

11. Select the Stop When All Data Collectors Have Finished check box. (This permits the data collector to complete recording the most recent values before the Data Collector Set is stopped.)

12. Click OK.

 LET ME TRY IT

Configuring Data Collector Sets to Delete the Oldest Log File When Starting Data Collection

You can also configure how your data is archived. If you log reports on a daily basis, log files generate automatically and start to consume disk space. You can define preset limits and actions to take with these files.

The following steps show you how to configure Data Collector Sets to delete the oldest log file when starting data collection.

1. On the Start screen start typing **Perfmon** (no particular place on the screen).

2. A Search box appears with the Perfmon app on the left side. Press Enter and Perfmon opens.

3. Expand Data Collector Sets in the left pane.

4. Click User Defined.

5. In the console pane, right-click the name of the Data Collector Set that you want to schedule and choose Data Manager.

6. Select the Maximum Folders check box.

7. In the drop-down below, choose 5.

8. Change the Resource policy to Delete Oldest.

9. Select the Apply Policy Before the Data Collector Set Starts check box.

10. Click Apply.

11. Click OK.

In this example, with the Maximum Folders check box selected, previous data will be deleted when the limit is reached. And since the Apply Policy Before the Data Collector Set Starts check box was chosen as well, previous data will be deleted before the Data Collector Set creates its next log file.

It's a good idea to know your Resource policy (Delete Oldest or Delete Largest) before making other data choices on the Data Manager tab. Minimum Free Disk Space, Maximum Folders, and Maximum Root Path all revolve around your policy. Here are some other points to understand when working with these features:

- **Minimum Free Disk**—This is the disk space that needs to be available on the drive where you store the log data. When you choose this, previous data will be deleted when the limit is reached.

- **Maximum Folders**—This is the maximum total of subfolders that can be in the Data Collector Set data directory. Like the Minimum Free Disk Space option, previous data will be deleted when the limit is reached.

- **Maximum Root Path Size**—This represents the total size (including subfolders) of the data directory for the Data Collector Set. Be advised that choosing this option causes your Minimum Free Disk and Maximum Folders limits to be overridden and previous data will be deleted when the limit is reached.

Unless you have a trained eye or have spent some time reading reports, you might not understand the results of the data you have collected. To help with this, Windows Performance Monitor provides assistance diagnosing your reports. These reports are easy to understand and contain a wealth of data that helps you pinpoint potential problems (see Figure 11.8).

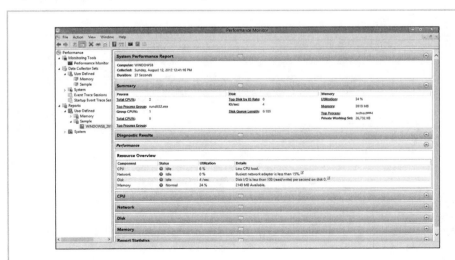

Figure 11.8   *Viewing a System Diagnostics report in Performance Monitor*

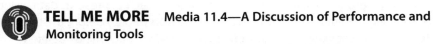

TELL ME MORE   Media 11.4—A Discussion of Performance and Monitoring Tools

Access this audio recording through your registered Web Edition at
my.safaribooksonline.com/9780789750518/media.

12

Managing and Troubleshooting

Using Administrative Tools

So here we are at the last chapter of the book. We hope you have enjoyed the adventure. So far we have talked about all the great improvements and cool features that you have at your fingertips with Windows 8. However, just like everything else in life, Windows 8 is not just fun and games. We must work on our operating system to get it to function the way we want and at times, yes, we must troubleshoot problems.

In this chapter we take a closer look at the Administrative Tools item in the Control Panel, and see how these tools can help you manage your Windows 8 operating system and troubleshoot any issues you might face.

After you go through Control Panel, you can see a shortcut to Administrative Tools located in the System and Security group that takes you to the list of shortcuts (see Figure 12.1). Some of the tools you see in the Administrative Tools section have been covered already in other chapters of the book. For example, Performance Monitor was covered in Chapter 11, "Performance and Monitoring Tools."

Figure 12.1 *The Administrative Tools section found under System and Security*

 **LET ME TRY IT**

Creating a Tile for Administrative Tools on Your Start Screen

Follow these steps to add a tile for Administrative Tools to your Start screen (see Figure 12.2).

1. From the Start screen type **Control** (in no particular location on the screen). A Search box appears on the right side and Control Panel on the left side. Press Enter and the Control Panel opens.

2. Click the System and Security link.

3. Right click Administrative Tools and select Pin to Start. You now have a new tile on your Start screen for Administrative Tools (see Figure 12.2).

If you want to remove the tile just right-click and select Unpin from Start that appears on the bottom left of your screen.

Figure 12.2   *Administrative Tools tile*

Tools You Might Never Use

There are some tools you might never need to work with. Others will be your best friend when it comes to administering your system. Let's first take a look at some of the more obscure tools.

Component Services

This is not a new feature in Windows 8. In fact, it has existed for some time. It is unlikely that you will ever need to use this tool. It is used to configure and administer your COM (Component Object Model) applications.

Data Sources (ODBC)

This allows you to add, delete, or configure data sources with DSNs (Data Source Names) for the current system and user. Again, not something the everyday user might ever work with.

iSCSI Initiator

This was an applet in Control Panel in Windows Vista, but it was appropriately moved in Windows 7 and remains in the Administrative Tools section in Windows 8. Internet Small Computer System Interface (iSCSI) uses TCP/IP for its data transfer over a common Ethernet network. But you need iSCSI devices to make it work, and the OS needs an initiator to communicate with the iSCSI devices. iSCSI devices are disks, tape drives, CDs, and other storage devices that you can connect to. In the relationship with the other device, your computer is the initiator and the device is the target.

In Windows 8 (as in Vista and Windows 7), the initiator is included. You can also download the initiator from Microsoft for 2000 (SP3), XP, or Server 2003. The shortcut under Administrative Tools lets you configure and control the interaction between your system and the device.

Local Security Policy

Although typically a security policy is something you configure on a network domain, there are times when you might want to create password policies, account lockout policies, and so forth on your Windows 8 standalone systems. This is the place to do that. You might be deploying Windows 8 in a school, a library, or as a kiosk system (or even at home); you can adjust these security settings to ensure they are enforced.

Print Management

Although you might not think of using your computer as a print server, it is a possibility. If you have multiple print devices on your network you can use the Windows 8 Print Management tool to add, remove, and manage the print queues. You can view the status of your print queues and see the print jobs being processed.

Windows PowerShell ISE

You will notice a slight difference from Windows 7 here with your selections for Windows PowerShell; you have three to choose from:

- **Windows PowerShell (x86)**—If you have used PowerShell in the past you will be familiar with this console (same as Windows 7).

- **Windows PowerShell ISE (x86)**—ISE (Integrated Scripting Environment) for 32-bit OS.

- **Windows PowerShell ISE**—ISE (Integrated Scripting Environment) is a new console that allows you to do much more within the one PowerShell console. More information can be found at http://technet.microsoft.com/en-us/library/dd315244.aspx.

Now we can move on to some tools that an everyday user may utilize for management and troubleshooting.

Working with Computer Management

The Computer Management tool is actually a collection of many tools that you can use to manage your operating system or troubleshoot issues you are experiencing. The tools are collected together within an MMC (Microsoft Management Console). MMCs are widely used for many tools that help you manage, monitor, or troubleshoot issues. Some application vendors take advantage of MMCs so their applications can be managed from within an MMC. You also have the ability to Add/Remove tools known as snap-ins. Computer Management is a preconfigured MMC (see Figure 12.3).

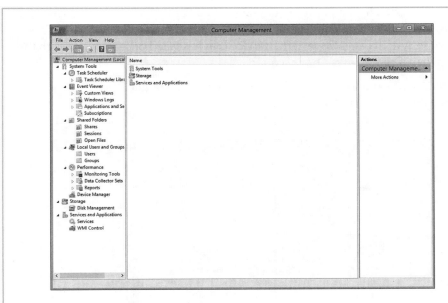

Figure 12.3   *Computer Management MMC*

 SHOW ME   Media 12.1—Using the Computer Management Tool
Access this video file through your registered Web Edition at
my.safaribooksonline.com/9780789750518/media.

Three top levels are defined:

- System Tools

- Storage

- Services and Applications

As you drill down into these areas you see the specific tools. One of the first tools you see under System Tools is Task Scheduler.

Task Scheduler

If you're coming to Windows 8 from the XP world you should know that Microsoft has significantly enhanced Task Scheduler over the last several Windows iterations. Under previous versions of Windows, you could use Task Scheduler to launch tasks at specific times or in response to minimal sets of conditions that might occur with the system. There was no way to maintain a task history or configure multiple actions to occur. It was still a great tool, but it was limited—thus forcing users to find other software to fulfill their needs.

Within Windows 8, you can configure Task Scheduler to perform tasks on a timed basis, but it can also respond to situations that occur on a variety of levels. The response system can even restart a service that has failed or send an email to the user when a certain event has occurred.

In addition, an entire Task Scheduler Library has preconfigured tasks for you to work with (see Figure 12.4).

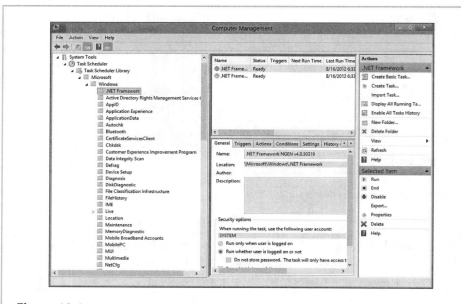

Figure 12.4   *Task Scheduler with the Library of tasks to choose from*

Task Scheduler makes use of triggers and actions. A trigger is what causes the task to run, and an action is what you have configured to occur in the event the trigger goes off. Some triggers are schedules that you put into effect. For example, if you want a specific action to occur each day at 1 p.m., then the trigger is the scheduled time. But a trigger can also be when a user logs in, when the system starts up, when a specific event occurs, and so forth.

An action can include running a program, sending an email, or even displaying a preconfigured message. The wizard provides a list of possible actions to take, including running scripts with the cscript.exe application, copying a file with robocopy, starting and stopping services, shutting down the system, and a host of others.

You can do this in several different ways. First, from the Task Scheduler console, in the Actions pane, you can click Create Basic Task. The Create Basic Task Wizard walks you through the following options:

- **Create a Basic Task**—Start with a Name and Description.

- **Trigger**—You can work from a schedule (Daily, Weekly, Monthly, One Time) where you set time parameters for the triggered event. Or you can select When the Computer Starts, When I Log On, or When a Specific Event is Logged. With that last one you can choose the Log, the Source, and even the Event ID that triggers the next step.

- **Action**—You can start a program (and choose which program that is), send an email (with the information for the email), or display a message (and write the message you want displayed).

- **Finish**—You can review your new task and tell it to open the properties of the task. When this happens, you can see a much more complicated tabbed view of a task. These options help you go beyond the basic task. You can create and manage your tasks in this way, or you can create a task from the more complicated tabs to start with.

One practical feature of Task Scheduler is its capability to open applications automatically for you at intervals you specify. For example, you might have Windows Backup and Restore configured to run over the weekend while you are away from your machine. As a reminder, you could set Task Scheduler to open Backup and Restore for you every Monday so you could verify the backup.

 **LET ME TRY IT**

Scheduling Backup and Restore to Launch Every Monday

The following steps show you how to use Task Scheduler to schedule Backup and Restore to launch every Monday and perform a backup.

1. Open Task Scheduler, which is found in the Computer Management Administrative tool, under System Tools.

2. In the right pane, click Create Basic Task. This opens the Create Basic Task Wizard (see Figure 12.5).

3. Type a Name and Description for this event. Click Next.

4. Choose Weekly. Click Next.

5. Specify a time for the task to start and select the Monday check box. Click Next.

6. Make sure Start a Program is selected and then click Next.

7. In the Program/Script text box type **%SystemRoot%\System32\control.exe**.

8. In the Add Arguments text box, type **/name Microsoft.BackupAndRestore**. Click Next.

9. Click Finish.

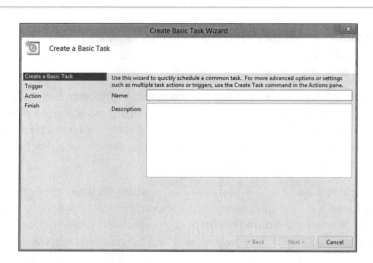

Figure 12.5   *Easily configure a task from the Create Basic Task Wizard*

Task Scheduler is integrated with Event Viewer now so that it can react to situations based upon events that occur. There is also a way to view the task history. You can see which tasks are running, have run, or are scheduled to run.

Using Task Scheduler on a Network

The capability to create tasks is not limited to the local computer you are working on. Task Scheduler gives you the opportunity to connect to another computer on your network and configure a task for it. You can connect to remote computers running Windows 2000, Vista, 7 or 8, as well as Windows Server 2003 or 2008.

There are a couple things to have in place before connecting, depending on the OS you are connecting to. Here are some reminders from Windows 8 Help and Support:

"If you are connecting to a remote computer running Vista or Windows Server 2008 from a computer running Vista or Windows Server 2008, you need to enable the Remote Scheduled Tasks Management firewall exception on the remote computer. To allow this exception, click Start, Control Panel, System and Security,

Allow a Program Through Windows Firewall and then select the Remote Scheduled Tasks Management check box. Then click the OK button in the Windows Firewall Settings dialog box."

 **LET ME TRY IT**

Connecting to a Remote Computer to Create a Task

The following steps show you how to use Task Scheduler to create a task on a remote computer. This exercise requires you to be connected on a network to another computer.

1. Open Task Scheduler.

2. In the left pane, click Task Scheduler.

3. In the Actions pane, click Connect to Another Computer. This opens the Select Computer dialog box.

4. Select the Another Computer radio button.

5. In the Another Computer text box, type the name or IP address of the remote computer or click the Browse button to browse for a remote computer.

6. Once you have selected a remote computer, click OK.

7. You can now create a task on the remote computer.

Creating an Advanced Task

To create a more advanced task, click the Create Task option in the Action pane. The Create Task dialog box offers the following five tabs to configure your tasks:

- **General**—Allows you to configure the name and description, which user account it should run under, and whether it should run only when that user is logged in.

- **Triggers**—Allows you to schedule an extensive list of triggers, starting with the time triggers you can set up. If you change the Begin the Task options, the settings will change. The most complex of the triggers involves Events.

- **Actions**—The same as the actions listed in the basic settings. Allows you to configure a program to run, send an email, display a message—or you can do all three. That is the benefit to using the advanced tabbed task creator. You can configure different actions to occur from here.

- **Conditions**—Allows you to specify conditions to your task. For example, you might want certain tasks to run only if the system is idle. Depending on whether the computer is running on AC power or battery, you might not want the task to run (or you might not want it to run if it isn't connected to a certain network).

- **Settings**—Allows you to determine whether you can start the task manually, what to do if your task couldn't run on schedule, and what to do in the event a task is running too long.

Every once in a while, a task that you have scheduled to start will not run as planned. When troubleshooting the cause of a failed task, keep the following in mind:

- Task Scheduler does not run while the computer is in Safe Mode.

- Verify the triggers for the task have been set correctly.

- Check the task history, making sure it ran correctly on previous occasions and there were no errors.

- A task will run only if all its conditions are met.

- Make sure the user who is logged on when the task is scheduled to run has the correct security level to run the task.

Event Viewer

Often you might have an error occur that crashes your system or simply crashes the application you are working with. Typically, if this happens once or twice, you might not think anything of it. But if it happens repeatedly, you might become concerned that there is a real problem you need to fix. The Event Viewer is invaluable for this because it can show you the incident in question and help you determine the cause of the failure.

The Event Viewer, shown in Figure 12.6, allows you to see more than the standard Windows logs (Application, System, and Security logs). There also are Applications and Services Logs, which include diagnostic logs, logs for specific applications within Windows 8 like your IE logs. In the past, you had to go hunting to find logs for certain applications, but Microsoft has tried to bring them all together here.

So many events come into the Event Viewer that it's almost impossible to track down the problem you are investigating without some form of filter. Views allow you to create filters that not only filter the events of one log, they allow you to select multiple logs to view. To create a custom view, select a log, click the Action menu, and then choose Create Custom View or Import Custom View. Keep in mind that you can still use filters, but custom views can be retained and quickly selected from the navigation section.

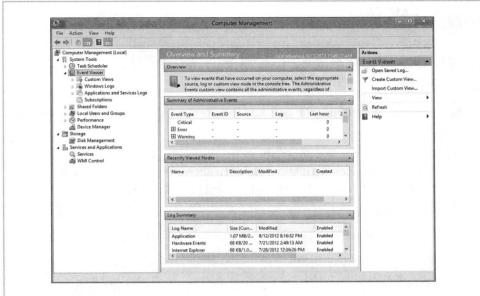

Figure 12.6   *Event Viewer offers enterprise monitoring functionality*

You might have noticed that there are different levels of events alerting you to possible issues. They are

- **Information**—This message occurs when there has been a change in an application or component. For example, a service started/restarted or an operation has successfully completed.

- **Warning**— When this message appears, an issue has happened that can impact a service or produce a bigger problem if action is not taken.

- **Error**—This message indicates that a problem has taken place that might impact functionality and is outside the application or component that triggered the error message.

- **Critical**—Usually the most serious event, a Critical event means that a failure has occurred where the application or component that triggered the event can't automatically recover.

 **LET ME TRY IT**

Opening Event Viewer and Viewing All Error Events Recorded

The following steps show you how to open Event Viewer and view all error events recorded.

1. From the Start screen type **Compmgmt.msc** and press Enter. This opens Computer Management MMC. (You can alternatively type **Eventvwr** and open an MMC with just the Event Viewer.)

2. In the Computer Management console expand Event Viewer.

3. After Event Viewer opens, in the left pane, double-click Custom Views.

4. Click Administrative Events.

5. In the main Operational pane, click Level to sort your events by type.

6. Using the scrollbar, scroll through any Error events recorded.

7. Click any Error event. In the General tab near the bottom of the pane, view more information about the event.

 **LET ME TRY IT**

Scheduling an Email to Be Sent to You in Response to an Event

Another nice feature in Event Viewer is the ability to attach a task to an event. This feature works with Task Scheduler in assigning events as triggers that require actions. This exercise builds off the previous one. After opening Event Viewer, you schedule an email to be sent to you in response to an event. Complete the following steps to accomplish this.

1. From the Start screen type **Compmgmt.msc** and press Enter. This opens Computer Management MMC. (You can alternatively type **Eventvwr** and open an MMC with just the Event Viewer.)

2. In the Computer Management console expand Event Viewer.

3. After Event Viewer opens, in the left pane, double-click Custom Views.

4. Click Administrative Events.

5. Locate an event that you want to be emailed about and right-click it.

6. Select Attach Task to this Event. This opens the Create Basic Task Wizard.

7. Create a description for this event.

8. Click Next.

9. Click Next again.

10. Choose Send an E-mail.

11. Click Next.

12. Fill out the email fields (From, To, Subject and Text) and the SMTP Server field.

13. Click Next and then click Finish. This creates the task and adds it to your Windows task schedule.

Shared Folders, Local Users, and Groups

As you continue to look through the Computer Management console, you see a Shared Folders section, followed by Local Users and Groups. With the Shared Folders tool you can manage and monitor any shared folders that reside on your workstations (unless you connect to a remote computer). There are three options for you to look at:

- **Shares**—This lists all the shared folders on your computer, including the administrative hidden shares.

- **Sessions**—Here you can view details on users that have a session (connection) to your computer.

- **Open Files**—All the open files are listed here and details include who is accessing the file. You can also force a file to close from here.

The Local Users and Groups tool allows you to add, remove, and manage user group membership on your local computer. In a domain users and group management is done on domain controllers. For the most part you may not be using this tool unless you share your computer with others and want them to use their own logon credentials. This would be useful as with each logon account a user gets his own profile and can keep his personal settings. Adding local user accounts is covered in Chapter 10, "System Configuration Settings."

The Performance Monitor was discussed in detail back in Chapter 11. Below Performance Monitor you see Device Manager.

Device Manager

Device Manager enables you to see what hardware devices are being used. As you drill down you see the specific devices under the main sections (see Figure 12.7). You also can see whether there are any issues with your hardware devices. If issues are present you see a yellow icon next to your device. Right-clicking on a device provides you with the following options:

- **Update Driver Software**—Update drivers for hardware installed.
- **Disable**—Turn off or disable hardware.
- **Uninstall**—Remove driver for hardware.
- **Scan for Hardware Changes**—Scan computer for any new hardware.
- **Properties**—Here you can perform some more advanced tasks.

The tool that you see next in Computer Management is under Storage, Disk Management.

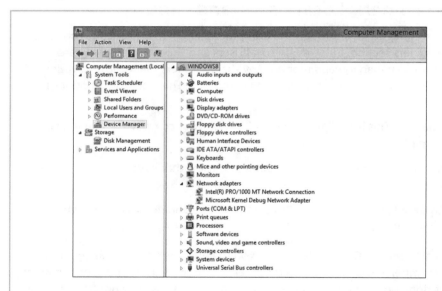

Figure 12.7   *The Device Manager is used to manage hardware*

Disk Management

With Disk Management, you can manage hard disks and their volumes and partitions (see Figure 12.8). There are a wide variety of options at your disposal. For example, you can initialize disks, create volumes, and format volumes with the FAT, FAT32, or NTFS file systems.

Because most configuration changes in Disk Management take place immediately, you can accomplish most disk-related tasks without restarting your computer. One of the most common tasks performed in Disk Management is to create a partition (volume) on a hard disk. To accomplish this, you need to be logged in as an administrator and there has to be either unallocated disk space or free space within an extended partition on the hard disk.

If you find that you don't have any unallocated disk space, you can create some in various ways. You can shrink an existing partition, delete a partition, or add an extra hard drive to the system.

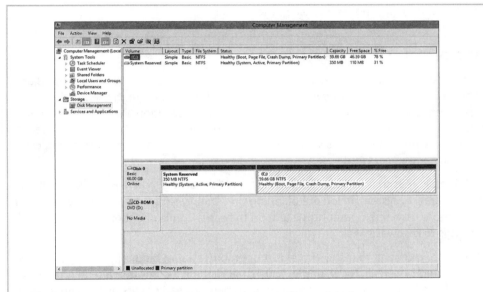

Figure 12.8 *Disk Management lets you configure all your disks from one spot*

 **LET ME TRY IT**

Creating and Formatting a New Partition

The following steps show you how to create and format a new partition. In this example, you create a new drive letter for you to access.

1. From the Start screen type **Compmgmt.msc** and press Enter. This opens Computer Management MMC.

2. In the left pane, under Storage, click Disk Management.

3. In the main pane, locate the hard disk you want to create the partition on. Right-click an unallocated region of it and select New Simple Volume. This opens the New Simple Volume Wizard.

4. Click Next.

5. Accept the maximum default size and click Next.

6. A default drive letter is provided for you. Accept this and then click Next. This opens the Format Partition dialog box.

7. Verify that you accept the default settings and click Next.

8. After reviewing your choices, click Finish.

Understanding Partitions

The first three partitions on a basic disk that is newly created will be formatted as primary partitions. Starting with the fourth, each partition (on the same disk) will be configured as a logical drive within an extended partition. Remember, formatting deletes any data you have on the drive, so make sure it is backed up if need be. Many times an error as simple as selecting the wrong drive for formatting can quickly erase years of data.

One main reason for creating a partition and formatting a drive is to prepare it for an operating system. If you are planning on creating a multiboot setup, where you run more than one operating system on the same computer, there are a couple of things to be aware of.

For one, you need to install the oldest operating system before installing the newer operating system. If, for example, you install Vista on a computer already running Windows 8, you can render your system inoperable; earlier versions of Windows don't recognize the startup files used in more recent versions of Windows and can overwrite them.

Another aspect to consider is making certain to use the NTFS file system on the partition or disk where you plan to install a new version of Windows. Although you have the option within Disk Management to select FAT or FAT32 when formatting a drive, these older file systems cannot utilize all the features in Windows 8, and they are not as efficient as NTFS. Unless you have a special requirement, stick with the NTFS file system.

Changing a Drive Letter

Changing the drive letter has become a simple task, thanks to Computer Management. Right-click your drive of choice and select Change Drive Letter or Path. A drop-down menu provides you with available options for your new drive letter (see Figure 12.9).

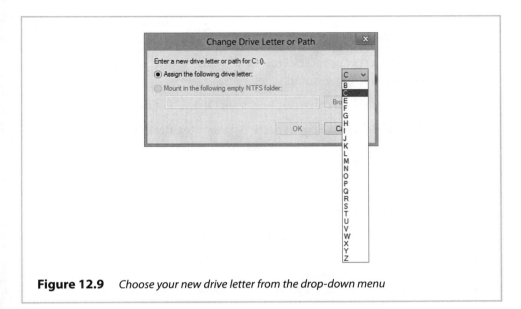

Figure 12.9   *Choose your new drive letter from the drop-down menu*

Working with Virtual Hard Disks

Computer Management also supports the Virtual Hard Disk (VHD) format. This style of file system can be used in conjunction with virtualization software such as the Hyper-V feature of Windows Server 2008 R2, Microsoft Virtual PC/Virtual Server or VmWare. From Disk Management you can create, attach, and detach virtual hard disks.

You will find that VHDs look just like physical disks in Disk Management. When a VHD has been attached, it appears blue. If the disk is detached, its icon reverts back to gray.

 LET ME TRY IT

Creating a VHD

Sometimes you want to work with virtual drives rather than physical hard drives within your system. The following steps show you how to do this by creating a VHD through Disk Manager.

1. From the Start screen type **Compmgmt.msc** and press Enter. This opens Computer Management MMC.

2. In the left pane, under Storage, click Disk Management.

3. Click the Action menu and then click Create VHD. This opens the Create and Attach Virtual Hard Disk dialog box.

4. In the Location text box, click Browse to choose the location where you want the VHD file to be stored.

5. In the Virtual Hard Disk Size text box, select the size of the VHD.

6. In the Virtual Hard Disk Format section, accept the default and click OK. You are returned to Computer Management, where your VHD is created. Follow its initializing progress in the lower right.

7. On successful completion, click the VHD in the main pane.

8. Click the Action menu and then click Attach VHD.

9. In the Location text box, click Browse to choose the location.

10. Click OK.

If you are having an issue creating a VHD, it might be due to the fact you're not meeting these requirements:

- The minimum size for a VHD is 3MB.

- The path specifying the location for the VHD needs to be fully qualified and can't be located in the \Windows directory.

- A VHD can be only a basic disk.

- A VHD is initialized when it is created. If you are creating a large, fixed-size VHD, it's going to take a while to finish creation.

Services

Services are the underlying core features that handle any number of operations on your system—from web service to print services and more. You might have seen the services console in previous versions of Windows.

The Services structure hasn't changed much in Windows 8 (see Figure 12.10). You might notice a few more services in Windows 8 depending on which older version of Windows you are comparing it to (from XP to Windows 8 there are new services to note), such as the BranchCache service, which was also in Windows 7).

One reason to open Services is when a service is not responding correctly. For example, you might send a print job to a printer that appears as if it went through correctly. However, there is nothing on the printer. If the hardware is on and working correctly, it's time to look at the software end of things. One possible solution would be to restart the Print Spooler service (see Figure 12.11).

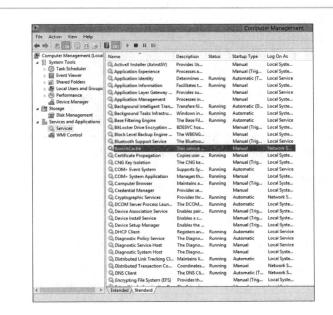

Figure 12.10   *Start, stop, and restart local services*

Someone might suggest that you just reboot the machine to fix it; that might work because it stops and starts all services. However, instead of stopping and starting all the services, why not just stop and restart the one causing the problem?

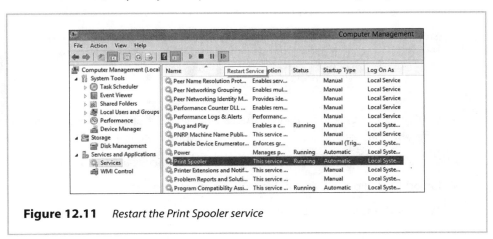

Figure 12.11   *Restart the Print Spooler service*

 **LET ME TRY IT**

Restarting the Print Spooler Service

The following steps show you how to stop and restart the Print Spooler service.

1. From the Start screen type **Compmgmt.msc** and press Enter. This opens Computer Management MMC. Alternatively you could type **Services.msc** and be taken directly into the Services console.

2. Under Services and Applications select Services.

3. Scroll through the Services names until you locate Print Spooler. Double-click it. This opens the Print Spooler Properties dialog box.

4. Under the lower section on the first tab called Service Status, click Stop.

5. A window opens, indicating Windows is stopping the service. Verify it is stopped by reviewing its service status. When it has stopped successfully, under Service Status, click Start.

6. A window opens, indicating Windows is starting the service. Verify it is started by reviewing its service status. When it has started successfully, click OK.

You also have the ability to quickly restart a service by clicking on the restart button in the toolbar while the service is selected.

From within Services you can do the following:

- Stop, start, pause, resume, or disable a service. You can also see the description of what each service does and what other services rely on it to work.

- Configure recovery actions in the event of a service failure (like restarting the service).

- Configure a service to run under the security context of a user account that is different from the logged-on user or the computer account.

- Configure hardware profiles that use different services enabled or disabled.

- Export your services information to a .txt or . csv file.

- Monitor the status of each service.

Setting Up Recovery Actions to Take Place When a Service Fails

If you have an issue where a service regularly fails and you are trying to troubleshoot it, the General tab in the Server Properties dialog box might have just what you need. On this tab, you can select the computer's response if a service fails. For example, the first time it fails, you might want to restart the service. If it fails again, you might want to automatically run an application in response to this failure. If it fails again, you might have the machine reboot to reset all services. For example, if you had multiple failures using Internet Connection Sharing and discovered a problem with the Network Connections service, you might want to start the Resource Monitor to see which processes are utilizing the network.

The following steps show you how to set up recovery actions when a service fails. In this example, a command is provided to start Performance Monitor when the Network Connections service fails.

1. From the Start screen type **Compmgmt.msc** and press Enter. This opens Computer Management MMC.

2. Select Services.

3. Scroll through the Services names until you locate Network Connections. Double click-it.

4. Click the Recovery tab.

5. From the Second Failure drop-down, select Run a Program.

6. In the Run Program area at the lower part of the tab, in the Program box, type **%windir%\system32\perfmon.exe /res**.

7. Click Apply.

8. Click OK.

When you click Run a Program, under Run Program, you need to type the full path for the specified computer. UNC names are not supported.

For example, type **C:\system32\dfrgui.exe** rather than **\\computername\c$\ system32\dfrgui.exe**.

It's not always clear which system drivers or applications depend on a service to function correctly. In narrowing it down, take advantage of the Dependencies tab on any service properties box. This tab reveals any services or drivers that depend on that service to run and services and drivers that the service depends on.

Task Manager

Another tool that you can turn to when you find that your computer is not performing well is Task Manager (see Figure 12.12). To open Task Manager you can type **Taskmgr** on the Start screen and press Enter. If you have used Task Manager in the past you see that there is a whole new look to it in Windows 8; there is also more functionality. Task Manager allows you to see what is going on with your computer from a number of different perspectives. It also lets you open up a couple of different consoles to troubleshoot further if needed.

Figure 12.12   *Task Manager*

When you first open Task Manager you may see just a list of applications that are running. You can forcibly close these applications by clicking on End Task with the application highlighted. The real power of Task Manager can be seen once you click the More Details down arrow. You can choose from seven tabs:

- **Processes**—When sorted by Name you see your applications and processes broken into sections (Apps, Background Processes, Windows Processes) in the left column. The right columns show the status and how many resources the process or application is utilizing. The great improvement here is that you can see utilization of CPU, Memory, Disk, and Network from one tab (see Figure 12.13). You can also sort by any of the columns, so if you want to see which application or process is utilizing the most CPU you can sort by the CPU column to easily find it. You have the ability to forcibly close applications and processes by using the End Task button. For those of you who might be familiar with Task Manager, you will readily see that you can now identify what actual functions the svchost.exe processes are doing by expanding the process in the list. This is a big improvement over past versions.

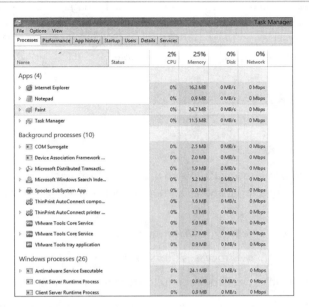

Figure 12.13   *See CPU, Memory, Disk, and Network Utilization*

- **Performance**—From this tab you can see a graphical display of CPU, Memory, Disk, and Network. Just click on each to see it displayed. On the bottom of this tab you see a link to Open Resource Monitor.

- **App History**—This is one of the new tabs in Windows 8 Task Manager. From here you can see the history of your applications' resource utilization. This is a great feature as now you can see what applications are using your resources the most over time.

- **Startup**—Another new tab that allows you to see what applications are set to run automatically when your operating system starts up. When you select an application listed the Disable button is activated. Disabling an application from here stops it from starting automatically when the operating system starts up.

- **Users**—Not only do you see a list of users here and have the ability to Disconnect them, but with Windows 8 Task Manager you can see the resource utilization for each of the users—another great improvement over previous versions.

- **Details**—Here you see a list of all processes that are running with details on Process ID (PID) and other information similar to what you may be used to from older versions of Task Manager Process tab.

- **Services**—Also new in this version of Task Manager, here you see a list of all the services running on your computer. Right-click on any of the services and you can Start, Stop, or Restart the service. By clicking on the Open Services link, you are taken to the Services console.

 **LET ME TRY IT**

Closing a Task

In the following exercise we assume that Internet Explorer is hung and use Task Manager to close the application. Open Internet Explorer before starting this exercise.

1. From the Start screen type **taskmgr** and press Enter.

2. If not already in the Processes tab, select the Processes tab.

3. Click on the Internet Explorer application to highlight it.

4. Click End Task. The application disappears from the list and Internet Explorer closes.

If you had multiple instances of Internet Explorer running you can expand the application in Task Manager and select the instance that you want to end.

 SHOW ME   Media 12.2—The New Task Manager
Access this video file through your registered Web Edition at
my.safaribooksonline.com/9780789750518/media.

System Recovery

From time to time you may install an application or a driver that causes your system to crash or not run very well. It may cause multiple errors in the event logs. You may not even be able to get Windows to start. If you can get into Windows, you may have tried to stop and restart services, kill processes, and even uninstall the application or driver, but to no avail. If you want to go back to before you even installed the driver or application you can do exactly that using System Recovery. To open the Recovery Tools, follow these steps:

1. From the Start screen type **Control Panel** and press Enter.

2. In the Search Box type **Recovery**.

3. Click on the Recovery link to display the Recovery Tools (see Figure 12.14).

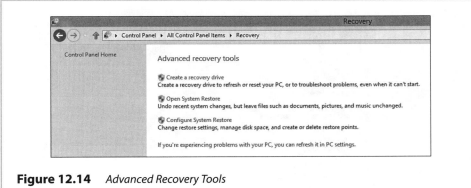

Figure 12.14   *Advanced Recovery Tools*

You see three options in the Advanced Recovery Tools item:

- **Create a Recovery Drive**—This operation allows you to boot from an external source and retrieve your recovery data. Clicking this link takes you through a wizard to create this boot disk, which must be done while Windows is still in working condition.

- **Open System Restore**—Use this link when you are having issues with your operating system. It takes you through the System Restore Wizard and offers you the opportunity to select a specific point in time restore.

- **Configure System Restore**—This option takes you to the System Protection tab of the System Properties dialog box (see Figure 12.15). From this screen, the System Restore button opens the System Restore Wizard (which is the same as clicking on the Open System Restore link). Listed in the Available Drives area you can see the drives that can be protected. With one of the drives selected, click Configure to access options that let you turn protection on/off and adjust the amount of drive space that is used for system restore files. You also have the ability to delete all restore points for the drive by clicking Delete (see Figure 12.16). With the Create button you can manually create a restore point of the system at that moment.

Figure 12.15   *System Protection tab of the System Properties dialog box*

Figure 12.16   *Configure your System Restore Settings*

LET ME TRY IT

Creating and Using a Restore Point

In the following steps you create a restore point and then go through the System Recovery Wizard to see that what you created is now available for you.

1. Type **Control Panel** from the Start screen and press Enter.

2. In the Control Panel Search box type **Recovery**.

3. Click the Recovery link.

4. Click the Configure System Restore link.

5. In the System Protection tab, click Create.

6. Type a name for the restore point (be as descriptive as you can).

7. Click Create. This creates a restore point for the drives for which you have protection turned on.

8. Click Close on the confirmation message that your System restore point was created successfully.

9. To see what you have created, click on System Restore in the System Protection tab. This opens the System Restore Wizard.

10. Click Next. You see the restore point you just created at the top of the list. You can also click the Show More Restore Points check box to see all the available restore points.

As you are not actually performing a restore, just click Cancel. If you wanted to perform the restore you would select your restore point and continue through the wizard.

You might have noticed that some restore points already are available that you did not create. Windows 8 automatically creates a restore point just before an update or application is installed, as well as every seven days if none of these things have happened during that time.

SHOW ME Media 12.3—**Understanding Recovery Options**
Access this video file through your registered Web Edition at
my.safaribooksonline.com/9780789750518/media.

Troubleshooting Items

Sometimes you just want someone else to do the work. Well, using the Troubleshooting item in Control Panel can do the work for you when it comes to figuring out what a specific problem is. You need to click through some wizards, but that's it. As you can see in Figure 12.17 there are four areas you can focus on.

Figure 12.17   *Four options to choose from when troubleshooting*

 **LET ME TRY IT**

Troubleshooting a Sound Problem

In this exercise we assume you are having a problem with your sound. (To make this example work, we disabled the sound device in Device Manager to simulate an actual problem.) Follow these steps to troubleshoot and fix the issue.

1. Type **Control Panel** on the Start screen and press Enter to open the Control Panel.

2. In the Search box type **Troubleshoot**.

3. Click the Troubleshooting link.

4. Click the Hardware and Sound link.

5. Click the Playing Audio link. This opens the Playing Audio Troubleshooting Wizard (see Figure 12.18).

6. Click Next and the device is checked.

7. You then see what the recommendations are if any. In this case you see Enable Device and a button to Apply This Fix or Skip This Fix (see Figure 12.19).

8. Click Apply This Fix and your sound device will be enabled. The next screen shows that the issue has been fixed (see Figure 12.20).

9. Click Close the Troubleshooter.

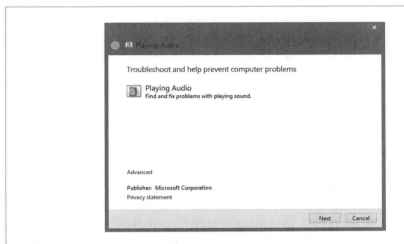

Figure 12.18   *Troubleshooting Audio with the Playing Audio Troubleshooting Wizard*

Figure 12.19   *Apply or skip the suggested fix*

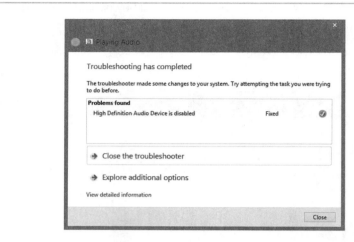

Figure 12.20   *Confirmation that suggested fix has been applied*

We did a pretty simple fix here, but you can see how powerful this tool can be. The Wizard options may change a bit depending on what option you choose to troubleshoot.

Looking back at the main Troubleshooting page you see some options on the left side:

- **View All**—Takes all the options from under the separate headings and lists them for you.

- **View History**—Lists past troubleshooting operations that were performed. You can see details on what was done.

- **Change Settings**—Here you can choose whether you want Windows 8 to check for routine maintenance issues and remind you when the system maintenance troubleshooter can help you fix problems. There is also an Allow Troubleshooting to Begin Immediately When Started check box.

- **Get Help From a Friend**—You can actually allow someone else to connect to your computer to assist you with your issue. Be careful and make sure it is someone you trust. From this page, you can also record the problem as you reproduce it; then you can send the recording to a friend.

The following steps allow someone to remotely access your computer to help troubleshoot a problem.

1. Type **Control Panel** on the Start screen and press Enter to open the Control Panel.

2. In the Search box, type **Troubleshoot**.

3. Click the Troubleshooting link.

4. On the left side, click Get Help from a Friend.

5. Click on Invite Someone to Help You. This opens the Windows Remote Assistant dialogue box.

6. Click on Save This Invitation As a File and a Save As dialogue box appears. You can browse to a location where you want to save this file, and then click Save.

7. You are presented with the Windows Remote Assistance window. The instructions there tell you to give your helper the invitation file and the password that is now viewable (you can send the invitation file via email).

8. Your helper can launch the invitation file and then be prompted for the password you provided, and will be connected to your computer.

 TELL ME MORE   Media 12.4—A Discussion of Windows 8 **Troubleshooting**
Access this audio recording through your registered Web Edition at ***my.safaribooksonline.com/9780789750518/media***.

index

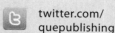

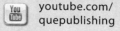

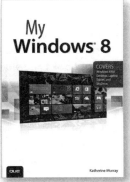

FREE
Online Edition

Safari
Books Online

Your purchase of *Using Windows 8* includes access to a free online edition for 45 days through the **Safari Books Online** subscription service. Nearly every Que book is available online through **Safari Books Online**, along with thousands of books and videos from publishers such as Addison-Wesley. Professional, Cisco Press, Exam Cram, IBM Press, O'Reilly Media, Prentice Hall, Sams, and VMware Press.

Safari Books Online is a digital library providing searchable, on-demand access to thousands of technology, digital media, and professional development books and videos from leading publishers. With one monthly or yearly subscription price, you get unlimited access to learning tools and information on topics including mobile app and software development, tips and tricks on using your favorite gadgets, networking, project management, graphic design, and much more.

Activate your FREE Online Edition at
informit.com/safarifree

STEP 1:   Enter the coupon code: YGSRUWA.

STEP 2:   New Safari users, complete the brief registration form.
Safari subscribers, just log in.

If you have difficulty registering on Safari or accessing the online edition,
please e-mail customer-service@safaribooksonline.com